The Politics of Economic Adjustment

Recent Titles in Contributions in Political Science

Trotskyism and the Dilemma of Socialism
Christopher Z. Hobson and Ronald D. Tabor

Policy Studies: Integration and Evaluation
Stuart S. Nagel

Open Borders? Closed Societies? The Ethical and Political Issues
Mark Gibney, editor

Dependence, Development, and State Repression
George A. Lopez and Michael Stohl, editors

Urban Minority Administrators: Politics, Policy, and Style
Albert K. Karnig and Paula D. McClain, editors

Papers for the Millions: The New Journalism in Britain, 1850s to 1914
Joel H. Wiener, editor

Government Response to Financial Constraints
L. R. Jones and Jerry L. McCaffery

Dilemmas of Social Democracy: The Spanish Socialist Workers Party in the 1980s
Donald Share

A Staff for the President: The Executive Office, 1921–1952
Alfred D. Sander

Hungary and the USSR, 1956–1988: Kadar's Political Leadership
Andrew Felkay

Trotsky and Djilas: Critics of Communist Bureaucracy
Michael M. Lustig

Isolation and Paradox: Defining the "Public" in Modern Political Analysis
Frank Louis Rusciano

The President and Civil Rights Policy: Leadership and Change
Steven A. Shull

Nominating Presidents: An Evaluation of Voters and Primaries
John G. Geer

A Right to Bear Arms: State and Federal Bills of Rights and Constitutional Guarantees
Stephen P. Halbrook

The Politics of Economic Adjustment

PLURALISM, CORPORATISM, AND PRIVATIZATION

EDITED BY

Richard E. Foglesong

and

Joel D. Wolfe

Contributions in Political Science, Number 237

Bernard K. Johnpoll, Series Editor

GREENWOOD PRESS

New York • Westport, Connecticut • London

Library of Congress Cataloging-in-Publication Data

The Politics of economic adjustment : pluralism, corporatism, and privatization / edited by Richard E. Foglesong and Joel D. Wolfe.
p. cm.—(Contributions in political science, ISSN 0147–1066 ; no. 237)
Bibliography: p.
Includes index.
ISBN 0–313–26627–1 (lib. bdg. : alk. paper)
1. Industry and state—Europe. 2. Industry and state—United States. 3. Privatization—Europe. 4. Privatization—United States. 5. Europe—Economic policy. 6. United States—Economic policy—1981– I. Foglesong, Richard E. II. Wolfe, Joel D. III. Series.
HD3616.E8P65 1989
338.94—dc20 89–2180

British Library Cataloguing in Publication Data is available.

Library of Congress Catalog Card Number: 89–2180
ISBN: 0–313–26627–1
ISSN: 0147–1066

First published in 1989

Greenwood Press, Inc.
88 Post Road West, Westport, Connecticut 06881

Printed in the United States of America

The paper used in this book complies with the Permanent Paper Standard issued by the National Information Standards Organization (Z39.48–1984).

10 9 8 7 6 5 4 3 2 1

Contents

Abbreviations

AFL-CIO	American Federation of Labor-Congress of Industrial Organizations
BDA	Bundesvereinigung der deutschen Arbeitgeberverbände (Federation of German Employers' Organization)
BDI	Bundesverband der deutschen Industrie (Federation of German Industry)
CDU	Christian Democratic Union (Germany)
CED	Committee for Economic Development
CERES	Center for Socialist Studies, Research, and Education
CFDT	Conféderation Française Démocratique du Travail
CFTC	Conféderation Française des Travailleurs Chrétiens
CGT	Conféderation Générale du Travail
CSSF	Chambre Syndicale de la Sidérurgie Française
CSU	Christian Social Union (Germany)
DGB	Deutscher Gewerkschaftsbund
ECSC	European Coal and Steel Community
FDES	Fonds du Développement Economique et Social
FDP	Free Democratic party (Germany)
FNE	Fonds National de l'Emploi
FO	Force Ouvrière
FRG	Federal Republic of Germany

FTC	Federal Trade Commission
GDP	gross domestic product
GIS	Groupement des Industries Sidérurgiques
GNP	gross national product
ICL	International Computers Ltd.
IG Chemie	German Chemical Workers' Union
IG Metall	German Metalworkers' Union
ISTAT	Italian Central Institute of Statistics
LICIT	Labor-Industry Coalition for International Trade
MIT	Massachusetts Institute of Technology
MITI	Ministry of International Trade and Industry
MoF	Ministry of Finance (France)
MoI	Ministry of Industry (France)
MP	Member of Parliament
NAM	National Association of Manufacturers
OECD	Organization for Economic Cooperation and Development
PCF	French Communist party
PME	petites et moyennes entreprises (small- and medium-sized firms)
PSBR	Public Sector Borrowing Requirement
RPR	Rassemblement pour la République (Rally for the Republic)
SDI	Strategic Defense Initiative
SPD	Social Democratic party (Germany)
UAW	United Auto Workers
UDF	Union pour la Démocratie Française (Union for French Democracy)
UN	United Nations

Tables and Figures

TABLES

FIGURES

1

Introduction

Richard E. Foglesong and Joel D. Wolfe

The topic of privatization, like that of corporatism, has generated a new growth industry. With the spread of privatization as a strategy for coping with economic decline in an increasingly interdependent world economy, the literature on the topic has proliferated.[1] At the same time, the corporatist literature that began in the mid–1970s has continued to develop in new directions.[2] Moreover, discussions of privatization and corporatism are increasingly found in popular journals and newspapers. Yet this burgeoning literature has thus far failed to provide an account of the determinants of this choice between privatization and corporatist strategies, or of the relationships between these strategies and the Keynesian ones that predominated in the post–World War II era. And despite all the debate over privatization and corporatism, there has been little explicit attention to how the choice between these strategies—by altering political and economic arrangements as well as the relationships among groups, classes, and the state—affects the character of democracy in the advanced industrial states. This book attempts to fill these gaps by considering both the determinants of the choice of an adjustment strategy and how that choice affects the nature of liberal democracy.

The emergent interest in privatization alongside the existing interest in corporatism reflects real world political and economic changes that have occurred in the 1970s and 1980s as the consensus backing the Keynesian welfare state collapsed. The triumph of Keynesian demand management in Europe and the United States after World War II generated economic growth, rising real incomes, shorter working hours, and improved working conditions. The success of Keynesianism also entailed a vast expansion of welfare services, notably in health care, education, and retirement benefits. All of this coincided with a period of U.S. geopolitical hegemony[3] and a system of production that maximized the provision of standardized goods and promoted mass consumption.[4] Politically, this period of unprecedented economic growth reduced social conflict and produced stable governments, since prosperity made it possible to satisfy most group demands.[5] Growth made possible a social convergence based on the diffusion of prosperity and the reduction, through technological advances, of manual labor; and this in turn generated a pluralist polity in which ideological conflict disappeared in favor of consensus on Keynesian-style management of the economy and an expanding system of welfare benefits. It was assumed that industrialism itself fostered this social convergence and the resulting evolution toward a pluralist polity.[6]

With the decline of U.S. geopolitical and economic dominance evidenced by the breakup of the Bretton Woods monetary regime and the OPEC-induced world recession, the consensus supporting the Keynesian framework has given way to renewed ideological and political conflict. The emergence of a more competitive and interdependent international political economy meant that the advanced states' economic problems have been more easily transmitted between nations, even as their terms of trade were eroded and their product markets undermined by a rising tide of exports from less developed nations.[7] As nations such as Taiwan, South Korea, Mexico, Venezuela, and Brazil have begun to produce manufactured goods, advanced industrialized nations have experienced a loss of manufacturing competitiveness, massive layoffs in manufacturing sectors, the economic decline of manufacturing regions, social pathologies associated with extended unemployment, and a sundering of community bonds—all components of what has been termed "deindustrialization."[8] Offering no solution to these problems, the Keynesian welfare-state formula lost credibility and created a vacuum that was filled by alternative public philosophies to the left and the right of the old consensus. The absence of growth meant that the material basis of compromise was no longer present, leading to a more divisive politics of winners and losers.[9]

As ideologies became polarized, political responses to economic crisis diverged. In some cases, the incremental bargaining and increasing prosperity characteristic of the pluralism of the 1950s and early 1960s became a crisis of pluralism in the 1970s and 1980s, as slower growth and overloaded governments proved unable to satisfy group demands.[10] In other cases, a restructuring of politics and policies occurred as governments embraced the strategies of corporatism and privatization. In general, advanced industrial states were faced with the need to increase their national competitiveness in the new, increasingly interdependent world economy and to reduce the influence of entrenched interest groups that had gained power during the Keynesian era. Constrained by their limited economic space for political discretion, governments could maintain the status quo and the crisis of pluralism, or turn to adjustment strategies like corporatism and privatization which promised to restore effective rule and economic confidence.[11]

The choices confronting what Samuel Beer[12] called "collectivist" democracy, with functional representation and party competition on the input side and state-regulated demand management and welfare on the output side, were as follows. Governments could adopt the privatization strategy and seek to revivify market forces by contracting regulation, cutting taxes, and casting off public enterprises. They could choose a corporatist strategy involving a more directive state role in the economy and attempt to organize a consensus between capital and labor on how to control inflation while stimulating the nation's competitiveness through state-sanctioned efforts. Or they could engage in some form of pluralist adaptation. Yet these choices were not made as technically determined responses to economic necessity. As the chapters in this volume relate, these adjustment strategies have political origins as well as manifold political effects. They represent attempts to alter government's role in the economy, block the imposition of economic losses, change the way groups and classes are incorporated into the political order, and reorganize the connection between public and private. In short, they represent shifts in the relationships among interest groups, classes, and the state that have characterized the Keynesian welfare state.

Importantly, the choice between a corporatist or privatization strategy may not be a choice for the entire state system. Just as different states adopt different strategies at the national level, there is also variation in response within a given state. The phenomenon of meso-corporatism, as emphasized in recent corporatist literature, is one example of internal variation.[13] In this volume, Christopher Allen and Jeremiah Riemer recount the evolution of meso-corporatism in West Germany. Instances of this phenomenon can also be found in the efforts of state governments in the United States to encourage high-tech development by the creation of corporatist-style boards and commissions.[14] Another example is the Thatcher government's urban renewal program, which shows a mixture of tripartite and market mechanisms at both national and local levels.[15] Thus, variation in strategy occurs not only at the macro level but between and across industrial sectors and regions.

The choice of an adjustment strategy has important implications for state-market relationships, too. In the United States, Ronald Reagan's privatization strategy is not a defense of the status quo, but an attempt to intervene in and alter the relationship between state and market. It is a form of intervention that seeks to restrict government (namely, government regulation and taxation) rather than business, albeit without necessarily weakening the state. In the terminology of Chalmers Johnson,[16] the Reagan administration opted for a strategy that is "market rational" rather than "plan rational." Indeed, this is a key issue in the debate over adjustment strategies—whether government policies should be "market reinforcing" or "market replacing," supportive of the market or directive.

The changing relationship between state and market occasioned by the choice of adjustment strategies raises anew questions about the character of democracy in advanced industrial states. On the one hand, the onset of economic crisis raises questions about the economic space for political choice. As the state's dependency on the performance of the economy increases with economic crisis, the space for political discretion and democratic debate correspondingly decreases. Tripartite planning arrangements based on democratic accountability may be presented as attempts to make democracy more real by placing investment decisions, arguably the most important decisions in any society, on the agenda of political democracy.[17] Yet, as Harvey Feigenbaum suggests in reviewing the experience of French nationalized enterprises in this volume, the state's reduced autonomy in periods of economic crisis may not make this choice very meaningful. If pluralist arrangements lead to excess demands and stagnation in societies undergoing the throes of deindustrialization, corporatist ones may involve trading nominal participation on the part of labor for acceptance of economic sacrifice.

On the other hand, the choice of an adjustment strategy may signify a change in the multiple ways in which democracy can be organized. As Claus Offe suggests, the shift from pluralism to corporatism constitutes a transition "from policy output and economic demand management to the shaping of political input and economic supply."[18] Following this insight, Joel Wolfe argues in his concluding chapter that such shifts from interest representation to modified state control of interest articulation imply fundamental changes in the character of democracy and the patterns of policy making. These changes in turn engender different types of policy responses, underscoring the importance of democratic practices for policy choices.

The choice of an adjustment strategy with all its manifold implications depends on the complex interaction between the democratic system and its economic and political environment. Special attention is paid in these chapters to the political determinants of the choices made. This awareness of political factors help correct the inaccurate and misleading way in which some adjustment strategies have been presented as technically determined responses to economic necessity—as when Japan's industrial policies are presented as solutions to America's economic problems. Further, the concern for the degree of economic space for political decision making leads to our addressing how domestic factors such as the role of intellectuals and political leaders, the organized power of classes, and the relative autonomy of particular states have influenced the choice of adjustment strategies.

This volume addresses the above issues by examining the divergent responses of liberal capitalist nations to the problem of economic decline. Included are chapters on the United States, Britain, France, West Germany, and Italy. They explain how these advanced industrial nations have experienced economic crisis differently and describe and explain why they have responded as they have. In so doing, they focus on whether and at what level a state has pursued (1) a corporatist approach involving a more direct government role in managing the economy with the assistance of private interest groups, (2) a privatization strategy involving a disengagement of state intervention and an increased reliance on market processes, or (3) a form of pluralist adaptation.

The first two chapters pose in stark terms the choice between corporatism and privatization. Wolfe argues that in contrast to corporatism, which has been much discussed as a possible solution to an overloaded system of interest representation, the political consequences of privatization have been neglected. He then develops a political analysis of privatization, showing that privatization, like corporatism, constitutes a strategy for reorganizing the system of group representation. Like corporatism, privatization promotes system rationality, entails state intervention, and benefits capital rather than labor. Unlike corporatism, which relies on authority or institutional controls, privatization relies on market processes. A case study of the Thatcher government's program demonstrates how privatization constitutes the functional equivalent of corporatism.

Foglesong develops further the contrast with corporatist strategies in his study of industrial policy in the United States, a nation comparable to Britain in its laissez-faire traditions. He explains the paradox that industrial policy proposals that in reality constitute system-maintaining reform have been promoted by policy intellectuals, liberal Democratic congressmen, and organized labor, against the opposition of most of the business community. It is because the former groups are dependent on the performance of the economy, a dependency accentuated by the problems of deindustrialization amid a changing world economy, that these groups seek to make American capitalism "work" in the sense of better providing for workers, consumers, and the disadvantaged. Yet capitalists remain wedded to the privatization strategy due to their anti-statist ideology, their recognition that market processes make disinvestment less politically costly, and their fear that present economic conditions do not permit material guarantees to noncapitalists.

The next two chapters are concerned with corporatist forms of adjustment in West Germany, a nation with a more statist corporatist tradition than Austria, Switzerland, or Sweden. Chris Allen and Jerry Riemer, in their analysis of the reindustrialization debate in West Germany, argue that the 1980s have witnessed a significant, if incomplete, shift toward meso-corporatism. By this they mean that the federal government has abandoned a leading role in industrial policy, with the slack being taken up by state governments and associations of capital and labor. Allen and Riemer thus add to the current corporatist debate, which focuses on middle-level corporatist processes rather than those involving the whole system.

Kathleen Thelen continues the focus on West German corporatist arrangements by considering the impact of growing unemployment and market competition on union participation in collective bargaining. Her focus is on the pacesetting German Metalworkers' Union (IG Metall) and its negotiations for working-time reduction as a means of reducing unemployment. She finds that employers are increasingly asserting their own agenda for expanding working-time flexibility. More generally, there has been a shift from bargaining over wages to bargaining over the terms and conditions of work, reflecting employers' market-oriented concern with rationalizing the use of labor in production. Ultimately, this shifts the defense of workers' interests from national to local organizations, which can better monitor employers' use of labor.

Chapters 6 through 8 suggest that economic crisis can limit state autonomy and its ability to organize interest representation, giving rise to pluralism as a political process for accommodating adjustment pressures and contradictory group goals. Moreover, these instances of pluralist power relations involve particularized benefits aimed at containing or dissipating the crisis. Lacking an overall strategy of adjustment, the state is reactive and defensive. As a result, it grants benefits and reassurances either to particular firms facing immediate collapse or undergoing large-scale restructuring or to the business community generally in recognition of the state's own dependence on economic success. In acceding to the imperatives of capitalist or union pressure to sustain ongoing enterprises, governments temporarily ease the process of adjustment to larger international market forces.

In his study of economic and industrial policy in France, Harvey Feigenbaum argues that the imperatives of international capital significantly limit the state's freedom of action. Recent policies of the right and the left converge, in spite of their different ideologies and domestic constituencies. The sources of convergence in economic policy are the international market and political forces and domestic capitalists. This revelation not only makes assertions about the strong, autonomous French state dubious; it means that democratically elected politicians have highly constrained options.

When industrial crisis turns into political crisis, at least in the case of the French steel industry, the state is compelled to assume responsibility for social and economic adjustment costs. Tony Daley's study of adjustment in the French steel industry shows that state intervention actually magnifies union influence. The crisis of the troubled steel industry up to 1970 had led to a mutual dependence between the state and employers, though labor was excluded. State restructuring plans were backed by financing and social guarantees, until the state took outright control in the 1970s. State intervention, plus the inability of capital and labor to negotiate successfully, led to a politicizing of relations within the steel industry, whereupon steel unions gained enhanced bargaining effectiveness through the use of direct action or protest methods. However successful, the French steel unions' protest strategy was carried out on a legal and political terrain defined by the state, Daley reminds us.

Like France, Italy has benefited from significant government involvement in promoting economic growth. Anthony Masi assesses these efforts by testing the Anglo-American concept of deindustrialization against the Italian case. His findings reveal trends in economic development that make Italy, which seems to be growing in spite of itself, an anomaly among advanced states. Italy displays no decline in manufacturing output as a share of national production and enjoys increased productivity, though there has been some decline in manufacturing employment since 1976, a higher than average deficit for Organization for Economic Cooperation and Development (OECD) countries, an export trade pattern that relies on standardized goods rather than high technology, and significant regional variations. The Italian government has promoted economic growth through a wide range of interventionist measures and has protected workers from economic collapse and rationalization, yet has recently experienced increased inflation, unemployment, and budget deficits, a combination reminiscent of the stagflation of the 1970s.

Finally, the concluding chapter offers an analysis of the meaning for democracy of divergent forms of economic adjustment. In doing this, Wolfe offers a characterization of adjustment strategies in terms of possible types of democracy, an examination of the three strategies of adjustment discussed in this book, and hypotheses concerning the sources of variation in patterns of democracy. Emphasizing democracy's multiform, flexible, and adaptive character, this comparative analysis portrays democratic political systems as both determined by social forces and determining of social and political development. Ultimately, this chapter underlines the diverse ways in which capitalism and liberal democracy can be combined.

NOTES

1. See John Kay, Colin May, and David Thompson, eds., *Privatisation and Regulation: The UK Experience* (Oxford: Clarendon Press, 1986).

2. Alan Cawson, "Varieties of Corporatism: The Importance of the Meso-level of Interest Intermediation," in Alan Cawson, ed., *Organized Interests and the State: Studies in Meso-corporatism* (London: Sage, 1985), pp. 1–21; Alan Cawson, *Corporatism and Political Theory* (Oxford: Basil Blackwell, 1986); Wyn Grant, "Introduction," in Wyn Grant, ed., *The Political Economy of Corporatism* (London: Macmillan, 1985), pp. 1–31; Wolfgang Streeck and Philippe C. Schmitter, "Community, Market, State—and Associations? The Prospective Contribution of Interest Governance to Social Order," in Wolfgang Streeck and Philippe C. Schmitter, eds., *Private Interest Government: Beyond Market and State* (London: Sage, 1985), pp. 1–29; Leo Panitch, "Recent Theorizations of Corporatism: Reflections on a Growth Industry," *British Journal of Sociology* 31 (June 1980): 159–87; Ilja Scholten, ed., *Political Stability and Neo-corporatism: Corporatist Integration and Societal Cleavages in Western Europe* (London: Sage, 1987).

3. Robert Keohane, "The World Political Economy and the Crisis of Embedded Liberalism," in John H. Goldthorpe, ed., *Order and Conflict in Contemporary Capitalism* (Oxford: Clarendon Press, 1984), pp. 15–38.

4. Michael Piori and Charles Sabel, *The Second Industrial Divide: Possibilities for Prosperity* (New York: Basic Books, 1984); Robert Reich, *The Next American Frontier* (New York: Penguin, 1983).

5. Joel Krieger, *Reagan, Thatcher, and the Politics of Decline* (New York: Oxford University Press, 1986).

6. Seymour Martin Lipset, *Political Man: The Social Bases of Politics* (Garden City, N.Y.: Anchor, 1960).

7. Keohane, "World Political Economy," pp. 27–36.

8. Barry Bluestone and Bennett Harrison, *The Deindustrialization of America* (New York: Basic Books, 1982).

9. Krieger, *Reagan, Thatcher*, chap. 2.

10. Samuel P. Huntington, "The United States," in Michel Crozier et al., *The Crisis of Democracy: Report on the Governability of Democracies to the Trilateral Commission* (New York: New York University Press, 1975), pp. 59–118.

11. John H. Goldthorpe, "The End of Convergence: Corporatist and Dualist Tendencies in Modern Western Societies," in Goldthorpe, *Order and Conflict*, pp. 315–43.

12. Samuel H. Beer, *British Politics in the Collectivist Age* (New York: Random House, 1969).

13. Streeck and Schmitter, "Community, Market, State."

14. Richard E. Foglesong, "Meso-corporatism, Sub-national Industrial Policies, and Florida High-Tech," paper delivered at the 1987 Meeting of the Florida Political Science Association.

15. Stephen Young, "The Nature of Privatisation in Britain, 1979–85," *West European Politics* 9 (April 1986): 235–52.

16. Chalmers Johnson, *MITI and the Japanese Miracle* (Stanford: Stanford University Press, 1982).

17. Joshua Cohen and Joel Rogers, *On Democracy: Toward a Transformation of American Society* (New York: Penguin, 1983), chap. 2.

18. Claus Offe, "The Attribution of Public Status to Interest Groups: Observations on the West German Case," in Suzanne Berger, ed., *Organizing Interests in Western Europe: Pluralism, Corporatism and the Transformation of Politics* (Cambridge, Eng.: Cambridge University Press, 1981), p. 127.

2

Reorganizing Interest Representation: A Political Analysis of Privatization in Britain

Joel D. Wolfe

Stagflation, declining productivity, and fiscal burdens among advanced nations compelled governments from the late 1960s to adopt policies designed to regenerate prosperity.[1] Yet, the futility of these policies posed questions about governability, leading to arguments about the excessive and negative influence of interest groups on economic growth and effective government.[2] The subsequent debate about how to restore state power and economic growth has focused on the ground rules of democracy by calling for a shift away from social-democratic Keynesianism. One solution—the corporatist strategy—calls for a state initiative to restructure relations between interest groups and the state. Another solution—the privatization strategy—proposes a withdrawal from direct intervention by the state in favor of the regulated use of the market.

The debate about economic and political adjustment has inspired a sizable body of literature dealing with corporatism as a solution to the problem of interest-group representation.[3] The analysis of privatization, on the other hand, has been limited to its contribution to economic efficiency,[4] its empirical manifestations,[5] and its contribution to advancing class interests.[6] Oddly, analysts of the dilemmas of pluralism have failed to consider privatization as a strategy for resolving the predicament of interest-group representation in advanced industrial states.

This chapter examines whether and how privatization constitutes a response to the problem of governability fostered by economic decline. It argues that privatization, like corporatism, constitutes a strategy for overcoming a political crisis created by incompatible and excessive group pressures. Like corporatism, privatization attempts to curb the excesses of interest-group influence in order to recoup authority and enable the nation-state to prosper in the fiercely competitive international political economy. The privatization strategy relies upon state-designed and state-imposed structures and requires disproportionate sacrifices from wage labor. Despite their significant difference in method, privatization and corporatism are both responses to an overloaded system of representation; they constitute equally radical departures from the Keynesian welfare-state policies that predominated after World War II.

To elaborate this argument, I first explore the relationship between corporatism and privatization and then offer a case study of the privatization policy of the Thatcher government in Britain. The case study examines the Conservative government's monetarist policy, the scope and rationale for the government's privatization program, and that program's differential consequences for capital and labor.

CORPORATISM AND PRIVATIZATION

Like corporatism, privatization is a strategy for reordering power relations, in particular those between interest groups and the state within complex systems of representation. While corporatism is seen by some as a mode of policy formulation, its more distinctive definition centers on what Philippe Schmitter has termed interest intermediation, referring to the state's role in shaping how associations represent and simultaneously control their members.[7] As Colin Crouch makes clear, "[the notion] . . . at the heart of corporatism is that interest organizations constrain and discipline their own members for the sake of some presumed 'general' interest as well as (or even instead of) representing them."[8] Privatization likewise seeks to compel interest organizations (and their members) to reorder both internal and external power relations. Conventional definitions of privatization ignore its role as a method of controlling interest representation, simply specifying how market discipline is used to shift the balance between the public and private sectors.[9] A more important feature of privatization is its consequences for power relations within and between interest groups in the democratic polity.

Comparing corporatism and privatization as power relations makes their similarities and differences apparent. Power relations in complex systems can be analyzed in terms of the values motivating collective action, the sources of these values, and the modes of control utilized.[10] From this perspective, both corporatism and privatization are strategies involving a state in rationalizing interest representation. Where these strategies differ is in the mechanism of effective control or implementation. Comparison of privatization and corporatism yields four major propositions.

First, as strategies of adaptation to economic decline, both corporatism and privatization promote a type of instrumental value orientation or rationality that enhances the rule of authorities and improves the capacity of capitalism to compete internationally. Corporatism draws upon the formal-legal rationality of organizational authority and appeals to individual self-interest and sentiments of trust and obligation.[11] It legitimatizes and strengthens the authority of leaders through an exchange in which groups are granted advantages and privileges by the state in return for promoting social stability and political authority. For privatization, the rationality of individual self-interest becomes the primary incentive for action, and the clash of self-interest in the market the major mechanism of discipline.

Second, as adjustment strategies, both entail the state acting to overcome economic and political stagnation. Rather than responding to interest-group pressures, these state initiatives attempt to reshape them. State officials seek to limit demands in order to enhance the political system's ability to cope with internal and external challenges.[12]

Third, the major difference between corporatism and pluralism lies in their mode of control. Whereas corporatism relies on organizational, representative, and inclusive processes of control to create a consensus on collective action, privatization turns to the impersonal, depoliticized, and preclusive discipline of the market, structured and regulated by the state.

The choice of control mechanism—representative authority or markets—depends on whether enlarging associational responsibilities or reducing the state's obligations to interest groups increases state power. Corporatism provides a response to the over-politicization of representative democracy arising from the development of functional interest groups capable of disrupting policy. It minimizes groups' potential for disruption by making them participants in the policy process.[13] The development of corporatist systems of private-interest government—self-regulating groups empowered with the public interest—emerges from mutually convenient or "meso-level" adjustments to the structural needs of interest groups and states.[14] In particular, corporatism responds to the failure of functional interests to serve their own or the state's interests in international competitiveness and to the state's need to maintain legitimate authority.[15] Thus, corporatism addresses the problem of demand overload by increasing the responsibilities of key organizational actors for ensuring system order.

The privatization strategy is a reaction to the over-politicization of the system of interest-group representation. With the option for increasing group obligations blocked, it attempts to lower the obligations of the state itself. Initiated by party and state officials, privatization, unlike corporatism, does not depend on "meso-level" agreements in which each party gets what it would not be able to obtain alone, though it does require their acceptance among those groups—firms, trade unions, consumer groups, and the public—which determine the politically acceptable limits of state action. The privatization strategy replaces corporatism's organizational form of effective control with a "commodification" of political and social relationships. By fragmenting interest-group power, forcing groups to compete according to impersonal and diffuse market criteria, and depoliticizing decision making through private ownership, privatization enables state authorities to enhance their power by avoiding or limiting the claims made against them.

Fourth, like corporatism, the privatization strategy benefits capital while disadvantaging labor. Because the power of capital and labor rests on their ability to withdraw from economic undertakings, Offe argues that the characteristics of capital enable it to exercise power even if it is not organized, whereas labor's power depends decisively on its collective organization.[16] The corporatist strategy thus binds organized labor to the state in order to harness its power for disruption. This entails subjecting groups to constitutional procedures and obligations which moderate the type and number of demands and make it more difficult to mobilize resistance.[17] The privatization strategy, however, enhances the power of capital by supplementing its negative potential (for withdrawing investment) with the positive element of increased profit opportunities while simultaneously curbing union power. Privatization undermines union strength by decoupling organized labor's political links to the state as employer and benefactor, making its bargaining position dependent on a firm's profit levels, and by attacking its collective strength through manpower reductions, the use of non-union labor, and the erosion of class solidarity as the basis for collective organization and action. Its aim is greater authority for management in rationalizing production and wage scales.

Thus, privatization does not mark a return to the nineteenth-century night-watchman state and laissez-faire economy, just as corporatism does not signify a return to fascist authoritarianism. Privatization, like corporatism, is a strategy for modifying a system of interest representation that erodes state power. Its ultimate purpose is to limit the type, number, and frequency of inputs that threaten system stability.

To present empirical support for these arguments about privatization, we now turn to a case study of the Thatcher government's privatization policy.

THE THATCHER GOVERNMENT'S PRIVATIZATION PROGRAM

After Margaret Thatcher became leader in 1975, the Conservative party became increasingly committed to breaking the postwar consensus on demand management, welfare services, and public-sector growth. The Thatcher instinct, evidenced in repeated declarations to rid the country of socialism, has been from the start to reorganize the faltering postwar system of collectivist representation, based on functional representation and party competition. In monetarism the Thatcherites found a political theory suitable to their needs. While the monetarist prescription for controlling the money supply gave way to privatization toward the end of Mrs. Thatcher's first term as Prime Minister, Thatcherite policy continued to be founded upon a political theory emphasizing individual self-interest, respect for authority and the state, restraint on the power of labor, and reliance on property and market mechanisms of allocation.

The Political Theory of Monetarism

The policy environment in which monetarism became fashionable was rising inflation and declining competitiveness. Control of inflation came to be seen as the key to reversing Britain's long-term decline. During the 1970s, when inflation became so important, the economy was still growing and unemployment was low by present standards.[18] According to monetarists, it was the pursuit of full employment through public expenditures and excessive wage increases that caused inflation. These practices increased the price of commodities without enhancing their value, reducing productivity and undermining competitiveness. The inflationary process, in turn, destroyed jobs and eroded entrepreneurial incentives.

While Keynesians held that governments could control the level of unemployment by careful use of monetary and fiscal policies, monetarists argued that governments had no such powers. In their view, the minimum level of unemployment was determined by the labor market; efforts to force unemployment below this level only produced inflation. Hence, the monetarists believed that trade unions caused unemployment by pricing people out of jobs.[19] In effect, monetarists attacked the coincidence of rising inflation and rising unemployment that halved Britain's share of world trade between 1955 and 1980.[20] These ideas gained force against the background of the global inflation of the early 1970s that was associated with rising commodity prices and a loss of markets to less developed countries, contributing to the identification of demand management as the source of decline.

Sir Keith Joseph and Margaret Thatcher believed that monetarist economic analysis provided a panacea for Britain's ills because the monetarist political assessment challenged the Keynesian governing formula. Attacking the collectivist power relations which had evolved after World War II, it pointed to how functional representation had suppressed individual initiative and interests. Unions in particular were seen as threats to liberty, because the sharing of public power with private interest groups through social-contract agreements seemed to establish a "corporate state" and displace parliamentary democracy. Ironically, state intervention created a powerful state but weakened its ability to govern in the interests of its citizens, obstructing individual ambitions and wasting resources, it was held. As one monetarist put it:

> A more exact analysis of this [postwar] consensus reveals an (understandable) bias towards agreement with the most powerful institutions in the land—the very groups who, through their ability to acquire and retain power and privilege, influence the "democratic" process, waste the nations' assets and yet receive continued accommodation from the public purse at the cost of the majority of responsible citizens.[21]

Past Tory acceptance of these concessions to power-grabbing interest groups was deemed to have arrested the entrepreneurial spirit and contributed to economic decline. By making concessions to unions, the Tories were put on the defensive, always working from a weak position. As William Keegan characterized this viewpoint, "by searching for the middle ground, the Tories were allowing the rules to be dictated by their opponents."[22] In consequence, the state-managed, welfare-oriented economy was seen as the source of Britain's most notable ailments—a bloated public sector, wasted subsidies for nationalized industry, and the failing competitiveness of private firms.

Monetarist political analysis prescribed a restoration of individual initiative and responsibility through a radical break with the postwar consensus and the Disraelian "middle way" tradition of Ted Heath, Francis Pym, and others who have argued for consent, compromise, and balance. Monetarist political theory sought to strengthen the market and Parliament, while enhancing the authority of property owners and social institutions generally. Taking a lead from Friedrich von Hayek and Joseph Schumpeter, its thesis that group power breeds economic and political stagnation ultimately gained the status of a public philosophy.

Significantly, monetarist political theory prescribed an activist state that shapes groups' ability to make demands on public authorities. Not simply proposing to restructure government, monetarism called for the state to determine the balance of group power by refashioning the environment that forms individual and collective motives for action. As Sir Geoffrey Howe asserted, "We place more emphasis on motivating and persuading people than in fiddling with the structure of institutions."[23]

To achieve this readjustment of group and individual behavior, a strong state must foster bourgeois values of individual rationality, economic aspiration, and material accomplishment. To eradicate the parasitical grasp of interest groups, establish a market order that will enrich society, and liberate individuals from bureaucratic constraint requires a state that consciously reconstitutes the social basis of power relations.[24] In his defense of monetarist politics, Rodney Atkinson argued that the state's task is to shape an environment that fosters innovations: "The market philosophy and the reduction of the state to its vital role as the controller of the strong, the protector of the weak, and the dissipator of power open up new and endless possibilities for individual and institutional initiatives."[25]

In short, the political theory of monetarism for Thatcherites prefigured a state-adjustment strategy. This doctrine posited that a strong, directive state can liberate rational self-interest and energize individual motivation by breaking up a stagnant, group-bound environment. If monetarism first captured attention as an enonomic policy that purported to control inflation, its more lasting contribution has been as a political vision that seeks to reconstitute state and managerial authority by restructuring the environment of politics itself.

Privatization: Monetarism plus Markets

The Conservative administration gradually adopted privatization as the central element of its strategy for restructuring the collectivist state. The privatization program grew in comprehensiveness and, at a time when monetarist economics proved ineffective and unpopular, became the symbol of the Conservatives' radical approach to the problem of governability. While retaining the monetarist commitment to individual self-interest, a strong state, and diminished union power, privatization replaced monetarism's narrow focus on control of the money supply with a broader concern for private ownership and competition, making it an effective instrument for dismantling the system of functional representation that had produced a stagnant bureaucratic order. As a strategy of adjustment to political disorder and industrial decline, then, privatization constitutes a type of state control of interest-group action equivalent to corporatism. It combines a state patterning of interest representation and social control through market mechanisms and discipline.

The comprehensiveness of the privatization program grew as leading Thatcherites adapted monetarism to developing political and policy imperatives. An important policy statement, *The Right Approach to the Economy*, published in 1977, contained a vague reference to privatization: "The long-term aim must be to reduce the preponderance of state ownership and to widen the base of ownership in our community. Ownership by the state is not the same as ownership by the people."[26] A Conservative party study group proposed a schedule for denationalization in 1978, and the party's election manifesto made few but specific commitments.[27] The election manifesto promised to deregulate busing and to privatize recently nationalized aerospace and shipbuilding firms, the National Freight Corporation and National Enterprise Board shareholdings.[28] At the time of the 1979 election, then, there was no hint of the political potential of privatization or of its future role in the Conservative government's program.

After its election, the Thatcher government first pursued a limited effort to roll back the state, even though this first stage itself exceeded manifesto promises. In the 1979–80 period, the government sold shares in British Petroleum, International Computers Ltd. (ICL), and the Suez Finance Company. Not until the 1980–81 fiscal year did the government sell a majority of its holdings in British Aerospace, and not until the 1981–82 fiscal year did it sell the National Freight Corporation to a consortium of employees as promised in its election manifesto, although in 1980 it also unloaded National Enterprise Board holdings like Ferranti and Fairey. British Shipbuilders remains to be privatized despite its inclusion in the 1979 manifesto. At the prodding of Sir Keith Joseph, the scope of privatization was broadened after 1979, leading to the historically unprecedented selling of part or all the government's interests in peripheral though sizable sections of the public sector. This stage involved the privatization of Britoil in 1982, Cable and Wireless in 1981, Amersham International in 1982, British Sugar in 1981, Associated British Ports in 1983, as well as the sales mentioned above.

Yet, from the start the Thatcher program found its aim of extending property ownership most achievable in the area of housing. By increasing council or public housing rents while providing tax relief on mortgage interest payments, the government has favored the growth of private-sector housing and attempted to reduce the public sector to a safety net. Most significantly, the 1980 Housing Act provided council tenants with an incentive to purchase their homes by establishing the right to buy and by making flats available at substantial discounts. As a result, the proportion of owner-occupied households rose from about 54 to 61 percent between the 1979 and 1983 elections as over 800,000 houses and flats were sold.[29] This represents a remarkable redistribution of capital from public to individual ownership.

After 1981 a second phase of privatization took shape, gaining momentum in the second and third terms of the Thatcher government. This involved broadening the program to a wider range of public-sector activities and firms. New initiatives were taken to sell off major public corporations, including British Telecom (1984), British Gas (1986), British Airways (1987), Enterprise Oil (1984), Royal Ordnance Factories (1987), Sea Link (1984), British Airports Authorities (1987), National Bus Company (1986), Water Authorities (1990), Electricity (1990) and parts of British Shipbuilders (1987), British Steel (1988), British Petroleum (1987), and British Leyland (1987). By early 1987, the government had raised over £11 billion from the sale of assets, which reduced the public sector by one-third since 1979 and transferred 600,000 workers to the private sector.[30]

The government used methods besides denationalization and liberalization to introduce private enterprise and competition to the provision of public services. As illustrated by a 1985 White Paper proposing the introduction of private pension schemes alongside a more limited state scheme, the private provision of some welfare and other public services became another aspect of privatization. This joined with the partial or complete substituting of user charges for tax financing, contracting out public-sector provision to private firms, and adopting private-sector decision-making practices in the public sector.[31] From a limited commitment to denationalization, the Thatcher government developed the idea of extending market processes and discipline into a major, systematic, and extensive program for realizing the monetarist ends of readjusting state-society relations and thus reshaping the power relations of civil society.[32]

As a form of state reorganization of interest-group behavior, privatization's justification relies on the purported advantages of market mechanisms of control. According to David Steel and David Heald's analysis of Conservative leaders' statements, four main arguments have been advanced in favor of privatization: that it will enhance economic freedom, increase efficiency, ease the problem of public-sector pay, and reduce public-sector borrowing.[33] Each justification is directed toward rolling back the power of organized labor and other interest groups and shows how the strategy involved changing the way civil society motivated associational interests and power.

First, freedom is increased because privatization prevents public enterprises with statutory monopoly powers and monopoly market strength from competing unfairly and thereby limiting consumers' freedom of choice.[34] Second, efficiency is enhanced because the private-sector firms have to confront the discipline of capital and product markets. Public-sector firms are insulated from these market forces and instead use political pressures, leading to inefficient allocation of resources.[35] Third, privatization ends unions' ability to hold the nation "by the jugular vein," since private-sector workers know that excessive pay agreements will lead to bankruptcy. Further, liberalization or deregulation prevents firms from passing on the cost of pay raises to consumers.[36] Finally, privatization contributes to restraining public-sector borrowing and slowing monetary growth.[37] The sale of assets directly contributes to the Exchequer, since the creation of hybrid companies (newly privatized firms in which the government retains a minority stake) permits the government to exclude the firm's external borrowing from the Public Sector Borrowing Requirement (PSBR), while imposing user charges on public services and contracting out cut public expenditure and reduce pressure on the PSBR.

The aim of privatization, then, is to replace political and bureaucratic pressures with an alternative mode of control: the commodification of social relations and the discipline of the market. Michael Beesley and Stephen Littlechild, leading academic proponents of privatization, argue: "The underlying idea is to improve industry performance by increasing the role of market forces."[38] While other factors like greater competition are necessary, the change in ownership is fundamental, they argue, because it changes the motivations of managers and employees to the benefit of consumers. Motivated by profit-seeking, privately owned firms are responsive to consumer choices.[39] Ultimately, privatization frees decision making from political influences, making increased competition possible.[40]

A policy of private ownership consequently became the main solution to the government's conundrum over how to manage the nationalized industries. Previous efforts to overcome the poor performance of nationalized industries, set out in White Papers in 1961, 1967, and 1978, had failed. The Thatcher government, being generally unsympathetic to the nationalized industries, initially chose to introduce management discipline by limiting their borrowing power, setting clear financial targets, and then assuming a hands-off relationship. But in the face of a recession, higher than expected public-sector borrowing needs were stimulated, and conflict emerged between industry ministers and industry chairmen—over price increases, the lack of investment, large deficits in some industries, and demands for greater freedom to borrow outside Treasury control.[41]

The government has also attempted to broaden share ownership and to foster a people's capital market in order to encourage positive attitudes about capitalism and strengthen the authority of management. The aim of these initiatives in newly privatized firms is to end traditional class conflict between workers and management by creating a synergetic harmony between management and workers. This required reversing a trend of declining individual and rising institutional share ownership. In 1984 only 7 percent of adults in the United Kingdom owned shares, compared to 25 percent in the United States, and the proportion of U.K. company shares owned directly by individuals fell from 54 percent in 1963 to 37 percent in 1975, and then to 28 percent in 1981.[42] Observing that "a new army of capitalists" was formed by the British Telecom sale in 1984, John Moore, the government minister coordinating privatization until 1986, believes that new attitudes are being created. He writes: "When employees commit their capital as well as their labour to the company for which they work, it becomes apparent that they and the management have a common interest in the success of the company."[43] By spreading ownership via the public sale of assets and employee-share schemes, the government, he says, intends to remove those illusory barriers between "them" and "us."

The idea of a people's capitalism is reflected in Margaret Thatcher's own rhetoric. She has said: "Don't talk to me about 'them' and 'us' in a company. . . . You're all 'we' in a company. You survive as the company survives, prosper as the company prospers—everyone together. The future lies in cooperation and not confrontation."[44] As Marxist academic Stuart Hall points out, in Margaret Thatcher's vision class conflict is ideologically displaced by a populist unity. Referring to her statement above, he explains:

> This [formulation] displaces an existing structure of oppositions—"them" versus "us." It sets in its place an alternative set of equivalents: "them and us equals we." Then it positions we "the people"—in a particular relation to capital: behind it, dominated by its imperatives (profitability, accumulation): yet at the same time yoked to it, identified with it.[45]

In short, privatization realizes Thatcher's instinctive readjustment of ideology, eliminating those interests which might impede capitalist rationality.

In addition to the ideological and cultural reasons favoring privatization, Margaret Thatcher, Sir Geoffrey Howe, and Sir Keith Joseph recognized the need for a policy initiative that would revitalize their free-market ideology when monetarism lost its appeal due to its excessively deflationary consequences during 1981. Not only did privatization respond to the party's natural constituency by increasing profit opportunities, it also provided a new direction in the face of the rapid contraction of industrial production and the dramatic increase in unemployment.[46] Approaching the 1982 budget, the Thatcher government was unpopular among its traditional supporters and the public at large. Yet, because they were unwilling to waver from Thatcher's vision of a society based on sound money, family virtues, and private enterprises,[47] the ministers on the Economic Strategy Committee turned to privatization and anti-union legislation in the hope of refocusing public attention on the future.[48] More than anything else, the political limits of monetarism, when faced with rising unemployment and increased government spending, turned the Thatcherites toward privatization.[49]

Finally, privatization helps to reduce the government's fiscal burden, assisting it in containing the PSBR. Although Samuel Brittan questions those who argue that denationalization was motivated only by a desire to raise funds,[50] central to Thatcherism is the idea that reduced public spending would permit tax cuts, allow interest rates to fall, help control inflation, and put an end to the "socialist ratchet effect."[51] Consequently, the Thatcher administration's privatization strategy became part of its effort to lower public-sector borrowing.[52] The decision in autumn 1981 to raise public spending by £5 billion more than originally planned made it imperative to challenge the power of entrenched functional interests to continue to gain state subsidies. What had necessitated the increased outlay, according to Peter Riddell, was the "inescapable upward pressures on expenditure exerted by the recession (increasing the deficits of nationalized industries and expenditure on unemployment)...[not] a successful campaign by the 'wets.' "[53] The sale of public assets would end obligations to nationalized industries and add resources to the Treasury. Other forms of privatization would also reduce the government's financial burden. Consequently, as it became clear that the recession was making it harder to cut public expenditures, the government gave greater impetus to the privatization strategy.[54]

Politically, privatization is a way of disaggregating the power of privileged groups and forcing market relations to act more fully as the allocative mechanism of society. Privatization, paraphrasing Samuel Brittan, added markets to monetarism.[55] The early focus on the control of money supply ignored mechanisms by which political influence and social rigidities could be dislodged. The privatization strategy proposes a widening of the market sector as a means of reorganizing incentives and discipline. By creating flexibility and rewarding individual self-interest, the greater use of market would relieve fiscal pressures on the government, force businesses to operate more efficiently, and enhance consumer sovereignty. As Sir Geoffrey Howe argued in a lecture in July 1982 setting out future government strategy, "the reform of the welfare state would be required on public spending grounds alone but also was required to devolve power and responsibility to the lowest tier in the delivery chain and would involve extending the use of charges and increases in private sector involvement."[56] In short, privatization is a mechanism for curtailing excessive demands on government by compelling interests to be expressed in commodity terms and disciplined by market forces.

Differential Consequences of Privatization

The differential effect of privatization on capital and labor is evident in the turnaround of public firms as they were readied for public sale. The nationalized industries during the 1970s performed below the level of private-sector firms, yet the preparation for privatization reduced losses and in some cases produced profits. During the 1970s and early 1980s the rate of return of the private industrial and commercial sector fell to a low 3 to 4 percent; yet the state sector did even worse, with a zero rate of return.[57] Now only coal and rail industries incur losses.

While privatization expands profit opportunities as well as profits, it also replaces (often ineffective) political control of public-sector unions with control by the market. The firm's product markets and the factors affecting productivity rather than the political leverage of unions determine the outcome of collective bargaining. As firms are prepared for sale to the private sector, they shed labor and reduce costs. Employment levels, for example, at British Steel, British Leyland, British Airways, and Rolls-Royce fell by 20 to 40 percent.[58] Moreover, the contracting out of ancillary operations like cleaning and maintenance in the public services directly attacks the power of unions by shifting work to non-unionized workers.

While the disposal of assets benefits the traditional large stockholders, such as pension funds and insurance companies, individual stock ownership provides a material incentive for building employee attachment to the firm which erodes class solidarity. The move toward a "share-owning democracy" or "people's capitalism," much publicized by the government, has been significant. Experience with the earlier disposal of British Aerospace assets revealed, for example, that the number of shareholders fell from 157,000 on flotation to 27,200 within a year, and the number owning 100 shares slumped from 30,000 to less than 3,300. By 1987, however, the number of shareholders in Britain had trebled to about 8.5 million, with British Telecom attracting 2 million private investors, 1 million of whom were first-time investors.[59] Furthermore, over 80 percent of the employees in newly privatized firms purchased shares, often in defiance of their union's recommendation.[60] Also notable has been the spread of property ownership through the sale of council-owned housing.

In most cases the sale of assets has been preceded or followed by a measure of deregulation, strengthening pressures on the unions. In the case of British Telecom, the limited competition provided by Mercury weakens union power by making Telecom's hold on its product markets uncertain, heightening the need to increase productivity and rationalize working practices. These pressures were evident in the 1987 British Telecom strike in which worker-shareholders finally conceded significant changes in working practices and increased redundancies in return for higher pay. And on long-distance coach routes, competition led to new firms that were not unionized and to lower fares, which forced British Rail to offer competitive prices and to reduce its workforce.

Finally, the strategy of contracting out particular public-sector services such as laundry or cleaning needs to private firms has aroused opposition from public-sector unions like the National Union of Public Employees, who see this practice as an attempt to circumvent their power. To defend their members, these unions have cited the failure of such firms to provide adequate substitute services at less cost, as well as the negative impact of contracting out on wage levels, working conditions, and employment. Although it provides profit opportunities, it is not clear that contracting out provides greater efficiency, as claimed by the government.[61]

This brief survey suggests that privatization differentially benefits capital and labor, often by reinforcing independent trends toward raising productivity via manpower reductions and more effective managerial strategies. Opening up new profit opportunities benefits business, while market processes attack workers' bargaining strength and enlist their support for the fate of the enterprises in which they work. The overall result is a diminution of the bargaining and organizational power of trade unions.

CONCLUSION

Privatization's emergence as the central adjustment strategy of the Thatcher government resulted from the failure of monetarism to achieve a satisfactory break with social democracy. This new strategy advances the monetarist political project of using commodity-exchange relations as a generalized mechanism of control. If Keynesian social democracy had improved the material well-being of society and sustained the authorities' ability to direct society, interest in monetarism and privatization would not have arisen. Privatization, in short, represents a solution to the problem of governability by consciously aiming to use property ownership and competitive markets to modify the power relations between interest groups (capital and labor) and between interest groups and the state.

By viewing privatization as a response to a crisis of governmental authority brought on by economic decline, one can better understand how the reshaping of state-society relations is occurring without mass political pressures from below or overt initiatives from a capitalist ruling class. The effort to recast domestic power relations in order to check excessive group demands required that politicians acquire new means of establishing control. The choice of the privatization strategy represents an effort by political elites to limit the scope of and disaggregate the concentration of interest representation. This strategy of reorganizing relationships between interest groups and the state contrasts dramatically with the processes of mass protest and group pressure that contributed to the development of the Keynesian welfare state.

Thus, privatization constitutes a functional equivalent of corporatism. Both are strategies for resolving a political crisis by reordering the system of interest-group representation. While corporatism draws on the rationality of organizational authority and privatization on the rationality of the market, they promote the same value orientation—instrumental rationality. Both strategies use the state to impose a structure of interest-group representation that will realize the instrumental values necessary for overall system integration. They differ, significantly, in the mode of control—formal-legal authority versus commodity-exchange transactions—used to restore system stability. Finally, corporatism and privatization affect the power of capital and labor differently.

Yet, privatization challenges corporatist theory, calling for its revision. It not only implies that the range of adjustment options open to the capitalist state is wider than corporatist theory acknowledges, but raises questions about the meaning of democracy in advanced industrial states. More fundamentally, this analysis of privatization shows that understanding the state's role in determining interest-group relations requires an understanding of the motives and processes shaping the internal power relations of interest groups, and how they in turn affect the interaction among such organizations. Ultimately, these questions demand that analysts move beyond corporatism to develop a more comprehensive theory of the power relations in complex representative systems.

NOTES

1. I am grateful to Gerard Braunthal and Richard Foglesong for comments on earlier versions of this chapter and to a Taft Grant from the University of Cincinnati for financial support. An earlier version was presented at the annual meeting of the Midwest Political Science Association, Chicago, April 1988.

2. See Samuel H. Beer, *Britain Against Itself* (New York: W. W. Norton, 1982); Robert A. Dahl, *Dilemmas of Pluralist Democracy* (New Haven: Yale University Press, 1982); and Mancur Olson, *The Rise and Decline of Nations* (New Haven: Yale University Press, 1982).

3. See Philippe C. Schmitter and Gerhard Lehmbruch, eds., *Trends Toward Corporatist Intermediation* (Beverly Hills: Sage, 1979); Suzanne Berger, ed., *Organizing Interests in Western Europe: Pluralism, Corporatism, and the Transformation of Pol-*

itics (New York: Cambridge University Press, 1981); J. H. Goldthorpe, ed., *Order and Conflict in Contemporary Capitalism* (Oxford: Clarendon Press, 1984); Wyn Grant, ed., *The Political Economy of Corporatism* (London: Macmillan, 1985); Alan Cawson, ed., *Organized Interests and the State: Studies in Meso-corporatism* (London: Sage, 1985); Wolfgang Streeck and Philippe C. Schmitter, eds., *Private Interest Government: Beyond Market and State* (London: Sage, 1985); and Alan Cawson, *Corporatism and Political Theory* (Oxford: Basil Blackwell, 1986).

4. The literature on this aspect of privatization is vast. See, for example, Michael Beesley and Stephen Littlechild, "Privatization: Principles, Problems, and Priorities," *Lloyds Bank Review* 149 (July 1983): 1–20; J. A. Kay and D. J. Thompson, "Privatization: A Policy in Search of a Rationale," *Economics Journal* 96 (March 1986): 18–32; David Steel and David Heald, "The Privatization of Public Enterprises, 1979–83," in Peter Jackson, ed., *Implementating Government Initiatives: The Thatcher Administration 1979–1983* (London: Royal Institute of Public Administration, 1985), pp. 69–91.

5. David Heald, *Public Expenditure: Its Defence and Reform* (Oxford: Martin Robertson, 1983), chap. 13; Stephen Young, "The Nature of Privatisation in Britain, 1979–85," *West European Politics* 9 (April 1986): 235–52.

6. Labour Research Department, *Privatisation: Who Loses, Who Profits* (London: LRD, 1983); Patrick Dunleavy, "Explaining the Privatization Boom: Public Choice Versus Radical Approaches," *Public Administration* 64 (Spring 1986): 13–34.

7. Philippe C. Schmitter, "Interest Intermediation and Regime Governability in Contemporary Western Europe and North America," in Berger, *Organizing Interests*, pp. 287–98.

8. Colin Crouch, "Pluralism and the New Corporatism: A Rejoinder," *Political Studies* 31 (September 1983): 452–60.

9. Heald, *Public Expenditure*, chap. 13; Young, "Nature of Privatization," pp. 235–52.

10. This framework is elaborated in Joel D. Wolfe, "Class Formation and Democracy: The Decline of Working-Class Power in Britain," *West European Politics* 9 (July 1986): 343–61; and Joel D. Wolfe, "Varieties of Participatory Democracy and Democratic Theory," *Political Science Reviewer* 16 (Fall 1986): 1–38.

11. Schmitter, "Interest Intermediation," pp. 291–93; Claus Offe, "Corporatism as Macro-structuring," *Telos* 65 (Fall 1985): 101–3.

12. Claus Offe, "The Attribution of Public Status to Interest Groups: Observations on the West German Case," in Berger, *Organizing Interests*, pp. 128–33.

13. Ibid., p. 131.

14. Philippe C. Schmitter, "Neocorporatism and the State," in Grant, *Political Economy of Corporatism*, pp. 38–40. For important discussions of meso-corporatism, see Wolfgang Streeck and Philippe C. Schmitter, "Community, Market, State—and Associations?: The Prospective Contribution of Interest Governance to Social Order," in Streeck and Schmitter, *Private Interest Government*, pp. 1–29; and Cawson, *Corporatism and Political Theory*, chap. 6.

15. Schmitter, "Neocorporatism," p. 42.

16. Offe, "Attribution of Public Status," p. 147. Also see Claus Offe and Helmut Wiesenthal, "The Two Logics of Collective Action—Theoretical Notes on Social Class and the Political Form of Interest Representation," *Political Power and Social Theory* 1 (1979): 67–115.

17. Offe, "Attribution of Public Status," pp. 148–50.

18. Francis Pym, *The Politics of Consent* (London: Hamish Hamilton, 1984), p. 138.

19. William Keegan, *Mrs. Thatcher's Economic Experiment* (Harmondsworth: Penguin, 1984), p. 42.

20. Rt. Hon. Sir Geoffrey Howe, *Conservatism in the Eighties* (London: Conservative Political Centre, 1983), p. 6.

21. Rodney Atkinson, *The Moral Basis of Monetarism* (Tyne and Wear: Compuprint Publishing, 1984), p. 8.

22. Keegan, *Mrs. Thatcher's Economic Experiment*, p. 84.

23. Howe, *Conservatism*, p. 5.

24. Andrew Gamble, "Smashing the State: Thatcher's Radical Crusade," *Marxism Today* (June 1985): 22–24.

25. Atkinson, *Moral Basis of Monetarism*, p. 18.

26. Cited in Peter Riddell, *The Thatcher Government* (Oxford: Martin Robertson, 1983), p. 35.

27. Keegan, *Mrs. Thatcher's Economic Experiment*, p. 127.

28. Cited in Jock Bruce-Gardyne, *Mrs. Thatcher's First Administration: The Prophets Confounded* (London: Macmillan, 1984), p. 80.

29. Riddell, *Thatcher Government*, pp. 154–55.

30. Guy de Jonquieres, "Privatisation: Irreversible, Warts and All," *Financial Times*, March 25, 1987, p. 18.

31. David Steel and David Heald, "The New Agenda," in David Steel and David Heald, eds., *Privatizing Public Enterprises* (London: Royal Institute of Public Administration, 1984), p. 13; Young, "Nature of Privatization," pp. 238–44.

32. Young, "Nature of Privatization," pp. 246, 247; Sue Hastings, "Privatisation, 1979–82," in Sue Hastings and Hugo Levie, eds., *Privatisation?* (Nottingham: Spokesman, 1983), pp. 16–45.

33. David Steel and David Heald, "Privatising Public Enterprise: An Analysis of the Government's Case," *Political Quarterly* 53 (April-June 1982): 333–49. Cp. Julian LeGrand and Ray Robinson, eds., *Privatisation and the Welfare State* (London: George Allen and Unwin, 1984).

34. Steel and Heald, "Privatising Public Enterprise," p. 337.

35. Ibid., pp. 339–40.

36. Ibid., p. 341.

37. Ibid., p. 342.

38. Beesley and Littlechild, "Privatisation," p. 1.

39. Ibid., p. 4.

40. Samuel Brittan, "The Politics and Economics of Privatisation," *Political Quarterly* 55 (April-June 1984): 120.

41. Riddell, *Thatcher Government*, p. 171.

42. John Moore, MP, "A People's Capital Market," speech given on December 5, 1984, para. 7; "Wider Share Ownership," *Economic Progress Report* 181 (November-December 1985): 1–2.

43. Moore, "People's Capital Market," para. 4.

44. Stuart Hall, "The Great Moving Right Show," in Stuart Hall and Martin Jacques, eds., *The Politics of Thatcherism* (London: Lawrence and Wishart, 1983), p. 31.

45. Ibid.

46. Brittan, "Politics and Economics of Privatisation," pp. 111–12.

47. Riddell, *Thatcher Government*, p. 231.

48. Keegan, *Mrs. Thatcher's Economic Experiment*, pp. 73–74.

49. Michael Bleaney, "Conservative Economic Strategy," in Hall and Jacques, *Politics of Thatcherism*, p. 145.

50. Brittan, "Politics and Economics of Privatisation," p. 113.

51. Martin Holmes, *The First Thatcher Government, 1979–1983: Contemporary Conservatism and Economic Change* (Brighton: Wheatsheaf Books, 1985), pp. 40, 105.

52. Riddell, *Thatcher Government*, p. 232.

53. Ibid., p. 46.

54. Ibid., p. 138.

55. Brittan, "Politics and Economics of Privatisation," p. 121.

56. Riddell, *Thatcher Government*, p. 139; Howe, *Conservatism*, pp. 10, 21–23.

57. Brittan, "Politics and Economics of Privatisation," p. 116.

58. Ibid., p. 120.

59. Peter Riddell, "An Instinct, Not an Ideology," *Financial Times*, March 23, 1987, p. 6.

60. H. M. Treasury, *Privatisation in the UK: Background Briefing* (London: H. M. Treasury, 1986), p. 18/1, p. 3.

61. Michael O'Higgins, "Privatisation and Social Security," *Political Quarterly* 55 (April-June 1984): 129–39.

3

The Politics of Industrial Policy in the United States

Richard E. Foglesong

Over the past decade, the U.S. economy has suffered from trade imbalances, lost international competitiveness, declining rates of productivity growth, and massive job losses in basic manufacturing sectors.[1] These problems have been interpreted as signs of the "deindustrialization" of the American economy, a term referring to the increasing technological obsolescence of basic manufacturing industries and their inability to compete successfully in world markets. The proposals put forward in response have ranged from expanding science education, to promoting consumer savings, to creating industrial planning like Japan's.

Underlying these proposals is a fundamental debate about government's role in the nation's industrial evolution. Is government responsible for the decline of basic manufacturing? Should government intervention be contracted or expanded? More to the point, should government take a supportive role or a directive role in the economy? Should there be more partnership among business, government, and labor? Should there be explicit quid pro quo agreements whereby firms that receive government assistance provide guaranteed returns to the public? These questions are at the heart of the "industrial policy debate," a debate taking place in policy think tanks, interest groups, and academic circles, and among forward-looking politicians across the country. Within the realm of presidential politics, this debate has been transformed into the "competitiveness debate," although the issues are much the same.

Disregarding specifics, two broad strategies have been put forward for adjusting to the decline of basic manufacturing and rekindling America's lost international competitiveness. The "privatization strategy" entails increased reliance on market processes through tax cuts, deregulation of business, reduced social spending, and, where relevant, selling off public enterprises. In contrast, the "industrial policy strategy" involves a directive governmental role in channeling investment to those industries and product areas thought to represent our economic future. This strategy can also be termed a state-planning approach, since it involves using political, that is, nonmarket, decision processes to decide on appropriate investments. It can further be termed a "corporatist" strategy, since most industrial policy proposals call for consensus-seeking forums in which representatives of business, labor, and government would participate in making industrial policy choices.

This chapter examines efforts to formulate an industrial policy in the United States, focusing particularly on the 1983–84 period, when industrial policy figured briefly on the Democratic party agenda. Besides being interesting in their own right, these proposals are interesting for what they reveal about the origins and potential of corporatist-style arrangements. For industrial policy proposals present a paradox. On the one hand, they are exercises in system-maintaining reform: they represent attempts to rejuvenate a faltering American capitalism. On the other, American capitalists by and large remain wedded to the alternative privatization strategy. The impetus and political support for an industrial policy have come from policy intellectuals with ambiguous partisan and class affiliations, liberal Democratic politicians from declining Rustbelt regions, and organized labor. In the congressional hearings on industrial policy examined below, one sees these actors seeking to convince businessmen that an industrial policy would be in their interest as well as the nation's. Thus, the politics of industrial policy challenge instrumentalist Marxist and elite-theory views that system-maintaining reforms begin in corporate suites.[2] Industrial policy politics also call into question the application to the United States of theories of corporatism, drawn from the European experience, that trace corporatism's originating impulse to business.[3]

To make sense of the paradoxical pattern of opposition and support for industrial policy proposals, I begin by examining congressional testimony on industrial policy in Part I. This provides a partial answer to the question of who is attempting to get what and how in the effort to formulate an industrial policy. Yet I want to go beyond this standard political science question, for this chapter shows how those who advocate and those who benefit from system-maintaining reforms are not always the same. Thus, I seek to explain the pattern of opposition and support for industrial policy in Part II. There I discuss the structural forces and constraints that have led policy intellectuals, liberal Democratic congressmen, and organized labor to promote industrial policy proposals against the opposition of most of the business community.

I. INDUSTRIAL POLICY POLITICS

The 1983–84 hearings on industrial policy before the Economic Stabilization Subcommittee of the House Banking, Finance, and Urban Affairs Committee are an excellent source on the politics of industrial policy. In all, over 120 individuals representing more than 35 organizations (exluding business corporations) testified.[4] Moreover, in the colloquy between congressmen and committee witnesses, the hearings provide revealing glimpses of the relationships between private interests and public policies, society and the state. Further, the Economic Stabilization Subcommittee is an important forum for the development of an economic adjustment strategy. Besides conducting these hearings, it was responsible for drafting the Chrylser and New York City loan guarantees—important forerunners of an industrial policy since they entailed agreements by loan recipients on necessary restructurings.

Business Opposition to Planning Approaches

There are exceptions to the pattern of business opposition to a state-interventionist industrial strategy. Investment banker Felix Rohatyn has been conspicuous in advocating a public development bank—probably the most "radical" stance on this issue taken by a major American businessman. Yet he wants a bank that is removed from political pressures and controlled by persons like himself, prompting criticism that his aim is to finance corporate bailouts with public tax dollars.[5] Chrysler chairman Lee Iacocca favors institutionalizing a system to provide the kind of governmental assistance given to Chrysler. Indeed, support for a planning and public banking apparatus like Japan's Ministry of International Trade and Industry (MITI) appears to be official Chrysler policy.[6] Among committee witnesses, Westinghouse chief executive officer Douglas Danforth called for government aid to specific industries, coordinating government assistance to achieve overall objectives, and requiring recipients to demonstrate how such assistance would benefit the public.[7] Yet Danforth spoke as a member of a labor-business organization, the Labor-Industry Coalition for International Trade (LICIT). While acknowledging these exceptions—and more could be cited—the facts do not support an assertion that business, or even big business, is promoting an activist industrial policy. Business opinion may yet move in this direction, but that seems unlikely to happen soon.

A good example is the statement of the subcommittee's lead witness, Robert Anderson, CEO of Rockwell International and a representative of the Business-Higher Education Forum. The latter organization, an offshoot of the American

Council of Education, was asked by President Reagan in 1982 to examine ways to improve the nation's economic competitiveness. Speaking for the forum, Mr. Anderson was emphatic about maintaining our "historic free market traditions."[8] Among the forum's recommendations were lowering capital gains taxes, relaxing antitrust constraints, and reducing the antibusiness stance of regulatory agencies through "greater interaction among interested parties early in the process"—all elements of the privatization strategy.[9]

Essentially the same strategy was defended by other business spokesmen, whether from conservative or liberal business organizations or from basic manufacturing or high-tech industries. Not surprisingly, the conservative National Association of Manufacturers (NAM) stated firm opposition to an activist industrial policy. Jerry Jasinowski, NAM's chief economist, recommended instead a "positive adjustment policy" aimed at improving market efficiency.[10] As a key element of this policy, he called for measures to encourage capital formation and reduce business's regulatory burden. Yet the "liberal" Committee for Economic Development (CED), which purportedly speaks for big business more than does NAM,[11] expressed a similar view. Testifying for the CED was J. Paul Lyet, former chairman of Sperry Corporation and head of the CED's Subcommittee on Industrial Strategy and Trade. He testified that the CED was moving toward recommending an "industrial strategy" but not an "industrial policy." The difference, he said, was that the CED opposes further government intervention, favoring instead a "greater reliance on the market system as a mechanism for adjustment to economic change." Interestingly, he observed that improving American productivity might require modifying the "consumption bias" of current policies. Although this would generate "enormous" political problems, it should not be construed as government intervention, he maintained.[12]

A similar perspective was presented by a spokesman from the machine tool industry, an older industry suffering from intense Japanese competition. William R. Jahnke said that his industry organization "did not endorse an activist industrial policy that would mimic the Japanese model." Government's role was to maintain the "macro-economic environment," leaving industrial adaptation to the "manager at the helm of his or her firm or the worker on the production line."[13] Yet, in the interest of "national security," he called for import quotas on Japanese machine tools. From the quintessentially high-tech semiconductor industry came a similar view. George Scalise, speaking for the Semiconductor Industry Association, expressed opposition to the kind of industrial targeting practiced by Japan. Any success of that strategy was because Japan had "American successes as a tail light to follow." Without the guidance of a nation "further down the road of economic development," a free-market economy is "far more likely to guide this country to the best solutions than is a government-led planning effort," he averred. Yet Scalise wanted the U.S. government to encourage nations such as Japan and France to open their markets to U.S. firms and play by free-market rules. He also sought more favorable treatment of capital gains in order to increase savings and investment.[14]

Business support for free markets should not be taken too literally, though. Some expressions of faith in the market system seem to be offered ritualistically, as code expressions for a kind of business patriotism, rather than as considered judgments. This is evident in the broad—or loose—definition of "free market" in some business statements. Robert Anderson was emphatic in opposing government planning. Yet, as Congressman Sander Levin (D-Mich.) noted during questioning, Anderson wanted government to develop a "comprehensive, coherent, long-term approach" to maintaining national competitiveness.[15] Saying that he favored a system like Japan's, Anderson described their system as one in which they "turn loose their industry and support them with the proper laws and regulations, and certainly the proper financing so that the industry can go out and do the job."[16] (He made no reference to MITI's role in Japan's industrial development.)

Sheldon Weinig, CEO of Materials Research Corporation and a representative of the American Business Conference, an organization of mid-size corporations with high growth rates, touted his company as the first U.S. firm to receive a plant construction loan from the Japan Development Bank. As committee chairman John LaFalce (D-N.Y.) noted during questioning, however, Weinig opposed a national development bank in the United States. Weinig responded that he opposed a public bank if it limited competitiveness—yet he seemed unaware of any contradiction between securing a Japanese government loan and criticizing government efforts to "pick winners." CED spokesman Paul Lyet also exhibited a degree of schizophrenia on the issue of government intervention. While asserting that some of our economic problems were attributable to government interference and that government's role in the economy should be reduced, he called for subsidizing exports through the Eximbank as a temporary measure.[17] These and related statements raise questions about what business leaders mean by "free-market" arrangements and whether they really understand how greater reliance on markets would affect their interests and the nation's interests.

Finally, business testimony does not evince much overt interest in organizing a consensual business hegemony. I refer to a hegemony in which business takes account of and seeks to guarantee the material interests of other groups in society, and in which nonbusiness groups in turn accept the interests of business as the general interests of society, as the motor-force for a universal expansion.[18] Robert Anderson, of Rockwell and the Business-Higher Education Forum, came closest to presenting a hegemonic argument. In calling for reduced taxes and deregulation of business, he opined that further loss of economic competitiveness would generate public service cutbacks in areas such as education and public safety, reduced support for the elderly, and fewer opportunities for the disadvantaged and minorities.[19] Yet, in defending the privatization strategy, he neglected what several congressmen termed the employment side of the issue—how to create equivalent jobs for displaced manufacturing workers. Another representative of the Business-Higher Education Forum, Edward Donley, chairman of Air Products and Chemicals, Inc., attributed our lost competitiveness to the high wages of American workers.[20] In response, Congressman Stan Lundine (D-N.Y.) asked whether the purpose of being competitive was not to "raise people's standard of living overall."[21] While professing to agree, Donley allowed that in the short term "givebacks [by labor] of the type that have been negotiated in the steel industry, will be helpful."[22] He then proceeded to discuss the need to robotize and further automate American industry.

Labor Support for a Corporatist Industrial Policy

Organized labor supports a corporatist industrial policy, one that would use political (i.e., nonmarket) mechanisms to target assistance to particular industries. This is apparent in the industrial policy proposals of both the AFL-CIO and the United Auto Workers (UAW). The AFL-CIO has called for a tripartite National Reindustrialization Board—it would include representatives from labor, business, and government—to identify industries that are vital to national economic growth and employment and that should receive targeted assistance. This tripartite body would also seek to aid geographic areas with unused capacity and high unemployment. It would provide policy guidance to a national development bank, patterned after the 1930s-era Reconstruction Finance Corporation, that would make and guarantee loans to finance approved reindustrialization efforts.[23] The UAW has created a "Blueprint for a Working America" that calls for four new institutions: a tripartite national strategic planning board to set overall performance standards; sectoral committees to develop strategies for specific industries; a national development bank to make loans to, or take equity in, companies undergoing restructuring as stipulated by the national strategic planning board; and a civilian technology agency to encourage the development of product and process innovations.[24]

Where the UAW proposal is most distinctive, however, is in calling for social accounting, "bargained development" (its term), and democratic accountability. In proposing social accounting, it wants industrial policy decision makers to consider the costs and benefits to society, not just the profitability of an individual firm or project, in making investment and loan decisions. It wants "bargained development" whereby government assistance would be conditioned upon a demonstrated benefit to the public. And it wants a democratically accountable policy process based on multipartite representation (consumers and minorities would be represented too), congressional oversight, and public field hearings.

As committee chairman John LaFalce (D-N.Y.) noted during testimony, labor's chief spokesman on the industrial policy issue has been Howard

Samuel, president of the AFL-CIO's industrial department and co-chair of the labor-industry coalition, LICIT. In his testimony, Samuel spoke of an "industrial policy gap"—a gap between the ad-hoc and indirect support given to certain industries by the U.S. government—and the "systematic or comprehensive intervention in support of specific industries" practiced by competitor nations. This gap exists between the Japanese and American robotics industries, he declared, and it may be economically disastrous not to play by the same rules as our competitors.[25] Thus, in this instance we find a labor representative urging government assistance to private industry in the name of enhancing America's economic competitiveness.

Like other labor representatives, Samuel did not express faith in the steering capacity of the market system. In discussing (in his joint statement with LICIT co-chair Douglas Danforth) how the industrial policy gap evolved, he observed that America's postwar economic strength was due less to our reliance on market processes than to particular historical conditions; World War II devastated the economies of our competitor nations, he noted, and we emerged from the war with unrivaled political and military strength to protect our access to foreign markets. In short, market competition worked for us because the war left us in a predominant competitive position. Conversely, the governments of war-torn Japan, France, and West Germany turned to interventionist policies to rebuild their economies and have continued to rely on interventionist policies, while the United States remains ideologically committed to market processes in the mistaken belief that competitive markets have made us strong.[26]

UAW president Owen Bieber presented a similar if less elaborate argument, stating, "Unlike the critics of industrial policy who want government out of the economy, we think our economy has performed best when government has played an active, supporting role."[27] Along the same lines, the LICIT testimony called for an "anticipatory" industrial policy, observing that trade reform was a reactive response to the competitiveness problem and that we need a method of industrial policy making that can anticipate problems and aid us in fulfilling long-term economic objectives.[28] In these and other proposals, we see organized labor exercising leadership in proposing new policies and new institutions that, without changing the capitalist character of the economy, would make the economy more responsive to the employment and consumption needs of the broader public. Notwithstanding business participation in LICIT, concern with making the economy "work" in this sense was much greater among labor leaders than among business leaders.

Educative Role of Intellectuals

The intellectuals who lecture and write about deindustrialization and industrial policy have played an important educative and legitimating role in the policy process. One is struck by the ubiquitous presence of certain individuals in this policy debate. There is a group of "usual suspects" who write, lecture, testify, and advise on industrial policy matters. Among the most prominent are Pat Choate, Lester Thurow, and Robert Reich. Choate is a policy analyst in economics at TRW; Thurow is a professor of economics and management at the Massachusetts Institute of Technology (MIT) and the author of a bimonthly *Newsweek* column; and Reich, an attorney, was formerly the director of policy planning at the Federal Trade Commission (FTC) and is now a lecturer at Harvard's Kennedy School.

Choate's influential advisory role was acknowledged by Chairman LaFalce during the subcommittee hearings. After describing Choate as the "best and most informative" of several experts who met privately with the subcommittee, he wryly noted that Choate must have been helpful to the Business-Higher Education Forum too, since their recommendations were remarkably similar to ones made by Choate.[29] Robert Anderson, representing the forum, responded that Choate had indeed been very helpful.[30] In contrast, Thurow and Reich have probably been more influential indirectly through their writing and public appearances. As a suggestive measure of Reich's influence, the colloquy between congressmen and himself following his formal testimony consumed 30 pages, longer than for any other witness.

The testimony of these and other policy intellectuals was distinctive in several ways. First, they were more likely to address systemic problems in diagnosing deindustrialization, and their proposals were more innovative and far-reaching.[31] A notable presentation in this regard was that of Harvard Business School professor Bruce Scott. He stated that American and European business executives may have to acknowledge the existence of a national strategy that is more competitive than pure private initiative in an unmanaged economy. Business rhetoric about gaining a "level playing field" misses the point that an active industrial policy is more competitive than an unfettered free market, he declared.[32] Similarly, Thurow asserted that America's era of "effortless superiority" is over. We can no longer effectively compete by relying on market processes, he maintained, listing five market defects that he believes justify an explicit industrial policy.[33] Choate rhetorically asked whether government's industry-specific interventions should not be rationalized and coordinated, and whether a few industries are not so critical (he offered five candidates) that they deserve special attention.[34] For his part, Robert Reich argued that our implicit industrial policy is neither rational nor effective because it has not been publicly formulated in a purposeful way.[35]

Second, the policy intellectuals who testified were more likely to address the needs of the broader society, at least in comparison with the business representatives. As a group, they were more society-minded and less overtly class biased than the business representatives. There were indeed a few businessmen who addressed how their favored privatization strategy would benefit the larger society—albeit without addressing the problem of displaced workers. Following a spate of business representatives calling for more investment capital to spur competitiveness and growth, it was, as one congressman noted, Ray Marshall and Russell Rumberger who first addressed the employment side of the reindustrialization issue. Marshall, President Carter's Labor Secretary who now teaches at Texas's LBJ School of Public Affairs, called for targeted labor market policies as part of any industrial policy. He recommended the 1930s-era Works Progress Administration and Civilian Conservation Corps, as well as the more recent Job Corps program, as models for retraining workers who are displaced by industrial change.[36] Rumberger, an economist at a Stanford research institute, addressed the misconceptions that high-tech industries need educated workers and that they will provide many jobs in the future. To reduce unemployment resulting from economic transformation, any industrial policy should have an employment policy supporting labor-intensive sectors of the economy, he declared.[37]

Leadership Role of Elected Officials

Elected officials have also played a leadership role in industrial policy politics. In this role, they do not appear to have functioned as the agents of other groups. Rather, they seem to have been responding to democratic pressures, trying to solve the problems of their constituents in order to protect and advance their political careers. Congressmen have sought to educate business leaders in particular about how their group interests and the national interest interrelate. In this connection, one finds congressmen talking not only about the need to increase competitiveness and generate growth (which businessmen like to discuss), but also about unemployment and job displacement (which businessmen are less interested in discussing). Further, the leading congressmen from the Economic Stabilization Subcommittee on this issue seem less committed to relying on market processes than do business representatives.

The subcommittee leaders on this issue have been Congressmen LaFalce and Lundine, both Democrats from New York State. LaFalce, the committee chairman, is from upstate New York; his district includes the industrial belt along the Niagara River near Buffalo. Lundine represents the state's economically depressed southern tier. Each of the congressmen has co-sponsored legislation (their bills differ slightly) calling for a national development bank. A former congressional leader on the industrial policy issue is Jim Blanchard, now governor of Michigan. Blanchard, who as chairman of the subcommittee initiated its deliberations on industrial policy, testified before the panel with two other governors, Bill Clinton of Arkansas and Richard Celeste of Ohio. Their testimony made clear that state governments are also responding to the effects of industrial decline.

Governor Blanchard urged the adoption of an explicit industrial policy for several reasons—to reduce unemployment, halt regional economic decline, assist fiscally stressed local governments, avoid creating a permanent underclass in the industrial Midwest, and guarantee national security. While noting the positive efforts of his state (state pension funds are being used to stimulate growth sectors of the economy), he declared that the underlying problems were international in dimension and therefore required a national government response.[38] Governor Celeste, director of the Peace Corps under President Carter, attacked the misconception that industrial policy is concerned with the "care and feeding of capital." The real focus, he maintained, should be on "enabling people to contribute to our country through their work, and head off the specter of a generation of unemployed."[39] For his part, Governor Clinton called for federal assistance to both emerging industries and dislocated workers. Among other things, he recommended that the federal government insure up to 10 percent of state pension funds that are reinvested within the state.[40]

Throughout the hearings one finds congressmen attempting to educate business leaders about government's necessary role in achieving a productive economy—and why business should support that role. As previously noted, Congressman Lundine challenged Edward Donley of the Business-Higher Education Forum when Donley blamed high wages for declining U.S. competitiveness.[41] Moreover, several committee members noted the contradiction between business leaders praising free enterprise and then requesting government assistance. Chairman LaFalce pressed witnesses on the "conditionality" issue, asking why they did not urge that government assistance to industry be conditioned upon changes in investment policies or management practices benefiting the public.[42] Lundine asked several witnesses what he termed the threshold questions for an industrial policy—first, whether "industrial policy combinations" of foreign firms and their governments were out-competing American firms, and second, whether government assistance should be conditioned upon guaranteed returns to the public.[43] To both questions he received affirmative responses, although often expressed reluctantly.

Regarding both the employment and national competitiveness issues, committee members seemed less concerned with the ideological implications of the measures proposed than with their likely results. Indeed, some rather surprising anti-market statements were made by congressmen. Democratic Congressman Dennis Hertel, who represents an auto-producing region of Michigan, praised the three previously mentioned governors for, in his words, "telling us . . . that you want central economic planning, you want it organized, and you want it to go forward now forthwith without further subsidies."[44] Congressman Stewart McKinney (now deceased), a Connecticut Republican, made one of the strongest anti-market statements. "The free enterprise system or laissez-faire," he declared, "may be great for McDonald's and Burger King, but it doesn't fit the steel, shipbuilding, and air freight industries of America, which are essential if we are going to remain leaders of the free world, whether economically feasible or not. Laissez-faire is forcing them to compete with other government policies instead of other corporations such as British-owned Rolls Royce and German Steel."[45] No business leaders made comparable statements.

II. INDUSTRIAL POLICY POLITICS INTERPRETED

What explains the stands taken by business representatives, organized labor, policy intellectuals, and elected officials on the industrial policy issue? Why does the political process appear biased in favor of the privatization strategy in the United States? What future course is likely in the United States?

Lester Thurow has said that the motivation that might lead to the adoption of a state interventionist adjustment strategy is "fear."[46] If that is so, then business is not yet fearful. Part of the explanation is that business views the world, including the problem of deindustrialization, through the lens of an anti-statist, pro-market ideology—an ideology conditioned on the historical fact that industrialization occurred in the United States without the direct state guidance practiced elsewhere. It is partly for this reason that the American bourgeoisie, as David Vogel has written, is the most reactionary in the industrialized world.[47]

Yet, business's faith in the market system is not entirely based on ideological delusion. Regardless of whether the market leads to appropriate investment decisions for society, it does provide two outstanding benefits for business. First, labor markets discipline workers and force them to accept sacrifices—out of fear of being made unwilling conscripts in the reserve army of the unemployed. This competition-forcing effect is accentuated through international product competition, which expands the size of the relevant industrial reserve army by putting American workers in competition with their foreign counterparts. Second, the market facilitates disinvestment from failing industries. In France, with its many nationalized firms, disinvestment becomes a political issue and threatens governmental stability, while in the United States the shutdown of a steel plant is regarded as a private decision for which public officials are not responsible. Tax laws abet this process of disinvestment by enabling firms to write off part of the cost of plant closures. U.S. Steel exemplified this disinvestment strategy when it purchased Marathon Oil—now only 50 percent of the company's investment is in steel. Similarly, Armco Company is no longer Armco Steel, having dropped "steel" from its name in recognition of its diversified operations.

Why did business not seek a corporatist industrial policy that took account of and sought to guarantee workers' material interests? Here, one must recall Marx's observation that capital is wasteful of labor, in spite of its dependency on human labor power, unless under compulsion from society to act differently.[48] Business on the whole was not interested in anything resembling an incomes policy, because in the prevailing political conjuncture, with labor poorly organized and welfare-state clients divided and on the defensive, it was not compelled to adopt such a policy. Normally, as Antonio Gramsci wrote, it is the task of intellectuals to educate dominant groups about the requirements for maintaining their position.[49] And indeed, one can see American intellectuals (wittingly or unwittingly) offering such advice. Yet business leaders will not heed this advice until it makes more political sense to do so—that is, until they are under more pressure, principally from organized labor.

A second and possibly more important reason for business leaders' failure to put forward a hegemonic program is, quite simply, that they do not think such a program is economically feasible in the context of deindustrialization. This interpretation is supported by business representatives' complaints about cross-national wage differences and the "consumption bias" of current policies. If rejuvenating American capitalism means asking workers and consumers who benefit from a consumption bias to make economic sacrifices, it will be difficult to organize a consensual business hegemony.[50] The attraction of the privatization strategy in this regard is that it substitutes governmental protection for corporatism's government-organized consensus: it offers governmental protection against the threats posed by workers, welfare-state clients, foreign capitalists, and foreign industrial policies. This in turn helps to explain how business leaders can defend "free-market" arrangements while requesting, as Edward Donley did in his congressional testimony, a closer business-government partnership.[51] They want a partnership with government—as modeled by President's Reagan handling of the air traffic controllers' strike—that forces workers and consumers to take what *Business Week* described in 1980 as a bitter pill: accepting less.[52]

Meanwhile, organized labor wants an industrial policy because it sees this as the best way to make American capitalism work—for workers, consumers, the disadvantaged, and Americans generally. Precisely because it is less mobile than capital, labor is more dependent on the performance of the U.S. national economy. It is also dependent on the economic fortunes of particular industries and particular regional economies. Labor is willing to support productivity improvements because it sees productivity as the critical intervening variable that makes it possible for capitalists and workers to both have more. Andrew Martin, based on his analysis of Swedish politics, has written that democratic control of capitalist economies is only possible if several conditions are present: a strong, ideologically coherent labor movement; high voter participation among wage earners; and a labor or social democratic party that is the party of government most of the time.[53] Clearly, these conditions do not obtain in the United States at present. Since organized labor cannot put in place its own program—a program organized around its interests—the best it can do is to get business to recognize its own interest by taking labor's interest into account.

Because its interests are harmed by the privatization strategy, organized labor has proposed an industrial policy involving government planning, a public bank, and tripartite bargaining arrangements. It presents this strategy as being in business's interest (especially insofar as it closes the industrial policy gap) as well as the nation's interest. There are dangers to labor, however, if business profits are treated as the only or the most important criterion for investment decision making, and if labor becomes imprisoned in tripartite arrangements that shape the nature of labor's participation and use labor's leaders to control the ranks of labor. In consideration, no doubt, of these threats, the UAW—but not the AFL-CIO—has called for social accounting techniques and democratically accountable decision processes. Yet there is a danger that labor, in order to win business support for planning, will trim its demands for a democratically accountable industrial policy. After helping to educate business on the need for a state interventionist strategy, labor may find itself a subordinate partner in a corporatist mediating structure.

The role of intellectuals in the policy process is typically to educate particular groups and the broader society about problems of collective rationality. Because of their presumed autonomy from other groups, intellectuals are better positioned to discern problems of collective rationality and to legitimate public policies in these or similar terms. The industrial policy strategies advocated by such policy intellectuals as Pat Choate, Lester Thurow, and Robert Reich are not yet politically winning ideas, however, because they lack a sponsor group willing and able to put them in place. As noted, organized labor lacks the political capacity to impose an industrial policy strategy, and business is not under effective pressure to embrace such a policy.

Consequently, neoclassical economists with their advocacy of the privatization strategy are politically ascendant. This, however, is not because their ideas have proven victorious in some free competition of ideas. The neoclassical economists' message is supported by business groups because it corresponds with the limited possibilities of the era. Unlike their classical brethren, they recognize neither that there are classes in capitalism, nor that maintaining the capitalist system depends on securing the consent of the class that sells its labor power for a wage.[54] Their criticisms of labor demands, "special interests," and the political process "make sense" to dominant groups at a time when there is a limited material base for securing working-class consent.

The liberal Democratic congressmen who have promoted industrial policy have certainly not acted as agents of the business class—at least not in any direct and interpersonal sense. Instead, they have acted out the logic of capitalist democracy, attempting to solve the problems of the economy not for the sake of rejuvenating American capitalism, but for the sake of solving the problems of their constituents and winning reelection. A group of congressmen, most of them Democrats from districts in the declining Rustbelt, has been in the forefront in developing an activist industrial policy involving a directive governmental role in allocating savings and investment, because relying on the market offers little hope for their constituents. They have also been more responsive to the industrial policy gap. Like labor leaders, their dependency on the fortunes of the economy gives them an interest in making that system work—work, that is, for more than business. And like intellectuals, their partial independence from business gives them a greater capacity to discern problems of collective rationality in the economy and society. This, along with the problems of their constituents, lessens their faith in the market system. Yet the anti-statism of the Republican party and of large parts of the Democratic party limits their options in responding to the problems associated with deindustrialization.

Late in the spring of 1984, congressional Democratic leaders became wary that advocacy of an industrial development bank would make the party vulnerable to Republican charges that it was proposing a big-government solution to the nation's industrial woes. Although LaFalce, chairman of the Economic Stabilization Subcommittee, was open to dropping support for the bank idea, Congressman Lundine and his labor allies were not. After a six-week search for a compromise, during which representatives of Walter Mondale's presidential campaign urged Economic Stabilization Subcommittee members to drop the bank proposal to avoid splitting the party, House Democratic Caucus chair Gillis Long and his supporters told Lundine that an industrial policy bill would be scheduled for House debate only if the bank proposal was dropped from the legislation. Lundine refused; for him and his labor backers, no bill was better than one without a bank. And so this industrial policy legislation died.[55]

In the end, the industrial policy idea played almost no role in the 1984 presidential election. As Jim Shoch has perceptively written, "The [industrial policy] concept had become divisive within the [Democratic] party, had demonstrated strong academic and business opposition, seemed unnecessary as the economy recovered from the recession, and conjured up images of bureaucratic central planning among voters—when they bothered to think about the issue at all."[56] In the ensuing four years, the industrial policy issue was transformed into the "competitiveness issue," terminology which focused on the economic problem rather than a proposed solution and which avoided the feared image of socialist state planning. With increased public attention to America's continuing trade deficit, it was forecast that the competitiveness issue would dominate the 1988 presidential campaign.[57] That contest was instead fought over largely irrelevant issues—prison furloughs, the pledge of allegiance, and the image of the national Democratic party as a proponent of big-government solutions.

From all this it appears that the United States may be trapped between, on one side, a privatization strategy that is unresponsive to the industrial policy gap and fails to ensure political stability and consensus and, on the other, a social democratic strategy that liberals and labor are powerless to implement. Shaping that choice will be the anti-statism found in both major parties, the political weakness of labor, the current retreatist posture of the liberal-labor coalition, and a popular distrust of government spawned in part by the institutional fragmentation of the American state system. If, as seems likely, economic events force the competitiveness issue onto the agenda in subsequent presidential elections, the choice will probably be between a renewal of the Republicans' privatization strategy and the adoption of a weak, market-reinforcing industrial policy, with political progressives and labor supporting the latter.

NOTES

1. I would like to thank Joel Krieger and especially my co-editor Joel Wolfe for their helpful comments on this chapter and Donata Gataletto for her invaluable typing assistance.

2. The view that the policy process begins in corporate boardrooms is presented, inter alia, in G. William Domhoff, *The Powers That Be* (New York: Vintage, 1978); see, e.g., p. 62.

3. One notable example is James O'Connor's *The Fiscal Crisis of the State* (New York: St. Martin's Press, 1973), which makes the mistake of attributing corporatism's originating impulse to business.

4. U.S. Congress, House Committee on Banking, Finance, and Urban Affairs, Subcommittee on Economic Stabilization, Hearings on Industrial Policy, Serial 98–39 (Washington: Government Printing Office, 1983–84); hereafter cited as "IP hearings." These hearings took place between June 1983 and January 1984 in Washington, Berkeley, and Chicago. The published proceedings fill six volumes totaling more than 4,000 pages.

5. See Felix Rohatyn, "Alternatives to Reaganomics," *New York Times Magazine*, December 5, 1982, pp. 72ff; for a more revealing look at Rohatyn's thinking, see also Jeremy Bernstein, "Profiles (Rohatyn)," *The New Yorker*, January 24, 1983, pp. 45–78.

6. Statement of Gerald Greenwald (vice-chairman, Chrysler Corporation), IP hearings, 3:3–16.

7. Statement of Douglas D. Danforth, IP hearings, 1:118–20.

8. Statement of Robert Anderson, IP hearings, 1:12.

9. Report to the President of the United States from the Business-Higher Education Forum, "America's Comparative Challenge: The Need for a National Response," Appendix; in IP hearings, 1:607–60; quotation pp. 619–20.

10. Statement of Jerry Jasinowski, IP hearings, 1:499–523.

11. See Domhoff, *Powers That Be*, chap. 3.

12. Statement of J. Paul Lyet, IP hearings, 1:135–56.

13. Statement of William P. Jahnke (representing the National Machine Tool Builders' Association), IP hearings, 2:457, 462.

14. Statement of George Scalise, IP hearings, 2:193–203.

15. Congressman Sander M. Levin, IP hearings, 1:65.

16. Statement of Robert Anderson, IP hearings, 1:66.

17. Statement of J. Paul Lyet, IP hearings, 1:137–38.

18. This concept comes of course from the writing of Antonio Gramsci, *Selections from the Prison Notebooks*, ed. and trans. Quintin Hoare and Geoffrey N. Smith (New York: International Publishers, 1971), pp. 181–82.

19. Statement of Robert Anderson, IP hearings, 1:11.
20. Statement of Edward Donley, IP hearings, 1:43.
21. Congressman Stan Lundine, IP hearings, 1:51.
22. Statement of Edward Donley, IP hearings, 1:51.
23. Statement of Milan Stone, IP hearings, 1:293–302.
24. Statement of Owen Bieber, IP hearings, 4:337.
25. Statement of Howard Samuel, IP hearings, 1:117.
26. Statement of Douglas D. Danforth and Howard Samuel in behalf of LICIT, IP hearings, 1:123–24.
27. Statement of Owen Bieber, IP hearings, 4:332.
28. Statement of Douglas D. Danforth and Howard Samuel in behalf of LICIT, IP hearings, 1:132.
29. Congressman John LaFalce, IP hearings, 1:53.
30. Robert Anderson, IP hearings, 1:53.
31. An exception was the polemical testimony of writer George Gilder. He offered sweeping generalizations (e.g., declaring France's industrial policy "a joke") yet had difficulty defending his assertions when questioned.
32. Statement of Bruce Scott, IP hearings, 1:419–44; quotation p. 431.
33. Statement of Lester Thurow, IP hearings, 1:168–72.
34. Statement of Pat Choate, IP hearings, 1:524–72.
35. Statement of Robert Reich, IP hearings, 5:212–44.
36. Statement of Ray Marshall, IP hearings, 1:310–27.
37. Statement of Russell Rumberger, IP hearings, 1:333.
38. Statement of Governor Jim Blanchard, IP hearings, 1:233–48.
39. Statement of Governor Richard Celeste, IP hearings, 1:249–61; quotation pp. 252–53.
40. Statement of Governor Bill Clinton, IP hearings, 1:262–74.
41. Congressman Stan Lundine, IP hearings, 1:51.
42. Congressman John LaFalce, IP hearings, 1:157.
43. Congressman Stan Lundine, IP hearings, 1:161–62.
44. Congressman Dennis Hertel, IP hearings, 1:287.
45. Congressman Stewart McKinney, IP hearings, 1:387.
46. Statement of Lester Thurow, IP hearings, 1:168.
47. David Vogel, "Why Businessmen Distrust Their State: The Political Consciousness of American Corporate Executives," *British Journal of Political Science* 8 (January 1978): 45–78.
48. Karl Marx, *Capital: A Critique of Political Economy*, vol. 1, trans. Samuel Moore and Edward Aveling (New York: International Publishers, 1967; orig. German ed. 1867), chap. 10.
49. Gramsci, *Prison Notebooks*, pp. 3–24.
50. This interpretation is supported by Gramsci's view that class leadership is founded upon an ever-changing balance of force and consent; the need for force increases in proportion as the material basis for organizing consensus diminishes. See Gramsci, *Prison Notebooks*, pp. 183–85.
51. Statement of Edward Donley, IP hearings, 1:50.
52. "The Reindustrialization of America," *Business Week*, special issue, June 30, 1980.
53. Andrew Martin, "Is Democratic Control of Capitalist Economies Possible?" in

Leon Lindberg, ed., *Stress and Contradiction in Modern Capitalism* (Lexington, Mass.: D. C. Heath, 1975), pp. 45–46.

54. On this point, see my article "Business Against the Welfare State," *Challenge* 26 (November/December 1983): 38–45.

55. "Industrial Policy Divides Democrats," *Business Week*, May 14, 1984; for an excellent analysis of the defeat of industrial policy legislation, see Jim Shoch, "The Politics of the U.S. Industrial Policy Debate, 1980–84: A Theoretical and Historical Perspective," unpublished paper, MIT Department of Political Science, February 1988.

56. Shoch, "Politics," p. 53.

57. *Newsweek* predicted in January 1988 that the competitiveness issue would dominate the presidential campaign: "The Quest for the '88 Issue," *Newsweek*, January 19, 1988, pp. 14–16.

4

The Industrial Policy Controversy in West Germany: Organized Adjustment and the Emergence of Meso-Corporatism

Christopher S. Allen and Jeremiah M. Riemer

Like the industrial policy controversy in the United States, the debate over what West Germans call "structural policy" has a history closely linked to the political fortunes of organized labor.[1] In both countries, left-of-center parties took to industrial policy as the limits of Keynesian macro-economic management became apparent in the 1970s. What then happened in the 1980s was different for each country. In the United States, Democratic party economists and politicians discovered the reindustrialization issue in the final years of the Carter administration, mulled it over during what they hoped would be a brief Reagan interregnum, and discarded it (in favor of a new theme—tax reform) soon after the failed Mondale campaign. In West Germany, Social Democrats turned their attention to industrial policy as a way of giving macroeconomic policy a new lease on life during Helmut Schmidt's last full term in office. When the Social Democratic party (SPD) was turned out of power in 1982, structural policy momentarily disappeared from the issue agenda. Yet it soon resurfaced in the guise of labor-market policy. Thus, in the transition from Schmidt to Kohl and from Carter to Reagan, left and right positions in the German industrial policy debate have sometimes seemed to converge with liberal and conservative positions in the United States. Yet this apparent convergence with developments in the United States conceals important divergences and ironic "role reversals" that go back more than 20 years.

Two decades ago, West German politicians and economists drew on the "New Economics" of the Kennedy-Johnson years to legitimate an essentially Social Democratic agenda of Keynesian reforms in economic policy.[2] By the late 1970s, "Model Germany" was held up for emulation by Americans who admired such various and vaunted aspects of the West German economy as a low inflation rate, labor-management cooperation, an extensive social welfare safety net, state promotion of industrial restructuring, and banks that planned investments in companies by careful scrutiny of long-range goals rather than short-term glances at the "bottom line." Ironically, two prominent proponents of a new American industrial policy—Robert Reich and Ira Magaziner—drew inspiration from the Federal Republic of Germany (FRG) at a time when their counterparts in West Germany were calling for a more coherent (and more Social Democratic) industrial policy under the Schmidt government.[3] By the mid–1980s, with right-of-center governments wielding power in both countries, some conservatives in the FRG government began to argue that German industry needed what the U.S. economy supposedly had already: job creation in high technology, nourished by bountiful funds from venture capital firms and fostered by close relations between research facilities loosely affiliated with major companies and engineers from elite universities. In short, within a space of 20 years, analysts of political economy in the FRG and the United States moved from a common point of departure (Keynesian economics) through periods in which the fashionable model of industrial policy was variously a Social Democratic version of organized capitalism or Reaganomics with a "human face."

This chapter explores the origins and development of the industrial policy controversy in West Germany. We argue that the debate over industrial policy inside the Federal Republic has proceeded with little reference to the charge of "Eurosclerosis" once leveled against West Germany from the outside. The practice of industrial policy in the FRG—under both Social Democratic- and Christian Democratic-led governments—has been clearly more successful than many observers realize. Yet the conservative version of an "organized and private-sector-led" industrial policy also presented the Social Democrats and the labor movement with fundamental challenges in the 1980s. Part I addresses the shift of terms in the industrial policy controversy that has disadvantaged the Social Democratic left toward the end of the FRG's macroeconomic era while giving the Christian Democratic right advantages that were easily exploited in the emerging "meso-economic" environment, more fully discussed in Part II. This shift—analyzed through the prism of the 1976 federal election, the 1978 debate on stimulating the West German economy, and the *Wende* (turnaround) that saw the Christian Democrats replace the Social Democrats as the leading government party in 1982—was accompanied by some important institutional modulations that strengthened private-sector forces in the West German political economy. Among these modulations were the increasingly sophisticated organizational characteristics of German capital (both banks and industry associations), the difficulty that unions have experienced in responding to labor-market segmentation, the more strident pattern of collective bargaining between business and labor, and the sharper political articulation of interests within the party system of the FRG.

West Germany's increasingly private-sector-led "meso-corporatist" industrial policy[4] has appeared to put the labor movement in a defensive position similar to the plight of the even weaker American trade unions. But, as we indicate in Part II, this appearance of weakness should be viewed as the limited damage inflicted by an entrepreneurial assault that has already been contained and may still be challenged. The possibility of an economy based on "flexibility without solidarity," a prospect especially troubling to the labor movement and the Social Democrats, may not prove particularly lasting, however. The challenge for the SPD and the unions by the late 1980s has been to build upon a vision of "flexibility *with* solidarity" that some unions have pressed in certain key, "fulcrum" sectors. They thereby hope to force the diffuse privatized, regionalized, and firm-specific issues of the industrial policy debate back into focus on the political stage center. Our argument rejects the conventional wisdom of the left that either more macro-economic policies at the national level—or reduced worktime for all—are the primary approaches. We argue that the debate within the West German political economy has shifted to one between different views of "flexibility" on the part of the right and left. But for the Social Democrats and the labor movement, their own version of flexibility must serve as a new foundation for any effective macro-economic policies.

PART I: INITIAL SHIFTS IN THE INDUSTRIAL POLICY DEBATE: THE BREAKDOWN OF THE MACRO-ECONOMIC ORDER

The economic and political role of the industrial policy debate within the larger context of a macro-economic policy can be traced in three identifiable phases: (1) the period before and after the general election of 1976, the first of two elections returning Schmidt to power; (2) the events surrounding the Bonn summit of 1978, a turning point in the Social-Liberal government's effort to balance economic stability against economic revival; and (3) the so-called *Wende* (turnabout) from Schmidt to Kohl since 1983. This section will analyze the limits of the macro-economic policies that were pursued under both the Schmidt and Kohl governments. Failed macro-economic policies were a prelude to the approach which emerged in the 1980s, namely, "meso-economic" policy. What amounted to a strategy of "organized private-sector-led" adjustment among banks, employer and industry organizations, some regional governments, and trade unions in the core industries took center stage. In effect, this meso-economic policy displaced the leading role of macro-economic policy in the Federal Republic during the 1980s.

Strukturpolitik, as industrial policy is more commonly called in the FRG, was promoted by many Social Democrats as a cure for their government's apparent helplessness about proper macro-economic responses to the recession of 1975. The occasion for the emergence of structural policy as a major issue was the worldwide recession of 1975, which West Germans initially viewed as the second of two postwar "stabilization crises" in the Federal Republic.[5] The first such "crisis" (in fact, a minor recession with larger political consequences) happened in 1966–67 and ushered in a "Keynesian Revolution" sponsored by SPD Economics Minister Karl Schiller (and his adherents in the government) in a "Grand Coalition" with the conservative Christian Democratic Union (CDU) and Christian Social Union (CSU) parties. The recession was followed by an export boom, inflation, labor unrest, and volatility in foreign exchange markets that plagued the Social-Liberal government of Chancellor Willy Brandt (1969–74). Attempts to stop domestic inflation by imposing tighter monetary policies and to ward off "imported inflation" by taking advantage of flexible exchange rates showed little promise of achieving results until 1973, when the prospects of greater coordination among European currency movements freed the Bundesbank (the FRG's central bank) to experiment with a drastic new austerity course. In spite of growing unemployment, even this "new monetary policy" did not take hold until a year after the first oil crisis, when all of the capitalist economies entered a prolonged recession.

Throughout this period, economists and policy makers were continually frustrated by the limited usefulness of their government's new countercyclical policy machinery—the instruments of fiscal and monetary policy written into the Stability and Growth Law of 1967. It appeared to many as though West Germany had tried both Keynesianism and monetarism within a short time span, and that both had failed. Among some Social Democrats and trade unionists, an alternative crisis diagnosis (intellectually traceable to the English left-Keynesian Joan Robinson) interpreting the troubles of the 1970s as structural rather than cyclical gained in appeal. The notion of a "structural crisis" seemed an attractive way out of the impasse marked by the exhaustion of those narrow macro-economic options once characterized by President Kennedy as "ever so slightly to the left"—and right.

The push for a "structural policy" to supplement or replace exhausted macro-economic options gained momentum from several interrelated developments in party politics—from the coalition partners in Bonn, within the SPD, and from the Social Democrats and the trade unions. In the cabinet shuffles accompanying the transition from Brandt to Schmidt (1974), the liberal Free Democrats (conservatives on economic issues) gained control of the Economics Ministry. Schmidt frequently used his coalition partners, with whom he sometimes seemed more at home than in his own party, as a reason for not pursuing employment policies more in line with Social Democratic priorities. The special circumstances of Brandt's fall from power in a spy scandal notwithstanding, Schmidt's accession was widely interpreted as an inevitable move by top party officials to place the government in the hands of a supercompetent crisis manager who enjoyed the confidence of business circles. The shift from Brandt to Schmidt and toward a less distinctly Social Democratic economic policy led to tensions between those who continued to view the SPD as a party of social reforms (*Reformpartei*), and those who cared more about the Social Democrats' longevity as the new party of government (*Staatspartei*).[6] Although these tensions were suppressed for the duration of the 1976 election campaign, the party's change of course after the Brandt era did have long-term implications for those party activists and trade unionists who raised the issue of structural policy during Schmidt's second term.

The party activists who pressed the issue of structural policy were former *Jusos* from the Young Socialist branch of the SPD, who had a prior and related interest in "investment guidance" (*Investitionslenkung*). In the prosperous Brandt years, investment guidance was the project of unorthodox economists and *Jusos* who hoped to increase political control over the economy and implement "quality of life" reforms in West German society. Although this form of *Investitionslenkung* was rejected as a hopelessly abstract scheme that frightened a conservative public and threatened the Social-Liberal government's established agenda, the recession of 1975 allowed the adherents of investment guidance to reformulate the issue in more practical terms—as industrial policy. In the jargon of the time, structural policy changed *Investitionslenkung* from a radical reform that would be "system transforming" (*systemüberwindend*) into a problem-oriented reform that remained "system inherent" (*systemimmanent*). In this new pragmatic guise, investment guidance became a program for sectoral change in the economy via "structural councils" involving some new kind of corporatist representation.

By 1977, an SPD subcommittee chaired by Wolfgang Roth—which also included trade unionists and Social Democratic technocrats associated with the Research Ministry who wanted to press for "humanization of work"—pieced together a new programmatic consensus on structural policy that had the approval of *Jusos*, unionists, and technocrats and that won at least a token endorsement from the party leadership. But the Roth committee's main institutional innovation—structural councils—had to be advanced cautiously because the unions and the party leadership had settled on another reform—the extension of codetermination (*Mitbestimmung*) on company boards—as the major new arena for trade union influence within the economy.

Although there was no inherent conflict between the sectoral perspective of structural councils and codetermination at the firm level, some party stalwarts had portrayed investment guidance as a threat to union and company autonomy at an important party congress in 1975. More important, extending the reach of sectorally organized unions into companies where their influence was restricted by law (and where unions were forced to court works councils—*Betriebsräte*—as shop-floor allies) had become the party's way of compensating the unions for the disappointments of macro-economic policy in the 1970s.[7] Structural councils, while portrayed by the Roth committee as a new sectoral layer of codetermination, threatened to disturb an intact agenda of Social Democratic labor legislation. The uncertain new sectoral emphasis of industrial policy enthusiasts also promised to shake up an established pattern of interest politics—enshrined in the principle of *Tarifautonomie* (autonomy of collective bargaining)—in which the state undertook responsibility for macro-economic aggregates but left wage, price, and investment decisions entirely to private-sector actors. In light of these institutional difficulties and governing anxieties, it was significant that the SPD even entertained industrial policy innovations in response to the recession then being reinterpreted as a "structural crisis." What made industrial policy so appealing, especially for the unions, was the growing problem of structural unemployment—persistent joblessness in troubled sectors of the economy that was hard to define in merely cyclical terms.

Coalition Politics and Industrial Policy in the Late 1970s

Why, then, did "structural policy" go nowhere in the latter half of the 1970s? The answer is found both in the political stalemate that developed over the terms of the industrial policy debate and in the brief revival of Keynesian options midway in the second Schmidt term. While the governments of the SPD and Free Democratic Party (FDP) paid lip service to the Social Democrats' new interpretation of crisis symptoms, a resuscitation of mild Keynesianism was the *treatment* applied after 1977.

Inside the Social-Liberal coalition, the limits of the industrial policy debate were set by market-oriented Free Democrats in the Economics Ministry on the right, and by statist Social Democrats in the Research Ministry just to the left of the ideological center. Post-Keynesian economists and reform-minded political scientists supplied the Social Democratic technocrats with intellectual ammunition, whereas the Kiel Institute on the World Economy provided the Liberals (FDP) with a coherent outlook on structural change in the economy. The debate centered on who or what would bear the burden of adjustment in an economy responding to changes in the international division of labor. The Social Democratic technocrats wanted the state to facilitate the emergence of an industrial structure that would support high-paying jobs in emerging "high-value-added" sectors. The Liberals wanted market forces to shape structural change and an accommodating, "flexible" workforce to meet the challenge of heightened international competition. Within this debate, groups like the Roth committee pressed for a stronger state presence in the shaping of structural change, while the Liberals around Economics Minister Otto Graf Lambsdorff resisted what they regarded as unwarranted "official" interference in setting sectoral growth targets. As a compromise, the government funded a research project in which the five major economics institutes (including the one at Kiel) would develop separate (and therefore unofficial) systems for reporting on structural trends in the economy.[8]

Structural policy proponents also pressed the coalition to incorporate elements of industrial policy into some of the recovery programs that the new Schmidt government was considering after the 1976 election. Here, too, a compromise was worked out: the government announced a major recovery program in 1976 relying on infrastructural investment, but the funding (DM 16 billion) was to be spread over four years and earmarked for programs with low follow-up costs. Along with Schmidt's reflationary commitments to the Carter administration at the Bonn seven-power summit in 1978 (in exchange for Carter's promises of monetary and energy austerity), this new spending effort showed how the West German government responded to calls for fundamentally new "structural" policies by reviving the moderately Keynesian policies practiced in previous stabilization crises.

Die Wende: From Social Democrats to Christian Democrats

As is well known, the partly successful recovery after the Bonn summit ground to a halt in another postwar recession roughly coinciding with Schmidt's victory over Franz-Josef Strauss in the 1980 election. Owing to a combination of domestic and foreign policy factors, the Schmidt government was turned out of power in 1982 and replaced by a Christian Democratic-led cabinet that retained Liberal control of the Economics Ministry. Under the new Kohl government, the Research Ministry began to replace the Social Democrats' targeted, project-specific funding of new technology with general, indirect incentives to businesses.[9] Despite the Kohl government's move to the right since the *Wende*, its policies have not been as right-wing as those of Reagan or Thatcher. There have been no massive "fire sales" of public assets and no attacks on the "evils" of the welfare state. And despite more restrictive policies toward the unions in the form of denying unemployment compensation to locked-out workers, there has been no equivalent in West Germany to Reagan's smashing of the air traffic controllers' strike or Thatcher's breaking of the miners' union. Both of these were watershed events which changed the balance of power to the detriment of the labor movement in these two countries.

In addition to resisting the government's attempts to change the labor law, the unions in the trade union confederation DGB (Deutscher Gewerkschaftsbund) have offered their own solution to the unemployment problem. For several years before, and continuing during and after the *Wende* of 1982, the unions have pushed for reducing the work week to 35 hours. In settling a 1984 metalworkers' strike, employers and employees compromised on a 38.5 work week (reduced still further in 1988). By the late 1980s, flexibility in job classifications and further reductions in worktime have become central issues in collective bargaining, shifting the focus away from the older controversy over structural change.

The shift of focus away from macro-economic policy issues also moved away from industrial policy in the context of the debate over "flexibility." In the late 1970s, economists debated whether the persistence of unemployment long after the recession meant that the FRG was going through a structual crisis or experiencing an unusually severe downturn in the business cycle. Data about the pace of structural change, evidence about sectorally concentrated pockets of unemployment, and statistical linkages between these factors and various points in the business cycle were all used to bolster both sides of the debate—with inconclusive results.[10] Neglected in this debate over cyclical versus structural (meaning "sectoral") versions of a macro-economic crisis was a third perspective emphasizing structural aspects of the *labor market* (i.e., flexibility).[11] For over a decade, students of labor-market segmentation drew attention to the importance of internal (firm-specific) labor markets in the FRG.[12]

Specifically, the segmentationists argued (1) that rigidities in internal labor markets (chiefly the tendency of firms to hoard an expensive core of employees during slack times and to avoid hiring more marginal workers during business pickups) frustrated macro-economic stabilization policy; and (2) that job retraining legislation (like the *Arbeitsförderungsgesetz* or Work Promotion Law of 1969) neglected to find opportunities for job mobility *within* companies because of an exclusive focus on presumed mismatches between available skills and vocational job categories.[13] The segmentationists dwelled on micro-level obstacles to macro-level problems and proved able to offer only a few micro-level stopgap solutions to such pressing problems of economic recovery as reviving aggregate demand.[14] Some Social Democrats and trade unionists feared their arguments would be used (or abused) by conservative opponents of any new employment initiative, precisely because it could drive a wedge between the needs of workers in one region or sector over those of another.[15] Nevertheless, the new theoretical awareness about labor-market flexibility issues has helped guide a debate no longer centered on "the state versus the market" but on competing visions of industrial relations in the late 1980s and early 1990s.

Finally, the terms of the industrial policy debate shifted in a geographic sense. In the 1960s and 1970s structural policy was virtually synonymous with regional policy. It was assumed that troubled regions—those with aging industries or insufficient manufacturing, or those isolated from markets—needed nationally administered compensation for their relative backwardness. However, by the late 1980s, it was developments in the *Länder* (states, or provinces) that overshadowed actions by the *Bund* (the federal government), as the locus of action on industrial policy shifted from the center to the periphery, from "Model Germany" to "Model Baden-Württemberg" and "Model Bavaria," to name two *Länder* credited with interesting experiments in forging new financial links among regional governments and regional banks in order to modernize manufacturing. There has also been a second shift of focus away from Bonn, notably the decline of supranational coordination in macro-economic policy. In this regard, the seven-power summits no longer produce macro-economic bargains like that negotiated at the 1978 Bonn summit. For example, in the summits of the mid–1980s, President Reagan has offered no concrete actions on the U.S. deficit but a great deal of rhetoric (pleasing to the ears of European conservatives) about the virtues of less "restrictive" labor regulations and American-style capital markets.

The movement of the central government away from industrial policy, together with the decreased effectiveness of national and international macro-economics (i.e., the increasingly ineffective summits) after Keynesianism's brief second wind in the 1970s, might suggest that the West German economy is going through a second Americanization, this time following the political and economic contours of Reaganomics instead of the Kennedy era's New Economics. The reasons we argue that such an analysis is unlikely are examined in the next part of the chapter.

PART II: A NEW MESO-ECONOMIC ORDER?

The first portion of this chapter has shown that the industrial policy options of both the last center-left Schmidt government and the present center-right Kohl government have not proved particularly important or effective. From the deterioration of the *Strukturpolitik* debate in *Modell Deutschland* during the late 1970s to the lack of clear macro-economic policy in the post-*Wende* Kohl government in the mid–1980s, the picture for macro-economic policy formulation in the Federal Republic has not appeared—at first glance—to be particularly coherent.

This lack of a clear government macro-economic policy has caused some observers to conclude that the Germans are no longer leading economic players. Specifically, this view holds that the more generous social spending and protection for workers there have created a kind of "Eurosclerosis" which has impeded flexibility and, thereby, economic competitiveness.[16] Among the factors often cited as part of this apparent deterioration are:

- the failure of the macro-economic policies of the past 10 years, precisely at a time when sharp differences among various sectors of the economy have intensified;
- the alleged uncompetitiveness of many German industries on world markets, much of which conservatives have blamed on increased union demands for shortened working hours and the public sector's "usurious" role;
- the apparent lack of a "high-tech industry" and all its accoutrements—venture capital and entrepreneurial spirit—or, more specifically, the alleged inability of the German economy to keep pace with the Japanese and the United States with respect to innovation; and lastly,

- the increased criticism within the government coalition, reflected in one official of the Konrad Adenauer Foundation calling Helmut Kohl's economic policy "*Konzeptlos*."[17]

The upshot of this view—in the minds of many of those who made this diagnosis in the mid–1980s—is that German policy makers would be well advised to again follow the lead of the Americans (just as they did with Kennedy's New Economics in the 1960s). In the 1980s, this emulation would call for a new privatization mirroring the strategy of Margaret Thatcher and Ronald Reagan. If the economy was not performing as expected and if policy makers were hard pressed to devise appropriate policy via traditional public-sector instruments, then unleashing the "magic of the marketplace" was seen as the most appropriate solution.

Yet things were not so bleak as they seemed for the German economy. A series of innovative developments have been under way with West German industrial policy that predated the 1980s. By using, at least to Americans, a different set of conceptual and practical tools and institutions, major actors in the German economy have embarked not on the privatization strategy of Reagan or Thatcher, but on a "decentralized—or meso—corporatism."[18] This "new" *Modell Deutschland* consists of a regionalized and sector-specific pattern of industrial policies in which banks, industry associations, regional governments, and industry-wide trade unions were the main actors. Thus, the pattern of West German economic adjustment—even after the *Wende*—looked very different from the Anglo-American patterns of individualistically oriented privatization. The different structures of capitalism, party organization, and patterns of labor-market segmentation in West Germany all positioned the Federal Republic for better performance than many (American) observers believed possible.

More important, the particular patterns of this "hidden adaptiveness"—hidden in the sense that the Kohl government seemed not to fully comprehend its precise nature—may yet allow the unions and the SPD greater opportunity for resurgence via a reconstructed left industrial policy than is commonly believed. Yet such resurgence would also require a clear strategy for reconciling the left's traditional emphasis on social equity with these new patterns of economic adaptation. Its primary economic task would thus be to fight the employers' quest for "flexibility without solidarity." Such a strategy would have to go beyond these defensive responses, transforming these regionalized and private-sector-led policies into something more universal, while simultaneously offering greater public accountability and control.

West Germany's "Invisible" Economic Growth

By any thorough comparison, the performance of the West German economy has been strong. In the mid–1980s it remained the leading economy of Western Europe, its unemployment rate (at 8 to 9 percent) was only slightly higher than the "successful" U.S. economy, its inflation rate was near zero, and most of its export-oriented industries did remarkably well, finding niches which they have retained as the dollar has decreased in value.[19] By the late–1980s, West Germany had become the world's leading exporter.

Careful examination of the performance of such sectors as machine tools, chemicals, automobiles, and industrial applications of the electronics business showed the Germany economy to be much less uncompetitive than the conventional wisdom would have it. The primary reason for this "invisible" economic strength lay with the nature of production in these industries. One would be hard pressed to find a "splashy" high-tech industry like those in Japan or the United States. Yet if one looked for high-technology applications in such "unexciting" sectors as those mentioned above, then there was much more innovation and change to be found. What these and other German industries have been doing well for many years has been the practice of "flexible system manufacturing"[20] with the goal of finding niches in world markets for high-value-added products. Their key has been to apply the advanced skills of their—mostly unionized—workers to produce high-quality products at the upper price range of their respective markets. These German industries thus stayed at least a step ahead of their low-cost, mass-assembly counterparts in newly industrializing countries. Moreover, the continued high quality of most of their products has allowed these German firms to retain their export markets during both high and low dollar/Deutschmark exchange rate levels.

The organizational pattern of German industry has also differed from that of the United States, causing misperception about Germany's possibilities for adaptation. Most influential actors in the West German private sector, rather than unabashedly celebrating the small firm, as their counterparts do, have realized the symbiotic relationship among small and large firms in the Federal Republic. However important in its own right, the small firm has been primarily important as a key supplier to some of the more well known large firms. The question of size has also been important in understanding Germany's dominant large-firm structure, which arose in the late nineteenth century due to the country's need to industrialize rapidly. While not all late industrializers were slow to innovate—witness the Japanese example—the German pattern of industrialization, in both its trajectory and its nature, obscured its particular pattern of innovation in the 1980s. German production has always emphasized industrial goods, an arena in which innovation has been less apparent than in mass-market consumer goods. If this link between the patterns of industrialization and the patterns of innovation still holds, then it might explain how German industry has been slow to innovate but, once mobilized, highly effective.[21]

The Importance of Meso-Economic Analysis

As outlined above, a major characteristic of the West German economy since 1975 (and of most other industrialized economies) has been a sharp difference in the performance of economic sectors. A premium was thus placed on policies which could address specific regions and sectors of the economy. The economic sectors found in industrialized countries fall into three groups. In the first are such industries as coal, steel, and textiles, which have been profoundly threatened and radically contracted. The second have been the spectacular and fast-growing newer sectors. Most of high tech falls in this group. Yet the West German economy has been dominated by a third group of what we call "fulcrum" sectors. These sectors are more "mature"[22] than more splashy high-tech industries, but they have needed to remain internationally competitive since they have represented such a major share of West Germany's gross national product (GNP) and export share. Not surprisingly, Germany's fulcrum sectors have remained machine tools, chemicals, automobiles, and industrial electronics. And as these industries adapted, they have taken similar paths to innovation: they have employed high-value-added manufacturing through flexible work organization aimed at finding high-quality niches in world markets.[23] For Americans, the most visible examples of this strategy—in the sense that they are consumer products—have been Daimler-Benz and BMW.

Clearly, the extent of innovation in these sectors has gone beyond the capacities of individual firms totally to control. By the same token, the industry-specific nature of innovation has been too delicate to be adequately encouraged by clumsy macro-economic policies, which would be less able to make such differentiation. These industries have only been successful in innovating when forces within—or close to—that sector assume responsibility for change at the industry level. This suggests that the division between micro-economics (the firm) and macro-economics (the entire economy) must be supplemented by an understanding of how change occurs at the meso-economic (industry) level.[24] The strength of these attempts at meso-economic analysis is that they go beyond the more static industry studies which have surfaced since the *Strukturpolitik* (and American industrial policy) debates arrived on the scene some years ago.[25] Hans-Rudolf Peters and Lee Preston attempt to see this level of analysis not in isolation but as a strategic linking of targeted policies to particular sectors, policies which resonate both downward to the micro level and upward to the macro level. These actions work so well in Germany because they are legally sanctioned by the country's "public law tradition"[26] and because they have been practiced in one form or another for over 100 years.

Economic Policy and "Organized Capitalism"

But if—as we argued in Part I—national macro-economic policy has been in disarray, who or what was responsible for the comparatively successful performance of firms in the above fulcrum industries through the mid–1980s? Clearly, there are actors at the meso level in Germany who understand that the most distinctive characteristic of the economy since the mid–1970s has been a sharp difference in performance among sectors. More important, these actors have understood that targeted programs are needed to make these key fulcrum sectors serve as foundations for the successful adaptation of the entire economy. But exactly who are these actors? This meso-economic policy is being executed—within existing German legal traditions—by such private-sector and/or regionalized institutions as banks, industry organizations, *Länder* governments, and some of the industry-specific trade unions.

First, as Andrew Shonfield pointed out some years ago, the structure of the West German banking system allows these vertically integrated institutions to own large blocks of stock in most major corporations in Germany.[27] Consequently, their elevated position allows them to stand above the (micro-economic) fray and understand how particular industries can best be shaped. The banks have also taken note of the complaint that West Germany supposedly has lacked venture capital. The response of the Deutsche Bank, for example, was to found five in-house venture capital operations, allow them to compete with one another, and then mobilize the bank's ample resources around the most promising possibilities.[28] The banks also see a major role for themselves in shaping the patterns of innovation in German industry. When asked how the Deutsche Bank had stimulated long-term innovation in Germany, an aide to Bank Chairman Wilfried Guth stated: "The Deutsche Bank was founded in 1870. Or, in other words, one year before there was a Germany there was a Deutsche Bank." He paused and continued, "Regimes come and regimes go, but we will always be here."[29] This suggests that patterns established at the turn of the century have not substantially altered.[30] More concretely, this trend indicates that the banks fully appreciate the importance of innovation, and that their institutional position gives them an important role in shaping sectoral change.

Second, the industry organizations play a crucial role in another variant of "organized capitalism," namely, shaping the framework within which an industry's firms can adapt.[31] The term *Rahmenbedingungen* (roughly, "framework policies") is frequently used to describe the role of these sectoral-level institutions. The fact that this word is commonly used in Germany yet is difficult to translate into English suggests an important distinction between U.S. and German industry organizations. In the United States, such organizations are often conceived as special-interest groups or lobbying organizations, whose main function is defensively to "limit the damage" of public-sector policies or to protect against "unfair" competition from comparable industries in other countries. In Germany, on the other hand, these institutions have a much more strategic, positive role. A key distinction made by these institutions is between *Strukturpolitik* and *Ordnungspolitik*.[32] The latter term can be roughly translated as "policies of order," referring to setting the "framework" for industrial "order," as contrasted to the merely defensive role of their counterparts in the United States. To the industry organizations,

Strukturpolitik is a policy to be avoided because the public sector would be too directly involved in making strategic decisions. *Ordnungspolitik* is far more preferable because here the firms and the industry organizations play the dominant role.

The third component of West Germany's decentralized meso-corporatism is the Land governments. As noted in Part I, the governments of Baden Württemburg and Bavaria have taken major industrial policy initiatives aimed at transforming their regional economies.[33] From creative public-sector financing arrangements to export promotion and support for vocational education, these regional governments realize the importance of the public sector in creating the proper framework for innovation and change. Significantly, the locus of this public sector change is the meso-political rather than the macro-political level. Oddly enough, the Kohl government seems unable to translate the regional successes of fellow conservatives—Baden-Württemburg and Bavaria are governed by the CDU and CSU, respectively—into comparable national-level policies. Although the Kohl government has not slashed the public sector as have Reagan and Thatcher, it is not ideologically predisposed to playing the role that the Christian Democrats have in the southern *Länder*. In fact, the SPD Land governments in North Rhine-Westphalia and Bremen seem more interested in adapting these regional policies for their ends than does the Kohl government for national purposes. And because the problems of industrial adjustment are so sector- and region-specific, it is that much harder for any national government to supplement general macro-economic policies with more specific meso-economic ones.

A fourth component of innovative economic adaptation in these regions and in fulcrum industries is the skill base of the German working class and most unions' support for increased productivity and export-led growth. Long a crucial factor in Germany's economic strength, the skill level of workers is often overlooked by those touting Anglo-American-style privatization. There is an important reason why West German employers and regional governments—if not the Kohl government—have refrained from the "union bashing" practiced in Britain and the United States. Despite attempts to change the labor law to prohibit locked-out workers from obtaining unemployment insurance, most German conservatives realize that unionized workers are skilled workers whose services are needed if Germany's fulcrum sectors are to adapt and remain internationally competitive. German unions—particularly the metal workers (IG Metall), who organize the auto, machine tool, and electronics industries, and the chemical workers (IG Chemie)—realize their important position in the economy and thus secure favorable collective bargaining results. In addition, the unions—together with firms and governments (national and regional)—shape both the content and curriculum of the vocational education system. Thus, when the ending of the super-growth years of the U.S. high-tech industries is juxtaposed to the "hidden adaptiveness" that West Germany achieves through employing skilled workers in flexible-system manufacturing, it is unclear whether the United States has the more successful model of adaptation.

In addition to the Michael Piore and Charles Sabel work,[34] a study by two German industrial sociologists, Horst Kern and Michael Schumann,[35] contends that skilled workers are the primary reason for innovation and adaptation in the chemical, automobile, and machine tool sectors. Kern and Schumann argue that the flexible and advanced skills of workers in these industries enable employers to produce the high-value-added specialty products which other countries find difficult to emulate. More important—and unlike Piore and Sabel, who stop short of speculation—Kern and Schumann argue that this favorable structural position for organized labor represents an opportunity for West German unions to build a "producer consciousness" to shape progressive economic and social change. Yet, ultimately, we question whether this general model could be effectively applied—in various forms—to the entire labor movement, or whether it would only prove viable in a few sectors. If the latter result obtained, it might spawn a "new aristocracy of the working class," thereby impeding the solidarity with less skilled or fortunate workers that would be crucial for carrying out a left-wing industrial policy.

CONCLUSION

The uncertainty about whether the Piore/Sabel or Kern/Schumann models of flexible-system manufacturing could be diffused beyond a few industries represents the major challenge to any resurgence of a union/SPD *Strukturpolitik*. As important as these meso-economic interventions have been for particular industries, regions, and groups of skilled workers, they will not facilitate a left-wing resurgence unless they can be applied to other industries and regions. The SPD struggled with these themes throughout the mid and late 1980s and had yet to transform its previous primary emphasis on macroeconomic policy.

In the mid–1980s, West German "organized capital" and the Christian Democrats—at least within the *Länder*—had acquired a better sense of the meso-dynamics of the West German economy. Before the election of 1987, Kohl sought to take credit for the successes of fellow Christian Democrats, without having developed any national model of their regional successes. The center-right coalition was further advantaged because comparatively few members of the left-wing opposition—SPD and Greens—understood the meso-economic changes in the economy. Further impeding the SPD's attempts to formulate a left industrial policy were the debates about aligning with the Greens in a possible left-wing coalition and the inconclusive debate within the SPD about writing a "new Bad Godesberg Program."

In essence, by the mid and late 1980s, the SPD faced a kind of "programmatic paralysis." The party executive was unsure whether it wanted a dramatic new long-term policy statement (replacing Godesberg) or a more noncommittal campaign for the January 1987 elections. They opted for the latter because the party executive seemed to have no stomach for reviving the "state versus market" debates, given its commitment before the 1987 election to avoid proposing large budget increases and thereby increasing state spending. While the Kohl government has been unable to generalize the strong regional CDU/CSU successes at the national level, the SPD has experienced a parallel problem. Its most notable leaders, Oskar LaFontaine and Johannes Rau, the Minister-Presidents of the Saar and North Rhine-Westphalia, respectively, have been able to make gains from regional economic weaknesses for which the national government under Kohl has been blamed. Yet this kind of *defensive* strength has been no more nationally generalizable than Baden-Württemberg's or Bavaria's positive strengths. The SPD in the Saar and North Rhine-Westphalia has done well by taking advantage of labor's defensiveness. For example, LaFontaine's handling of the restructuring of ARBED, the troubled publicly held steel firm, was seen as a partial SPD success, and the party's defense of the unions on the issue of labor-law reform gained the SPD points because a majority of West Germans believe this CDU proposal to be unfair. But while this kind of defensive bargaining and mobilization has worked well in state elections—where sectoral issues are more salient—it has not been translated into national politics for the SPD any better than it has for the CDU.

Historically, the success of Social Democratic and trade union movements has turned on their ability to project themselves as representatives of the powerless majority. To the extent that wage bargaining in mass-production economies, Keynesian macro-economic policies, and distributive welfare state benefits were able to "deliver the goods" to their constituency during the postwar years, then these policies were successful. Yet the fragmentation brought on by sectoral and regional divergence—itself intensified by the new international division of labor—has dramatically undercut the effectiveness of these left-wing macro strategies. And simple defense of old macro strategies is no longer enough. More important, however, this fragmentation has deprived the left of a crucial tool—a universalism, and thus, a solidarity—for responding to these tendencies.

Any successful SPD/union *Strukturpolitik* must go beyond either defensive responses or the current macro-economic emphasis on a shortened work week for all. Clearly, a shortened work week might be part of a left *Strukturpolitik*. But unless the unions and the SPD challenge the employers' version of flexibility and push for their version of how the shorter work week would be implemented, the 35-hour movement will prove much less effective in producing new jobs than many of its adherents think.[36] We are arguing that a successful left *Strukturpolitik* must apply the "producer consciousness" of the Piore/Sabel and Kern/Schumann approaches to a wide variety of sectors. Such a strategy would establish the unions and SPD as major agents of progressive structural change, rather than as drags on a precarious economy. Although the policies pursued in particular industries and regions might differ, the unifying principle would be the belief that a union/SPD *Strukturpolitik* had a right and an obligation to challenge the conservative pattern of privatization. This left *Strukturpolitik* would need to have as its overarching mission the shaping of progressive economic and social change.

NOTES

1. Jeremiah M. Riemer is largely responsible for the introductory material and Part I; Christopher S. Allen for Part II and the Conclusion. Riemer wishes to thank Andy Markovits and the Harvard University Center for European Studies for providing a congenial work atmosphere. Allen wishes to thank the Division of Research at Harvard Business School for its travel support as well as Johns Hopkins University's American Institute for Contemporary German Studies, where he spent the 1988–89 academic year as the Hoechst Celanese/Siemens Research Fellow. He also acknowledges the helpful comments on earlier drafts of this chapter from Volker Bahl, Angelika Bahl-Benker, Angelika Christ, Gøsta Esping-Andersen, Gary Herrigel, Charles Sabel, and J. Nicholas Ziegler.

2. See Jeremiah M. Riemer, "Alterations in the Design of Model Germany: Critical Innovations in the Policy Machinery for Economic Steering," in Andrei S. Markovits, ed., *The Political Economy of West Germany: Modell Deutschland* (New York: Praeger, 1982, pp. 53–89.

3. On this point, see Jeremiah M. Riemer, "West German Crisis Management: Stability and Change in the Post Keynesian Age," in Norman J. Vig and Stephen E. Schier, eds., *Political Economy in Western Democracies* (New York: Holmes and Meier, 1985).

4. For a theoretical exposition of this concept in a comparative context, see Wolfgang Streeck and Philippe Schmitter, eds., *Private Interest Government: Beyond Market and State* (Los Angeles: Sage, 1985); and Alan Cawson, ed., *Organized Interests and the State: Studies in Meso-corporatism* (Los Angeles: Sage, 1985); and for analysis with respect to the Federal Republic, see Christopher S. Allen, "Corporatism and Regional Economic Policies in the Federal Republic of Germany: The 'Meso' Politics of Industrial Adjustment," *Publius* (forthcoming, 1989).

5. This section draws on Riemer, "Alterations," and Riemer, "West German Crisis Management." Consult the latter for references to further literature. A fuller account of developments before the 1982 *Wende* may be found in Jeremiah M. Riemer, "Crisis and Intervention in the West German Economy: A Political Analysis of Changes in the Policy Machinery During the 1960s and 1970s," Ph.D. dissertation, Cornell University, 1983. On the perspective since 1983, see Jeremiah M. Riemer, "Parties and Economic Policy in the Federal Republic of Germany: Has There Ever Been a *Wende*?" paper presented at the APSA Meeting, 1984; and Douglas Webber, "Combating and Acquiescing in Unemployment? Crisis Management in Sweden and West Germany," *West European Politics* 6 (January 1983). For a parallel account emphasizing changes in industrial production, see Michael Piore and Charles Sabel, *The Second Industrial Divide* (New York: Basic Books, 1984), esp. pp. 142–51, 229–34. Chapters 7 and 10 of

Piore and Sabel offer valuable background on the strengths and weaknesses of international Keynesianism.

6. See Wolf-Dieter Narr, Hermann Schneer, and Dieter Spöri, *SPD: Staatspartei oder Reformpartei?* (Munich: Beck, 1976).

7. On the SPD's posture toward the unions and reform, see Mary Nolan and Charles F. Sabel, "Class Conflict and the Social Democratic Reform Cycle in Germany," *Political Power and Social Theory* 3 (1982): 158–69.

8. For a review of the current status and different emphases of the five institutes' reports, see *Wo steht die deutsche Wirtschaft heute? Stärken und Schwächen im strukturellen Anpassungsprozess.* Vorträge des Symposiums zur Strukturberichterstattung, September 24 and 25, 1984, Frankfurt am Main. Kreditanstalt für Wiederaufbau.

9. Josef Esser, "State, Business and Trade Unions After the 'Political Wende,' " *West European Politics* 9 (April 1986): 198–214.

10. See Riemer, "Crisis and Intervention in the West German Economy," chap. 4, for details of the debate.

11. Werner Sengenberger, *Die gegenwärtige Arbeitslosigkeit: auch ein Strukturproblem des Arbeitsmarkts* (Frankfurt: Campus 1978).

12. See the collection of essays in Werner Sengenberger, *Der gespaltene Arbeitsmarkt. Probleme der Arbeitsmarktsegmentation* (Frankfurt: 1978). In English: Frank Wilkerson, ed., *The Dynamics of Labor Market Segmentation* (London: 1981). Important differences between West German and American theories and structures of labor-market segmentation are reviewed in the introduction to Sengenberger's *Der gespaltene Arbeitsmarkt* and in a recent study of Sengenberger and Christoph Köhler comparing the U.S. and West German automobile industries, *Konjunktur und Personalanpassung* (Frankfurt: 1983).

13. On the barriers to effective stabilization policy, see Burkhart Lutz, "Sieben magere Jahre—oder: Ist Unterbeschäftigung unvermeidlich?," in Ulrich Borsdorf et al., *Gewerkschaftliche Politik: Reform aus Solidarität* (Cologne: 1977), pp. 489–510; on vocational training, see Burkhart Lutz and Werner Sengenberger, *Arbeitsmarktstrukturen und öffentliche Arbeitsmarktpolitik* (Göttingen: 1974).

14. However, see Sengenberger, *Die gegenwärtige Arbeitslosigkeit*, and Lutz, "Sieben magere Jahre," for some preliminary suggestions. Also thought-provoking is Burkhart Lutz, *Der kurze Traum immerwährender Prosperität* (Frankfurt: 1984), and the historical overview provided by Piore and Sabel, *Second Industrial Divide*.

15. According to one observer of labor-market policy: "The findings of segmentation analysis on the hardening of structural unemployment during and due to the present labour slack were taken to support arguments against the expansion of final demand to meet the medium term 'bulges' in the labour force. Ex post facto, this alliance between segmentationists and neoclassical policy makers has proved to be one of the major obstacles to creating an active employment policy." Jürgen Kühl, "Employment Policy in Germany: Analytical Aspects and Empirical Evidence," in Frank Wilkinson, ed., *The Dynamics of Labor Market Segmentation* (London: Academic Press, 1981), p. 278.

16. Bruce Nussbaum, *The World After Oil* (New York: Basic Books, 1983).

17. Interview with Olga Wilde, June 10, 1985, Bonn, FRG.

18. See Streeck and Schmitter, *Private Interest Government*, and Cawson, *Organized Interests and the State*.

19. Robert M. Grant, "Adjusting to the Strong $: Lessons from the European Ex-

perience," *California Journal of Management* 28 (Fall 1985): 82–97; Henry Ergas, "Why Do Some Countries Innovate More than Others?" *Centre for European Policy Studies*, Paper No. 5, 1984.

20. See Charles Sabel, *Work and Politics* (Cambridge, Eng.: Cambridge University Press, 1982), particularly the concluding chapter.

21. The relationship between size and innovation is analyzed thoroughly in Joseph Schumpeter, *Capitalism, Socialism, and Democracy* (New York: Harper & Row, 1976), particularly in the chapter on monopolies. Two divergent theoretical positions on this theme are those of Mancur Olson, *The Rise and Decline of Nations* (New Haven: Yale University Press, 1982), and Albert O. Hirschman, *Exit, Voice and Loyalty* (Cambridge, Mass.: Harvard University Press, 1970). The implications of Olson's argument are that large institutions are incapable of innovation, while Hirschman points to conditions under which they could innovate.

22. The term was first popularized in 1983 when the Massachusetts state government established an agency to address these issues of industrial adjustment. See Commonwealth of Massachusetts, *Governor's Commission on the Future of Mature Industries*, 1984.

23. See Piore and Sabel, *Second Industrial Divide*.

24. The best theoretical treatment of this issue is Hans-Rudolf Peters, *Grundlagen der Mesooekonomie und Strukturpolitik* (Bern and Stuttgart: P. Haupt, 1981). For a good overview of the literature on meso approaches—including those of Streeck, Schmitter, and Cawson—see Lee E. Preston, "A Perspective on Mesoeconomics," Discussion Paper, Wissenschaftzentrum Berlin, October 1984.

25. For a review of the major approaches in the U.S. debate, see Christopher S. Allen and Harvey Rishikof, "Tale Thrice Told: A Review of Industrial Policy Proposals," *Journal of Policy Analysis and Management* 4 (Winter 1985): 234–49.

26. See Peter Katzenstein, *Policy and Politics in West Germany: The Growth of a Semi-Sovereign State* (Philadelphia: Temple University Press, 1987).

27. Andrew Shonfield, *Modern Capitalism* (New York: Oxford University Press, 1965).

28. For an analysis of the role of the Deutsche Bank, see "Markt und Herrlichkeit der Deutschen Bank," *Der Spiegel*, February 11, 1985.

29. Interview with Jochen Degkwitz, Deutsche Bank, Frankfurt, June 16, 1985.

30. For the major reference work on this theme, see Rudolf Hilferding, *Finance Capital* (London: Routledge and Kegan Paul, 1981).

31. Here we are distinguishing between organizations of "collective capital" in the macro-economic sense, such as the Bundesvereinigung der deutschen Arbeitgeberverbände (BDA) in West Germany, which represent the interests of *all* industry, and those which represent the interests of *specific* industries in the meso-economic sense. The former were analyzed in the 1960s by Gerard Braunthal; see *The Federation of German Industry in Politics* (Ithaca, N.Y.: Cornell University Press, 1965). The latter have been studied more recently in Wolfgang Streeck, "Neo-corporatist Industrial Relations and the Economic Crisis in West Germany," European University Institute Working Paper No. 97, 1984, and Philippe Schmitter, "Democratic Theory and Neo-corporatist Practice," *Social Research* 50 (Winter 1983): 885–928.

32. For a distinction which one industry association makes between the two terms, see Verband der Chemischen Industrie, "Die Rolle der Verbände im Wirtschafts- und Gesellschaftsystem der Bundesrepublik Deutschland," January 14, 1985.

33. "Fingerhackeln im Suden," *Wirtschaftswoche*, May 24, 1985, pp. 36–50.

34. See Piore and Sabel, *Second Industrial Divide*.

35. See Horst Kern and Michael Schumann, *Das Ende der Arbeitsteilung?* (Munich: Beck, 1984).

36. For a more complete articulation of this argument, see Christopher S. Allen, "Trade Unions, Worker Participation, and Flexibility: Linking the Micro to the Macro," *Comparative Politics* (forthcoming, 1989); and Christopher S. Allen, "Worker Participation and the West German Trade Unions: An Unfulfilled Dream?," in Carmen Sirianni, ed., *Worker Participation and the Politics of Reform* (Philadelphia: Temple University Press, 1987), pp. 174–97.

5

Neoliberalism and the Battle over Working-Time Reduction in West Germany

Kathleen Thelen

After 13 years in opposition, West Germany's conservative Christian Democratic Union (CDU) reclaimed the Chancellory in 1982, promising major change (*Die Wende*).[1] As elsewhere, the conservative refrain was to revitalize the economy through deregulation and privatization, offering less state and more market control. Since then, German unions have confronted not only employers emboldened by high unemployment, but also a conservative government committed to neoliberal, supply-side solutions to the country's economic stagnation.

This chapter explores how the "crisis" of Keynesianism and this combination of high structural unemployment and neoliberal adjustment have affected collective bargaining in West Germany. The effects have been threefold. First, the content of bargaining between labor and capital has shifted and echoes the dominant political agenda. It focuses increasingly on labor as a factor of production rather than as a constituent of demand.[2] Second and related, the political priority given to deregulation (especially of the labor market) is paralleled in collective bargaining by conflicts centering on flexibility in the deployment of labor at the plant level. In Germany's still comparatively collaborative labor relations, such conflicts focus not on whether there will be such flexibility, but on different types of flexibility with different implications for the continued viability of central unions. Third, the current "crisis" of labor relations has introduced new strains into the machinery of centralized bargaining, but it has also shown how the resiliency of West Germany's "dual system" (discussed below) has been a stabilizing factor in labor relations.

This chapter focuses on recent negotiations between the German Metalworkers' Union (IG Metall) and the employers' organization (Gesamtmetall) over the union's demand for a 35-hour work week. The IG Metall's campaign for working-time reduction provides a good window on broader trends in West German labor relations for several reasons. The IG Metall occupies a pivotal position within the West German political economy. As by far the largest of Germany's multi-industrial unions, it has traditionally served as the informal leader of the nation's labor movement as a whole. For this reason, and because it organizes the full range of Germany's metalworking industries, which comprise the core of the postwar German economy, its battles reverberate politically and economically throughout the country. Working-time reduction is an especially key issue, the union having cited it as their number-one priority for the 1980s. The resources the IG Metall has already devoted to this goal (including the largest strike in the history of the Federal Republic) indicate the centrality of this conflict to labor-capital relations generally.

By 1987 the IG Metall had reached an agreement with Gesamtmetall reducing the work week to 37 hours by 1989. The compromise, achieved in two bargaining rounds—in 1984 and 1987—called for working-time reduction, but with flexibility in its implementation at the plant level. The contracts established parameters for a second round of bargaining between works councils and individual employers. Such "opening clauses" in central contracts, devolving responsibilities to plant works councils, are not unprecedented. However, the agreements on working-time reduction do delegate to works councils important new responsibilities on the working-time issue.

Negotiations over working-time reduction reveal a trend toward "flexibility" in central contracts. Through much of the 1960s and 1970s, under conditions of full employment and under the cyclical strain of inflationary pressures, collective bargaining primarily revolved around wage issues. Central contracts established universally binding "floors" on wages and working conditions. In contrast, central negotiations over working-time reduction in the 1980s have produced no single, universally binding regulations, but instead set parameters for a second round of plant-level negotiations.

Wolfgang Streeck's insightful analysis provides a starting point for interpreting these pressures toward greater flexibility in central bargaining.[3] He argues that the deterioration of labor's market power and the changing character of international competition in the 1980s have produced pressures for a decentralization of bargaining. According to Streeck, continuing high unemployment encourages employer efforts to relax the "rigidities" imposed by central bargaining and to exploit labor's market weakness to "restore flexibility to a bargained economy" through the reintroduction of market pressures into neo-corporatist arrangements.[4]

Streeck argues further that these tensions for the decentralization of bargaining from without are exacerbated by tensions within the working class itself. He cites an "emerging 'wildcat co-operation' of individual workforces in workplace-based productivity alliances [that] parallels and reinforces... the pressures from employers for a relaxation of corporatist controls over the workplace."[5] Germany's "dual system" of labor relations—in which plant-level works councils are formally autonomous from the overarching industrial unions—provides particularly fertile ground for such developments. Although works councilors are in fact overwhelmingly (80 percent) union members, this structure and the relatively strong rights works councils enjoy encourage syndicalist tendencies, or what in Germany is often called "plant egoism" (*Betriebsegoismus*).[6]

An analysis of negotiations over working-time reduction confirms some of the tensions Streeck cites. But it also demonstrates the resiliency of centralized bargaining and the dual system. Similar pressures for decentralization have elsewhere translated into the breakdown of pattern bargaining, or the fragmentation of labor interests by "hiving off" particular plants or industries for exemption from central contracts. In Germany, in contrast, signs of decentralization (via plant-level flexibility) coexist with signs of continued centralization or even recentralization (as in the peak-level negotiations that produced the 1987 compromise on working-time reduction). Decentralizing pressures have been resolved within the context of central bargaining, by incorporating flexibility into the central contracts themselves. Central bargaining itself is not at issue in Germany, but rather the "balance" between central agreements and flexibility at the plant level. And finally, when viewed in a broader comparative perspective, it is clear that while plant egoism may be strong in Germany's dual system, the "superego" of central unionism is not weak.

The remainder of this chapter is divided into three parts. First, I will examine the macro-economic and political shifts that have provided the context for the current renegotiation of labor-capital relations in central collective bargaining in West Germany. Second, I will describe the evolution of union strategy on unemployment and the campaign for weekly working-time reduction. The focus is on the two collective bargaining rounds in which the union and employers clashed over both the working-time and the flexibility issues. Finally, I will examine the implications of these developments in collective bargaining, looking particularly at what the crisis of Keynesianism and the ascendance of neoliberalism mean for relations both between labor and capital and between the union's central leadership and the shop floor.

THE CHANGING CLIMATE OF LABOR RELATIONS IN WEST GERMANY, 1975–84

The political and economic context has shifted decisively in Germany over the last decade and a half. In the late 1960s and early 1970s, the Social

Democrats premised their economic and industrial policies on the inclusion and active cooperation of organized labor.[7] In this period, the government drew the unions into moderately corporatist arrangements (such as Germany's informal incomes policy, *Konzertierte Aktion*) and inaugurated aggregate-demand management and active labor-market policies. For the Social Democratic government, the incorporation and cooperation of Germany's industrial unions was crucial in macro-economic steering.

As early as 1975, however, strains in the "German model" were beginning to show.[8] Although in less dramatic form than in Britain or the United States, the German government gradually abandoned the Keynesian demand-management model of the early 1970s in favor of a strategy emphasizing monetary stability and fiscal austerity.[9] Policy in Germany shifted from the promotion of full employment through macro-economic demand stimulus toward efforts to restart growth by spurring investment and removing obstacles to capital accumulation.

In the late 1970s, German unions not only watched rising unemployment erode their market power; they also saw their political power wane as the Social Democrats shifted course. Thus, neo-corporatism was faltering well before the Social Democrats lost power in 1982, something the unions made explicit when they withdrew from *Konzertierte Aktion* discussions in 1977. So long as the SPD held power, though, the unions had nowhere to go, and found themselves trapped into tacit cooperation with a government that grew less and less responsive to labor's demands.[10]

The IG Metall Responds

The prevailing mood within the IG Metall in this period seemed to be one of waiting out the storm, banking on an economic upswing to reverse labor's weakened position.[11] The idea that better times were just around the corner died slowly. Employer strategies and the union's own assessment of the likely effects of wage militancy in the face of increasingly restrictive monetary policy sustained wage restraint in central bargaining, even after *Konzertierte Aktion* broke down.[12]

However, relations between the government and the unions (and particularly the IG Metall) were becoming increasingly strained. Chancellor Helmut Schmidt's austerity programs rolled back many of the gains that labor had achieved in the reforms of the late 1960s and early 1970s. Thus, the union's wait-and-see attitude was foundering by the late 1970s, and in 1978 the IG Metall went on the offensive, waging two bitter strikes—the first in the metalworking industry in Baden-Württemberg and later in the steel industry.[13]

These two battles preview the important aspects of labor politics in the 1980s. They foreshadow the growing importance of "qualitative" issues in labor-capital relations and mark a shift in the union's agenda, from (primarily) wage to nonwage issues.[14] Demands to alleviate the negative effects of technological change and reduce unemployment lay at the heart of the two strikes in 1978.

While the union did not walk away from either struggle empty-handed, the 1978 conflicts did reveal the difficulties of the union's new strategy of self-reliance. In the Baden-Württemberg conflict, the union won 18-month income guarantees for individual workers demoted to lower-level jobs. It failed, though, to achieve its more far-reaching demand for income security.[15] And the union's attempt to generalize the results of negotiations in that district to other bargaining districts foundered on employer resistance. The settlement in the steel industry increased paid vacation time to six weeks and secured extra paid working days for night-shift and older workers, but the union did not achieve its original demand to reduce weekly working time for steelworkers to 35 hours.

The union's weakened market position no doubt contributed to its limited gains in these two major conflicts.[16] Yet the character of the demands themselves evoked particularly strong resistance by employers. In both cases, employers responded to the strikes with major lockouts. In addition, a document of the German Employers' Organization (BDA: Bundesvereinigung der Deutschen Arbeitgeberverbände) surfaced during the steel strike, which further heightened tensions between the union and employers. The document listed issues on which the BDA counseled its member organizations against even negotiating with the unions.[17] This so-called *Tabu-Katalog* named working-time reduction with full wage compensation, along with other issues (such as restrictions on overtime), as "nonnegotiable." In short, what became clear in 1978 was not only that employers were in a stronger position than before, but that they would systematically resist centrally imposed agreements on issues they saw as restricting managerial discretion over the organization of production.

The 1978 strikes in many ways previewed precisely those conflicts that have become central in the 1980s. Employers are still willing to negotiate central wage bargains in the metalworking industry. But as the union turned its attention to unemployment and other "qualitative" issues, they ran up against employer taboos. The IG Metall's experience in 1978 provided a jolt that forced the union to rethink its strategy. But unlike their counterparts in some other Social Democratic countries, German unions could not really count on decisive government action on the unemployment problem. Indeed, the union's political clout appeared to be waning in tandem with its labor-market strength.

Die Wende

In 1982, the Free Democrats put an end to the strife-torn center-left coalition by forming a new alliance with the CDU. Like conservatives elsewhere in Europe and North America, Chancellor Helmut Kohl called for the revitalization of market forces to stimulate growth. But while the rhetoric sounded the same themes as the Thatcher and Reagan administrations, the West German neoliberal *Wende* turned out to be milder in many ways than in either Britain or the United States.[18] Werner Sengenberger's characterization of a shift from "socially controlled welfare capitalism" to "unrestricted market capitalism" may be thus somewhat overdrawn, although the general direction is certainly right.[19]

Peter Katzenstein explains how institutional and political arrangements that bias German politics against abrupt and dramatic policy reversals have constrained German neoliberalism. His analysis thus illuminates why Kohl's promised policy changes were not as extensive and thoroughgoing as those orchestrated by conservatives elsewhere.[20] For example, Kohl's attack on the welfare state has been far less ambitious in its intent, and less comprehensive in its effects, than Thatcher's in Britain. Moreover, because German unions are institutionally and legally anchored at virtually every level of the political economy, a frontal attack on their power is politically impossible.

The comparative moderation of neoliberalism in West Germany is important because this political moderation has undoubtedly helped temper industrial conflict. The compromises the metalworkers and employers reached in 1984 and 1987 would have been less likely in a more polarized national political context. German labor's still relatively strong position is thus both cause and consequence of that country's milder dose of neoliberalism.

This, of course, is not to say that nothing has changed. Among other things, neoliberalism has brought cuts in unemployment insurance and social spending as well as changes in immigration law and in labor-market policies. The latter has been particularly important in the government's deregulation agenda. As Streeck and others have pointed out, Germany's heralded system of codetermination and the job security it provides have made labor a kind of fixed cost for employers.[21] The rigidities this implies have been the target of the conservatives' labor-market policy.

Such rigidities, argued the government's economic advisers, not only act as a drag on firms struggling to keep pace in the highly changeable international markets of the 1980s; the job security enjoyed by the presently employed has the nefarious side effect of discouraging employers from hiring new workers. For the government, then, the culprit in West Germany's high unemployment rate was the market-distorting effects of codetermination and strong unions. The antidote was to "restore worker competition" through changes in labor-market policy.[22]

The cornerstone legislation in this strategy was the Employment Promotion Act of 1985 (*Beschäftigungsförderungsgesetz*).[23] By and large, the new law did not tamper extensively with works councils' existing codetermination rights. Rather, its main thrust was to offer employers a broader palette of options to increase the flexibility of their workforces in ways that were less regulated under either existing collective bargains or codetermination laws, thus partially circumventing union and works council influence.[24]

The Employment Promotion Act increased employers' options in several ways.[25] First, the law allowed employers, without special justification, to hire new workers on a fixed-term basis for up to 18 months (in plants with fewer than 20 workers, for up to 2 years). Second, it extended the maximum tenure of subcontracted or "temporary" workers (*Leiharbeiter*) from three to six months.[26] Third, the law sought to promote part-time work and job sharing by clarifying and regulating certain elements of their legal status. And finally, it impinged on codetermination by redefining some of the conditions under which employers must negotiate a "social plan" with their works councils over major layoffs not brought about in connection with changes in the plant. In sum, the government's new labor-market policies aimed at facilitating greater flexibility in plant personnel policy by making it easier for employers to use workers whose status is less regulated through collective bargaining and codetermination.[27]

The government's approach to unemployment further confirmed the unions' political isolation. Not only was unemployment still rising steadily; the conservatives' answer to this was to encourage labor-market flexibility in its most neoliberal form. Although the Employment Promotion Act did not go into effect until 1985, the gist of the government's plans for the labor market was clear long before that time. It is against this political backdrop that the union's campaign for working-time reduction must be understood.

THE BATTLE FOR WEEKLY WORKING-TIME REDUCTION

The IG Metall has taken a leading role among unions in the advanced capitalist countries in striving for working-time reduction through collective bargaining in the 1980s. However, the foregoing analysis shows that this vanguard role is as much a sign of German labor's political weakness as of the metalworkers' industrial power and self-confidence. Between 1978 and 1983, the IG Metall watched unemployment double, rising from just under 1 million to 2.3 million. Despite the unions' entreaties, the Social Democratic government had not acted decisively to stem the unemployment problem, which had reached postwar highs by the time the SPD left office. The incoming conservative government only promised to make things worse for the unions by addressing unemployment through its attack on labor-market "rigidities." The unions were not convinced that this approach would reduce unemployment. Worse still, to the extent that it did create jobs of a certain type, it would also reinforce divisions within the working class between full-time and various kinds of "irregular," less-than-permanent workers. Such divisions could only weaken the union over the long run.

At their 1983 congress, union delegates voted to pursue a 35-hour work week (with full wage compensation) in the metalworking industries as a whole, and indeed to make it the union's number-one bargaining priority. With that, the stage was set for a showdown with Gesamtmetall, since in demanding a 35-hour week, the union was targeting an employer taboo.

The 1984 Bargaining Round

For the IG Metall even more was at stake in the 1984 bargaining round than working-time reduction.[28] The issue for the union was its very ability to represent and defend workers' interests at a time when its political and market strength was low. On the eve of the 1984 strike, the head of collective bargaining, Hans Janßen, stated: "We openly admit that . . . we are also defending our capacity to defend workers' interests. . . . [This] strength cannot be sealed up in a bottle and saved for better times."[29]

From Gesamtmetall's perspective as well, the stakes were very high in the 1984 conflict. The National Employers' Association had declared weekly working-time reduction to be nonnegotiable. Employers feared that concessions to the union would impose unbearably high labor costs on German industry, which was still struggling in the midst of a recession.[30] A settlement in the all-important metalworking industries would surely open the floodgates for working-time reduction in all of German industry.

Both sides thus saw the looming battle as a test of resolve and of strength that would set the tone in labor relations for a long time to come. The conflict that ensued did indeed turn into the biggest strike in the history of the Federal Republic.[31] Yet unlike the British miners' strike (which occurred at the same time), this struggle was not to be a fight to the death. When the dust had settled from this historic confrontation, the compromise was working-time reduction with flexibility in its implementation at the plant level. The union had achieved the breakthrough it sought on working time (though a more modest one than it had hoped). And employers, concerned about their ability to respond "flexibly" in the increasingly volatile markets of the 1980s, secured greater latitude in working-time arrangements.[32] The compromise assigned a crucial role to plant works councils in implementing the central agreement.

The early stages of the conflict made clear that the struggle would be long. The IG Metall held strike ballots in Baden-Württemberg and Hessen in May 1984, and employed a "mini-max" strike strategy which targeted a few selected plants on whose production the entire automobile industry depended.[33] Gesamtmetall countered with massive lockouts. Four weeks into the strike the bargaining partners had made little progress toward a compromise, and Gesamtmetall still opposed all proposals for a general reduction of weekly working hours.

Negotiations were still deadlocked in the fifth week of the strike, at which point both sides—under considerable public pressure to end the dispute—

agreed to impartial mediation. Georg Leber, former head of the (moderate) construction workers' union, chaired the proceedings.[34] After almost a week of negotiations, he announced a compromise proposal calling for a 3.3 percent wage increase for 1984 and a 1.5 hour reduction in the work week beginning April 1, 1985. To maintain wages in a shorter work week, Leber proposed a 3.9 percent raise beginning on April 1, 1985, and a 2 percent wage increase beginning on the same date for the duration of the contract.[35] His proposal allowed for some flexibility in applying the bargain within the individual plants, to be worked out in negotiations between works councils and employers. Thus, the core of the Leber compromise, which became the basis for the central agreement, was working-time reduction to 38.5 hours per week with "flexibility" in its plant-level implementation.

The contract established parameters for working-time reduction which gave employers new flexibility in two forms, what in Germany are referred to as differentiation and flexibilization.[36] First, the contract's *differentiation* clause allowed employers (in negotiations with plant works councils) to distribute working-time reduction unevenly across the workforce. Some workers could continue with a regular 40-hour week, while others worked fewer hours, so long as a plant average of 38.5 hours was maintained. Gesamtmetall was particularly eager to exempt skilled workers from working-time reduction, anticipating skill shortages and higher production costs associated with hiring additional qualified workers.

Second, the contract's *flexibilization* clause created new leeway for varying working hours over time. Daily or weekly working-time reductions were only one possibility. Another was to cumulate reduced hours into free days, which many workers preferred and many employers viewed as less disruptive to production. Various combinations were allowable, so long as the 38.5 hour per week average was achieved within a two-month "balancing" period (*Ausgleichszeit*).[37]

While the union billed the outcome as a great victory (a "broken taboo"), employers heralded the retreat from "rigid central agreements" as an important step forward. The door was now opened to the 35-hour work week, but another door was also opened—to reduced but more flexible working times. A shift in the balance between the central union and works councils facilitated a compromise under highly politicized and polarized conditions. At the same time, it thrust works councils onto center stage in industrial relations and union bargaining.

Denouement in the Plant

The "opening clause" in the central contract on working-time reduction meant that the 1984 bargaining round was not over when union representatives and employers shook hands in the various bargaining regions. As soon as they signed the contract, both sides began counseling their respective constituencies on how to proceed. The IG Metall advised works councils not to negotiate without first receiving instructions and feedback from the union.[38] Above all, union leaders hoped to thwart employer efforts to exploit the contract's differentiation clause. Under the motto "38.5 hours for *all* workers," they urged works councils to resist attempts by employers to split the workforce by negotiating different base working times for different groups of workers.[39] In the union's preparation for the second round of plant bargaining, the question of flexibilization (flexibility over time) seemed to take a back seat to the goal of blocking differentiation among workers.

The peak business association meanwhile launched its own offensive, encouraging individual employers to take full advantage of both kinds of working-time flexibility won in the 1984 round. In a brochure distributed to its members, the BDA detailed several models for reducing working time which showed how firms could use the flexibilization and differentiation clauses to avoid skill shortages and maximize investment returns by introducing or expanding shift work.[40]

Plant negotiations over the implementation of the central agreement ran from July 1984 to April 1985. Early on it became clear that despite the entreaties of the BDA, very few employers were taking advantage of differentiated working times for different categories of workers. Singling out their most valuable (usually skilled) workers for longer regular working hours (and thus also depriving them of some overtime pay) quickly proved to be politically unworkable.[41] And, in general, the complicated differentiation formulas worked out in the BDA brochure were simply too complex and unwieldy to spark great interest, especially in small- and middle-sized firms lacking a personnel department to administer them.

In the end, only 13 percent of all plants concluded agreements using the contract's differentiation clause. And even in the plants that did, the number of workers affected was generally very small. All told, only 5.7 percent of all workers in the metalworking industries ended up with regular working times either above or below 38.5 hours.[42]

Where considerable variation did emerge in the second round of plant negotiations was in working-time flexibility across time. Here a variety of models emerged. A survey of over 3,300 plants in the metalworking industries conducted by a union research institute found that just half (47.7 percent) had concluded *weekly* working-time reductions, which was what the union originally had in mind.[43] Another 8.3 percent distributed working-time reduction over several weeks. Thirty percent of all plant agreements called for cumulating working-time reduction into free days, often situated on "window" days between holidays and weekends.[44]

The 1984 bargaining round was a turning point in many respects. The union mobilized enormous financial and political resources and achieved concessions on an issue that employers had considered nonnegotiable. But the IG Metall also paid a price for what it achieved. In conceding flexibility, the union ceded some control over plant outcomes. Establishing parameters rather than a single uniform level of working-time reduction opened up possibilities for different working times for different workers, and for variation across plants. The critical task of actively implementing the agreement in the plants (as opposed to simply enforcing centrally defined rules) fell to the works councils.

Of the two kinds of flexibility the contract allowed, differentiation is arguably the more insidious from the union's perspective. Uniform, all-encompassing minimum standards are crucial to reducing competition among workers in the market and maintaining unity and solidarity in the labor movement.[45] Differentiation directly threatens a weakening of labor through fragmentation. It breaks with the principle of a single uniform working week that applies to all workers, and makes it possible for different workers to be covered by different working-time minimums. Moreover, newly hired workers employed at less than 38.5 hours per week would not be entitled to full wage compensation for their shorter hours, and this would permit working-time-based income differences among workers as well.[46] The union's emphasis on thwarting differentiation in the second round of plant negotiations reflects its fear of such working-time-based fragmentation.

Flexibilization (flexibility across time rather than among workers) contains its own dangers (discussed below), but its direct effect on working-class unity appears to be more ambiguous than differentiation. The union, of course, fundamentally opposed all employer proposals for flexible working times throughout the 1984 conflict. However, Karl Hinrichs and Helmut Wiesenthal note that delegates to the IG Metall's 1983 congress had considered (though ultimately rejected) a proposal that would have allowed for a degree of such flexibility by defining the demand for the 35-hour work week as an average to be maintained over an eight-week period. These authors also cite instances in the course of the 1984 conflict itself in which union representatives expressed a willingness to negotiate over possible concessions on this kind of "collective" working-time flexibility.[47] At no time did the union express a similar willingness to discuss differentiated working times for individual workers or groups of workers. Differentiation, unlike flexibilization, appears to have been less a point of compromise in 1984 than a straightforward victory for Gesamtmetall, though one that ultimately proved less useful to employers than the organization had thought.

The 1987 Bargaining Round

The 1984 agreement had indeed set a precedent. The contract had stipulated that the issue of further working-time reduction could not be opened for three years. Throughout 1985 and 1986, however, the union emphasized that it considered the 1984 agreement only the first step toward its goal of a 35-hour work week. And when the IG Metall opened negotiations over further working-time reduction in 1987, Gesamtmetall came armed with demands for more flexibility.

Although the union's demand was the same as in 1984, the tenor in both camps was very different leading up to the 1987 bargaining round. In June 1986 the union's collective bargaining department issued a position paper that criticized employers' flexibility demands while acknowledging that many workers prefer more flexible working times.[48] Working-time flexibility, the document argued, should serve workers' interests. In addition, while the union still adamantly opposed working-time differentiation, statements by the union's president, Franz Steinkühler, seemed to signal a willingness to discuss certain varieties of working-time flexibilization.[49]

For their part, employers still opposed in principle a further reduction of the work week. Yet the pre-negotiation intransigence that had heightened tensions prior to the 1984 bargaining round was absent. They made it clear that they were willing to discuss further working-time reduction, provided additional flexibility was also part of the package. Referring to a trade-off between the two, Hans-Peter Stihl, head of Gesamtmetall's Baden-Württemberg district, said, "[The union] cannot have one without the other."[50]

For the first time ever, Gesamtmetall went into the 1987 bargaining round with its own set of demands.[51] First, employers wanted to use negotiations over working-time reduction to contractually establish Saturday as a regular work day, something most existing regional contracts neither specifically ruled out nor encouraged. Second, employers sought to win greater flexibility in the distribution of work across time. As discussed above, the 1984 contract required employers to arrange working times so that an average of 38.5 hours per week was maintained over a maximum two-month period. In 1987, employers wanted to relax this constraint to twelve months, to enable them to adapt working times to seasonal fluctuations in demand while avoiding the expense of overtime.

The bargaining process in 1987 turned out to be in some ways more centralized than ever. When negotiations in the regional bargaining districts reached an impasse, Steinkühler called Gesamtmetall president Werner Stumpfe on April 6 and declared that he was prepared to discuss a possible resolution to the conflict "any day from now on."[52] Peak-level negotiations between the top IG Metall and Gesamtmetall leaderships replaced the usual region-led "pattern" bargaining. Thirteen hours of negotiations produced a skeletal agreement between the two sides that each handed down to its regional representatives as the basis for settlements in the individual bargaining districts.

The bargaining environment had provided strong incentives for both sides to settle without another strike. Recent new legislation affecting benefits to workers locked out under certain circumstances threw the potential success of the union's "mini-max" strike strategy into question.[53] More surprisingly, perhaps, employers were equally wary about testing the new legislation.[54] In addition, a business upswing at the time gave employers further incentives to avoid the interruption in production that a strike would entail.

Again in 1987, the compromise hinged on the trade-off between working-time reduction and plant flexibility in its application. The agreement also called for an (unprecedented) three-year working-time and wage contract.[55] The contract provided for a reduction of average weekly working hours to 37 in two steps over two years, and for nominal wage increases of 3.7, 2.0, and 2.5 percent for the next three years.

The peak agreement widened flexibilization and narrowed differentiation possibilities. Employers won an extension in the maximum "balancing" period from two to six months, giving them greater leeway in adapting working times to production requirements and seasonal fluctuations in demand.[56] The union, for its part, secured concessions on two "differentiation" issues. First, the 1987 agreement narrowed the contractual parameters for differentiated working times for different workers.[57] Second, on one of the most contentious issues in the negotiations, the IG Metall succeeded in extending some working-time reduction to apprentices.[58] Trainees had been passed over in the previous round and still worked a regular 40-hour week. Although relatively few metalworkers were affected by these two points, the union's bargaining priorities reflected concern over how differentiation would adversely affect labor unity. On the question of apprentices, for example, Steinkühler argued that excluding the union's youngest and often most active members from working-time reduction threatened to fragment both individual workforces and the IG Metall itself.[59]

Negotiators in the individual bargaining districts all adopted the central guidelines as the basis for subsequent regional contracts. On issues such as Saturdays and overtime (on which no central guidelines were established), regional bargaining produced a variety of settlements.[60] Most of these do not place further limits on overtime as the union had hoped, but on balance the union prevailed on the issue of Saturday.

The settlements reached in plant negotiations followed the same trends as in 1984. As of April 1988, regular working times dropped to 37.5 hours (the last step in the new agreement, to 37 hours, will take effect in April 1989). Flexibility in working hours over time has again been far more prevalent than differentiation among workers. The vast majority of employees work a regular 37.5-hour week (on average and before overtime); only 5.7 percent have regular working times above or below that.[61]

The 1987 compromise in many ways is simply an extension of the 1984 settlement. In both rounds, the union subordinated wage demands to the working-time issue.[62] And in 1987 the key trade-off was between further working-time reduction and the renegotiation of the parameters for its "flexible" implementation in the plant. As in 1984, opening clauses leave to a second round of negotiations how working times will be arranged at the plant level. Again, it is up to plant works councils to implement decentrally the terms of the contract.

CONCLUSIONS AND IMPLICATIONS

The outcome of the conflict over working-time reduction certainly signals a decentralization of bargaining, as other authors have emphasized.[63] Yet works councils have until now not been as passive as some versions of this argument imply. Thus, in order to assess the theoretical significance of this bargaining experience, one must first be clear on what has and has not changed. One thing that is not new is plant-level deviation from central collective contracts. Works councils in thriving plants, for example, have long been able to supplement centrally defined wage minimums in an informal "second round" of plant negotiations, often in exchange for concessions on overtime or other plant issues. The resulting "wage drift" has for decades made "rigid" central bargains upwardly flexible at the plant level.[64] Nor are "opening clauses" unprecedented that explicitly mandate supplemental bargaining between works councils and employers to fit the central agreement to plant conditions. The union's 1973 contract in Baden-Württemberg over "humanization of work" issues is an example of where the central contract specified guidelines for plant bargaining.[65] Finally, works councils have long determined aspects of plant working times, some of which have implications for working-time flexibility.[66]

What *is* new is that the current agreement institutionalizes a second round of plant bargaining on working-time arrangements that moves not forward from a collective and universally binding minimum (40 hours per week for each and every full-time worker), but both forward and backward within centrally defined parameters. As emphasized above, the new flexibility employers won takes two analytically distinct forms that have different implications for labor. The contract's flexibilization clause gives the works council much more discretion on the distribution of work over time. This form of flexibility is not different in kind from that allowed before, but it is vastly expanded and allows for qualitatively different strategies for organizing work. Employers now have more leeway to arrange working schedules so as to maximize machine-operating times and adapt to seasonal fluctuations in demand.[67] The differentiation clause, in contrast, is itself qualitatively new. It recasts the very definition of full-time work from a single, uniform time (40 hours) to a range of times (now 36.5–39 hours) and allows employers to hire workers with different base working times.

The IG Metall's campaign for working-time reduction will almost certainly go down as the most important conflict in West German labor relations in the 1980s. The outcome confirms Streeck's observation that national unions may increasingly find themselves confronted with pressures to decentralize bargaining.[68] An analysis of the context and course of the conflict over working-time reduction allows us to go a step further as well, and specify more precisely the conditions under which such pressures have emerged and the way they have been resolved in West Germany.

The significance of the conflict and its outcome can be tentatively evaluated in terms of (1) the link between the content of negotiations and its impact on the machinery of collective bargaining; (2) the conflict over the varieties of working-time flexibility as well as its limits; and (3) the comparison between the battle over working-time reduction in West Germany and union politics under neoliberalism in other countries.

First, there is a connection between the content of conflict and its implications for the machinery of centralized bargaining. Employers have pressed for decentralization and flexibility in central contracts when union demands affect the supply of labor and the conditions under which it is employed. But they continue to agree to "rigid" and encompassing central agreements in bargaining rounds involving traditional wage demands.[69] Thus, while plant flexibility was a theme in the 1984 and 1987 bargaining rounds over working-time reduction, it was not an issue in the 1986 round, which focused on wages.

In short, the decentralizing pressures that characterized central bargaining over working-time reduction are related to the nature of the demand itself. However, such strains are likely to become more prominent in the current period, as conflicts over production issues and other qualitative demands increasingly replace wages as the locus of conflict between labor and capital.[70]

Second, the conflict between the IG Metall and Gesamtmetall over *flexibility* in working-time arrangements was not only a struggle over its limits. An important subplot in the drama involved strategic trade-offs among different "varieties" of flexibility, with different political implications. I have argued, for example, that the two kinds of flexibility in the agreements on working-time reduction—flexibility over time (flexibilization) and flexibility among workers (differentiation)—have different effects on labor unity, which is critical to continued union strength. Of the two, differentiation goes most directly to the heart of union solidarity, by allowing different categories of workers to be covered by different minimum standards. Such "differentiation-based" fragmentation (which influences not just working-hours, but also wages) threatens to drive a wedge into the labor movement.

The different political implications of flexibilization and differentiation may help explain the IG Metall's behavior and bargaining priorities in the course of the conflict over working-time reduction. While both flexibilization and differentiation pose problems for the union, it appears that the IG Metall consistently found compromise on the former preferable to concessions on the latter. Indeed, the union sometimes devoted considerable political capital to making sure certain groups of workers (e.g., apprentices) were not left behind on the working-time issue.

My emphasis on the political meaning of different types of flexibility is part of a more general point: in the end, the union does not really have a choice between flexibility and no flexibility, only what kind and under what conditions. As pointed out above, the Conservative government is promoting its own variety of labor flexibility through recent changes in labor-market policy. This neoliberal approach to employment exacerbates divisions within the working class between full-time and various "irregular" workers, complicating labor solidarity in a different way. And, of course, continuing high unemployment is itself a major source of "dualism" in the labor market and the greatest threat to labor unity of all. In sum, highlighting the varieties of flexibility provides a more nuanced picture of both the choices the IG Metall confronted (and confronts) and the strategic concessions the union has made on the working-time issue.

Third, the analysis needs to be situated in a broader comparative context. While this chapter has focused largely on the union's concessions in the 1984 and 1987 bargaining rounds, this emphasis should not obscure the significance of the IG Metall's accomplishment. Whatever else happens at the plant level, workers in Germany's metalworking industries now have a shorter regular work week than they did five years ago. The union was able to win significant concessions from employers under what were arguably the most difficult political and market conditions labor had faced in the postwar period.

Shifting the emphasis in this way reveals that the IG Metall is weathering the crisis of Keynesianism and the ascendance of neoliberalism better than unions in many other countries. In the United States, neoliberalism has meant an attack on labor's institutional position, further decline in union membership, the breakdown of pattern bargaining in key industries, and the introduction of other, arguably more insidious forms of "flexibility," such as two-tiered wage systems and a large pool of underemployed workers.[71] In Britain, neoliberalism has also taken a heavy toll on organized labor, and when Margaret Thatcher finally exits 10 Downing Street, she will leave the British labor movement a great deal less formidable than she found it.

Again, it is important to realize that German unions have weathered the neoliberal storm better in part because it has been less extreme there. At the same time, however, union strength is not reducible to labor's political and economic environment, and the IG Metall's own actions have contributed as well to the union's continued relative strength. Orchestrating a national campaign for a 35-hour work week not only demonstrated this strength, it reaffirmed and reinforced it by showing that the union is still capable of defining a national agenda and mobilizing its membership in support of that agenda.

The outcome of the conflict over working-time reduction demonstrates new strains in central bargaining in West Germany, but what is equally striking is the resilience of central bargaining there. Pressures for decentralization have not led to a "breakdown" so much as to a modification of central bargaining and a shift in the balance between the central union and works councils. A new layer of bargaining at the plant level has enhanced the importance of works councils. Centralized bargaining itself, however, is not at issue in Germany. Indeed, as pointed out above, the 1987 bargaining round was in some ways more centralized than ever, with peak-level negotiations preceding and establishing guidelines for subsequent regional bargaining.

The relative stability of central bargaining in Germany is due in part to union defenses. However, it also owes something to continued support for it from German employers. Hans-Peter Stihl (head of the Baden-Württemberg branch of Gesamtmetall) still speaks for much of the German business community when he says that employers still want "strong unions . . . who are capable of enforcing the rules they agree to."[72] In other words, German employers still want centrally defined rules, only more flexible ones.

The outcome of recent negotiations over working-time reduction in the German metalworking industries thus combines elements of both stability and change: stability in the continued viability of central bargaining, change in the balance between it and plant-level bargaining. For this reason, attempts to "classify" unambiguously the outcome of this conflict—as a union victory or defeat, as a sign of the breakdown or persistence of centralized collective bargaining—distort one of its defining features, which is the way it combines all of these. Indeed, the shifting balance between the central union and works councils, and compromise *within* the "dual system" may have helped to avert an attack *on* that system.

Speculation on the future fate of labor relations in Germany is risky. Neoliberalism and new market pressures have changed the content of conflict and placed new strains on the machinery of bargaining. But so far the characters themselves are the same, and all are still basically intact. The balance between stability and change in German labor relations will ultimately be decided politically, and depends on how labor, capital, and the state interact in the future.

NOTES

1. I would like to thank Richard Foglesong, Stephen Silvia, Ben Schneider, Wolfgang Streeck, Lowell Turner, and Joel Wolfe for their valuable comments on earlier versions of this chapter.

2. Benjamin Coriat, "Labor and Capital in the Crisis, 1966–82," in Mark Kesselman and Guy Groux, eds., *The French Workers' Movement: Economic Crisis and Political Change* (London: George Allen and Unwin, 1984), p. 45. For a more general discussion of the crisis of Keynesianism and its implications for labor, see Michael Piore and Charles Sabel, *The Second Industrial Divide* (New York: Basic Books, 1984), and Charles Sabel, "Struktureller Wandel der Produktion und neue gewerkschaftliche Strategien," *Prokla* 62 (March 1986): 41–60.

3. Wolfgang Streeck, "Neo-corporatist Industrial Relations and the Economic Crisis in West Germany," in John H. Goldthorpe, ed., *Order and Conflict in Contemporary Capitalism* (New York: Oxford University Press, 1984). Streeck's argument is part of

a larger (and growing) literature on the "crisis" (or "breakdown") of neo-corporatist bargaining. See also Scott Lash, "The End of Neo-corporatism? The Breakdown of Centralised Bargaining in Sweden," *British Journal of Industrial Relations* 23 (July 1985): 215–39.

4. Streeck, "Neo-corporatist Industrial Relations," p. 298.

5. Ibid., p. 297.

6. See also Paul Windolf and Hans-Willy Hohn, *Arbeitsmarktchancen in der Krise: Betriebliche Rekrutierung und soziale Schließung* (Frankfurt: Campus, 1984), and Shigeyoshi Tokunaga and Joachim Bergmann, eds., *Industrial Relations in Transition: The Cases of Japan and the Federal Republic of Germany* (Tokyo: University of Tokyo Press, 1984.)

7. Werner Sengenberger, "West German Employment Policy: Restoring Worker Competition," *Industrial Relations* 23 (Fall 1984): 323–43.

8. Andrei Markovits, ed., *The Political Economy of West Germany: Modell Deutschland* (New York: Praeger, 1982); Sengenberger, "West German Employment Policy"; Fritz Scharpf, "Economic and Institutional Constraints of Full-Employment Strategies," in Goldthorpe, *Order and Conflict in Contemporary Capitalism*.

9. Sengenberger, "West German Employment Policy."

10. Andrei Markovits and Christopher S. Allen, "Trade Unions and the Economic Crisis: The West German Case," in Peter Gourevitch et al., *Unions and Economic Crisis: Britain, West Germany and Sweden* (London: George Allen and Unwin, 1984).

11. Andrei Markovits and Christopher Allen, "The 1978–79 Steel Strike: German Unions at a Crossroad," unpublished manuscript (1979), provides an especially good account of union-government relations and of union behavior in this period. This section draws on their analysis.

12. Scharpf, "Economic and Institutional Constraints," pp. 285–86.

13. Markovits and Allen, "1978–79 Steel Strike," pp. 9–10.

14. Ibid., esp. pp. 14–15.

15. The union's demands were elaborated in IG Metall Bezirksleitung Stuttgart, "Arbeitsmaterialien zum Tarifvertrag zur Sicherung der Eingruppierung und zur Verdienstsicherung bei Abgruppierung," Stuttgart, July 1978.

16. Disagreement within the IG Metall over whether to strike for working-time reduction in the steel industry also contributed to the outcome of that conflict, which the union entered quite disorganized and somewhat half-heartedly. See Markovits and Allen, "1978–79 Steel Strike," on which the rest of this paragraph also draws.

17. A text of the document appears in *Die Zeit*, February 2, 1979.

18. Peter Katzenstein, *Policy and Politics in West Germany: The Growth of a Semisovereign State* (Philadelphia: Temple University Press, 1987), esp. chaps. 2 and 8.

19. Sengenberger, "West German Employment Policy," pp. 323, 326.

20. Katzenstein, *Policy and Politics*, chaps. 2 and 8.

21. Wolfgang Streeck, "Co-determination: The Fourth Decade," in B. Wilpert and A. Sorge, eds., *International Perspectives on Organizational Democracy* (New York: Wiley, 1984).

22. Sengenberger, "West German Employment Policy," 323.

23. For a text of the law, see *Bundesblatt*, No. 21, 1985, pp. 710–17. This section draws as well on Michael Kittner, *Beschäftigungsförderungsgesetz* (Frankfurt: Bund, 1985), and Gerhard Bosch and Hartmut Seifert, "Das geplante Beschäftigungsförde-

rungsgesetz: Ein arbeitsmarktpolitisches Notstandsgesetz," *WSI Mitteilungen* 10 (1984): 581–87.

24. See the special issue of *WSI Mitteilungen*, August 1988, on the Conservative government's labor-market deregulation program. Articles in that volume by Wolfgang Däubler and Ulrich Zachart outline the trend toward the erosion of "normal" full-time working relationships (legally defined), and the growth of "atypical" working relationships such as part-time, temporary, and fixed-contract employment.

25. See especially Bosch and Seifert, "Das geplante," and Kittner, *Beschäftigungsförderungsgesetz.*

26. A recent study shows that the number of subcontracted and fixed-contract workers has grown since the law passed. Fixed-contract work, for example, has almost doubled since 1984, rising from 4.2 percent of all workers to 8 percent by November 1986. See Wilhelm Adamy, "Deregulierung des Arbeitsmarktes: Zwischenbilanz des Beschäftigungsförderungsgesetz," *WSI Mitteilungen* 8 (1988).

27. Adamy's description of the law's intent complements mine. He stresses how it promotes plant personnel policies based on external rather than internal flexibility (*unternehmensexterner Flexibilität*). See Adamy, "Deregulierung," p. 481.

28. For a more detailed account of the 1984 strike, see Reinhard Bahnmüller, *Der Streik: Tarifkonflikt um Arbeitszeitverkürzung in der Metallindustrie* (Hamburg: VSA, 1985), and the special issues of *Gewerkschaftliche Monatshefte*, July and November 1984. For different interpretations of the conflict and its outcome, see Hajo Weber, "Desynchronisation, Dezentralisierung—und Dekomposition?" *Arbeitsberichte und Forschungsmaterialien*, No. 19, Universität Bielefeld, Fakultät für Soziologie, May 1986; Karl Hinrichs, William K. Roche, and Helmut Wiesenthal, "Working Time Policy as Class-Oriented Strategy: Unions and Shorter Working Hours in Great Britain and West Germany," unpublished manuscript, University of Bielefeld, October 1984; and Karl Hinrichs and Helmut Wiesenthal, "Arbeitszeitverkürzung als Klassenstrategie: Die Arbeitskämpfe des Jahres '84 als Versuch einer Verbesserung der Klassenposition," unpublished manuscript, University of Bielefeld, May 1985.

29. Quoted in Bahnmüller, *Der Streik*, p. 31.

30. Katzenstein, *Policy and Politics*, p. 354.

31. All told, 150,000 workers went out on strike, 60,000 were locked out, and another 300,000 workers were idled due to parts and supply shortages related to the strike (the so-called cold lockout). See I. Kurz-Scherf, "Tarifpolitik und Arbeitskämpfe," in Michael Kittner, ed. *Gewerkschaftsjahrbuch 1985* (Cologne: Bund, 1985), p. 113.

32. *Die Zeit*, February 17, 1984, p. 32.

33. Stephen J. Silvia, "The West German Labor Law Controversy: A Struggle for the Factory of the Future," *Comparative Politics* 20 (January 1988): 164.

34. *Die Zeit*, June 29, 1984, p. 18.

35. *International Herald Tribune*, June 27, 1984, p. 1.

36. The terms of the contract are laid out in Kurz-Scherf, "Tarifpolitik und Arbeitskämpfe," pp. 76–81.

37. *Handelsblatt*, July 2, 1984, p. 3.

38. *Handelsblatt*, July 16, 1984, p. 1.

39. *Frankfurter Allgemeine Zeitung*, August 27, 1984; *Handelsblatt*, August 21, 1984.

40. Bundesvereinigung der deutschen Arbeitgeberverbände, *Flexibilisierung der Arbeitszeit: Neue Tarifregelungen als Chance* (Cologne: BDA, 1984).

41. *Handelsblatt*, August 27, 1984.

42. Wirtschafts- und Sozialwissenschaftliches Institut des DGB, "Informationsblätter Arbeit, Gesundheit, Humanisierung," November 1986.

43. Ibid. These agreements reduced weekly working times variously—through daily reductions of 18 minutes, or other combinations such as one hour on Fridays and another one-half hour on Thursdays, or one and a half hours off on Fridays.

44. Ibid. The remaining 14 percent of all plants in the survey had adopted various "mixed models," involving a combination of forms.

45. Gösta Esping-Anderson, *Politics Against Markets* (Princeton, N.J.: Princeton University Press, 1985), esp., pp. 31–36.

46. Hinrichs, Roche, and Wiesenthal, "Working Time Policy," p. 17.

47. Hinrichs and Wiesenthal, "Arbeitszeitverkürzung als Klassenstrategie," pp. 22 and 23, n. 10. Hinrichs and Wiesenthal also see the union's concessions on working-time flexibility as strategic. However, their characterization of the trade-offs the union faced has a different emphasis. They argue that concessions on "collective" working-time flexibility were less odious from the union's perspective than outright defeat on either reducing the work week or settling for less than full wage compensation. While this interpretation is not incompatible with my own analysis, it does not distinguish the "varieties" of flexibility (and especially the difference between flexibilization and differentiation) emphasized here.

48. IG Metall Abteilung Tarifpolitik, "Arbeitszeitflexibilisierung und Arbeitnehmerinteressen: Positionspapier der IG Metall," Frankfurt, June 1986.

49. *Nürnberger Nachrichten*, November 7, 1986.

50. *Handelsblatt*, February 23, 1987.

51. *Manager Magazin*, January 1987.

52. *Spiegel*, April 13, 1987, p. 130.

53. For a discussion of the new law, see Silvia, "West German Labor Law Controversy."

54. Ibid., n. 50; see also *Frankfurter Allgemeine Zeitung*, April 23, 1987, p. 1.

55. Contracts governing such issues as working times, payment systems, and other working conditions are regularly multiyear agreements; however, wage contracts only very rarely exceed twelve months. For a description of the agreement as a whole, see *Frankfurter Allgemeine Zeitung*, April 23, 1987.

56. *Frankfurter Rundschau*, April 23, 1987.

57. The 1984 contract had allowed a maximum span of 3 hours (between 37 hours for some workers and 40 hours for others). The 1987 contract cut this to 2.5 hours (36.5–39 hours). This not only ensured working-time reduction for all workers (since 39 hours is the new maximum); it also put a floor of 36.5 hours on the definition of full-time work. The latter is important to keep the wages of workers with fewer hours from slipping far behind that of workers with more. (Interview with Klaus Lang, head of the IG Metall collective bargaining department, 1987.)

58. See *Spiegel*, April 27, 1987, p. 44.

59. *Frankfurter Allgemeine Zeitung*, April 23, 1987.

60. IG Metall Abteilung Tarifpolitik, "Auszüge aus den regionalen Verhandlungsbewegungen 1986/87," May 26, 1987.

61. *Presse und Funk Nachrichten*, October 14, 1988.

62. Indeed, in agreeing to nominal wage increases (and moderate ones, at that) stretching over the next three years, the union was taking something of a chance with workers' real wages.

63. See, for example, Weber, "Desynchronisation, Dezentralisierung."

64. Eckart Teschner, *Lohnpolitik im Betrieb* (Frankfurt: Campus, 1977).

65. H. Schauer, H. Dabrowski, et al., *Tarifvertrag zur Verbesserung industrieller Arbeitsbedingungen* (Frankfurt: Campus, 1984).

66. Paragraph 87 of the Works Constitution Act gives them codetermination rights regarding the following issues: setting the beginning and end of daily working times; determining how working time will be distributed across the days of the week; scheduling overtime and short-time work (*Kurzarbeit*); and making changes in plant working times such as the introduction of shift work. For a text of the Works Constitution Act, see Michael Kittner, ed., *Arbeits- und Sozialordnung*, 9th ed. (Cologne: Bund, 1984).

67. Flexibilization can thus result in increased pressure on works councils to approve more shift- and weekend work. In addition, employers' skillful use of flexibilization to adjust working schedules to match demand cycles over a longer time frame could deprive workers of overtime pay in peak production periods to which many have grown accustomed.

68. Streeck, "Neo-corporatist Industrial Relations."

69. West German employers, like their counterparts elsewhere, sometimes talk about wage differentiation, but in Germany they never really act on it.

70. Charles Sabel, "Struktureller Wandel der Produktion und neue gewerkschaftliche Strategien," *Prokla* 62 (March 1986): 41–60.

71. Bob Kuttner, "The Declining Middle," *Atlantic Monthly* (July 1983); Barry Bluestone and Bennett Harrison, *The Deindustrialization of America* (New York: Basic Books, 1982).

72. Quoted in Bahnmüller, *Der Streik*, p. 24.

6

Democracy at the Margins: The International System and Policy Change in France

Harvey B. Feigenbaum

Conservative nostrums rarely lose their appeal among professional economists and are remarkably durable among politicians.[1] Thus, when Keynesian interventionism had failed to conquer the novel conditions of low growth and high inflation that characterized virtually every capitalist economy in the 1970s, conservatives opined that these unfamiliar problems could be solved by returning to familiar—indeed, ancient—solutions. If Keynesian state intervention failed, they maintained, the logical solution was to reduce the role of the state. Contracting the size of the public sector thus became the order of the day, and "privatization" became a common policy in such disparate countries as West Germany, Italy, Japan, and the United States.

The French Socialist government, unsurprisingly, was different. In 1981 France discovered Keynes as well as Marx. The original Socialist policy combined nationalization and reflation, with disastrous results. Inflation rates galloped beyond those of France's principal trading partners (already deflating), and by 1982 a balance-of-payments crisis forced retrenchment and austerity. Eventually, the French industry minister discretely implied the possible denationalization of at least some of the Socialist project,[2] and a French version of Thatcheresque enterprise zones, *pôles de conversion*, was proposed.[3] Finally, "denationalization" became the rallying cry of France's right-wing opposition; for indeed, there was very little else to distinguish their economic policies from those of the Socialists. After the legislative elections of March 16, 1986, denationalization became the centerpiece policy of the new conservative majority.

Within the framework of examining France's response to the economic stagnation of the last two decades, this chapter has several purposes. The first part is essentially descriptive, examining the broad lines of macro-economic policy as practiced by right and left, from Valery Giscard d'Estaing, to François Mitterrand, to the subsequent projects of the right-wing parties in parliament. Special attention is then given to the record of French nationalized industries and to the right's privatization strategy, for the size (if not necessarily the performance) of the public sector became the major issue in the debate over macro-economic policy.

Examining the French case historically demonstrates interesting similarities between the programs of the left and right, and between the practices of nationalized and private industry. The question then becomes more theoretical: What does an examination of French policy tell us about the autonomy of the state in the era of advanced capitalism? Most important, can the recent academic debate about the role of the state offer an adequate understanding of French economic policy?

In the last decade or so a large literature has been generated over the issue of the relationship of state to society. This question of whether policy-making institutions operate independently of social forces (classes, interest groups, etc.) has divided social scientists on both sides of the political spectrum. Marxists have split into two camps, one arguing that the state is necessarily the instrument of a unified ruling class ("the executive committee of the bourgeoisie"). The other argues that the ruling class is necessarily composed of fragments whose interests conflict (e.g., energy corporations versus automobile producers), and thus capitalist survival depends upon a state which can rise above the specific needs of individual fragments to pursue policies that are in the general interest of the class as a whole. In parallel fashion, non-Marxists divide into pluralists who see state policies as simply reflecting the demands of victorious interest-group coalitions, while neo-mercantilists argue that (at least some) state institutions have a life of their own and that they have the potential to pursue policies deemed in the public interest. "Strong states," the neo-mercantilists contend, may pursue such policies even in the face of severe domestic opposition.[4]

I shall argue that both notions, Marxist and neo-mercantilist, of an autonomous state are relatively uninstructive, and that the French state is constrained by both domestic interests and the international environment. In brief, the argument to be presented here is that

1. The policies of the successive right- and left-wing French governments have converged, despite conflicting ideologies and mandates.

2. The principal source of this convergence lies in the constraints upon state behavior arising from the international political-economic system. Moreover, state policies are further constrained by domestic private investors.
3. Both sources of constraint cast doubt on "autonomous-state" theories.
4. While policy variation has been extremely limited, there have been significant opportunities for previously weak constituencies to influence state decisions. These may result in incremental, but real, policy change over the long term.

BACKGROUND: POLICY FROM GISCARD TO MITTERRAND (1974–81)

Politics matters and political choices are real. This is certainly true of the choices between right and left in France. Nevertheless, a brief look at policy similarities between right and left in that country suggests an underlying set of structural constraints within which politics takes place. This structure sets the limits of democracy under advanced capitalism.

The policies of Giscard's presidency were in many ways the precursors of Mitterrand's. While Giscard's immediate reaction to the 1973–74 oil shock was a policy of deflation (*refroidissement*), he almost immediately switched to a Keynesian reflation in 1975. This was called the *relance Chirac*, after Giscard's first prime minister (and eventual rival), who directed the program. Real wages rose and were accompanied by increased purchases of imported goods, causing a balance-of-payments crisis. This in turn triggered an austerity program.

The *relance Chirac* gave way to the *plan Barre*, which aimed at controlling inflation and restoring profitability by depressing real wages.[5] The intention was to relieve pressure on the balance of payments by reducing domestic consumption (curtailing the demand for imports) and to encourage investment by bolstering profit margins. The latter, then, had an implicit "supply-side" aspect in its assumption that larger profit margins would encourage greater investment. This did not happen, however. With the exception of the 1975–76 *relance*, investments continued the sectoral decline that had started under Georges Pompidou in 1970.[6] Volkmar Lauber argues that the failure to encourage exports via a devaluation of the franc reduced the incentive for businessmen to invest.[7] However, since many of France's imports, especially oil, had to be paid for in dollars, a devaluation almost certainly would have had an immediate inflationary effect. This might have encouraged borrowing, but eventually would have reduced foreign demand for French products. More subtly, Raymond Barre used a plethora of targeted subsidies to stimulate exports, resulting in what amounted to a system of multiple real exchange rates.[8]

None of this, however, seemed to work. Nor did massive government spending in telecommunications and nuclear power produce the kind of spread effects (i.e., effects which encourage growth in other sectors) devoutly wished by the Giscard-Barre tandem. Economic stagnation quickly alienated much of the French electorate. Barre, in fact, became the least popular prime minister of the Fifth Republic, a dubious honor which he took to be a measure of his efficacity.[9]

Had Giscard or Barre been better politicians, they might have been able to survive in the 1981 elections. Disunity on the left had offered them a reprieve in the 1978 legislative elections, but disunity on the right, coupled with the lackluster results of the *plan Barre*, eventually spelled electoral defeat. The split in the right-wing camp was only partially due to differences over economic strategy. To the extent that economic differences could be discerned, Gaullists championed economic nationalism (read: statism and protectionism) in contrast to Giscard's liberal internationalism. However, Jacques Chirac, leader of the neo-Gallist *Rassemblement pour la République*, seized upon the perceived popularity of U.S. supply-side rhetoric in the last stages of the French presidential campign. The traditions of Gaullist *dirigisme* ceased to figure in the voters' choice. Moreover, eyeing the 1988 presidential campaign, the ambitious Chirac distanced himself from the unpopular Giscard in the latter's bid for reelection in 1981. Division on the right allowed François Mitterrand to become the Fifth Republic's first Socialist president.

POLICIES UNDER THE SOCIALISTS

The Socialist program included both a Keynesian demand-stimulus package and an ambitious project with extended nationalizations to account for over 13 percent of gross domestic product (GDP), giving France the largest public sector of any advanced capitalist country.[10] This stimulus on the demand side was modest, with a government deficit targeted at less than 3 percent of GDP and the minimum wage augmented by only 10 percent.[11] Ironically, the Socialists shared a principal assumption of the right: that a rise in real wages would deter investment. Yet, unlike Barre, Thatcher, or Reagan, the Socialists' solution was to have the state take over the investment process.[12] Thus, not only were five of France's largest industrial corporations nationalized, but so were most of the nation's banks.[13] Financial institutions were considered crucial to the nationalization project because it was felt that the banks in private hands directed their funds to ventures offering short-term profitability, rather than investments with long-term spread effects, and especially because much of their money went into real estate.[14] Indeed, it was argued, banks were to be nationalized so as to increase the availability of credit to export-oriented firms and to small- and medium-sized firms (PMEs: petites et moyennes entreprises) where job creation was likely to be most promising.[15]

The emphasis on providing a supply of capital for private investment gave the Mitterand experiment a "supply-side" quality, as did its subsequent cuts in the corporate and capital gains taxes. The Socialists were also, of course, concerned with the supply of labor, their principal constituency. Cuts in the work week to 39 hours (and eventually, it was hoped, to 35 hours), early retirement programs, and a fifth week of paid vacation were intended to increase opportunities for France's growing numbers of unemployed. Yet decisions not to reduce wages commensurately and to increase social changes paid by employers not only affected productivity rates (at least statistically) but provided strong disincentives for new job creation.[16]

The initial results of Socialism's Year One were mixed, but ultimately negative. Just as with the *relance Chirac*, the Keynesian injections stimulated the demand for products faster than the French economy could supply them. The resulting deficit was then filled by easily available imports. The world recession meant that the demand for French goods abroad was low, and France was soon importing much more than it was exporting. Depleted foreign exchange reserves forced the government into expensive international borrowing to prop up the franc, which in fact had been overvalued under Giscard d'Estaing.[17] It was the international payments crisis that finally brought about two successive devaluations of the franc and accompanying austerity programs. The Common Program of the Left (i.e., the original platform of the Socialist-Communist alliance) gave way to *rigueur socialiste* (a euphemism for austerity) in 1982. The 1982 turnabout, however, was insufficient to meet the gap in inflation rates between France and its trading partners (France's inflation rate was more than double that of West Germany), and the screws were turned again in 1983.

While the austerity program got high marks from the OECD,[18] it did not prove popular with the left's constituency or with the Communist party. The latter left the government in July 1984. Amid soaring unemployment levels and plummeting public approval, Mitterrand named centrist-leaning Laurent Fabius as prime minister. With Fabius' emphasis on returning French industry to profitability, the policies of the Socialists became increasingly indistinguishable from those of the right.

INDUSTRIAL POLICY UNDER THE SOCIALISTS

If the broad lines of macro-economic policy illustrate the narrow range of maneuver for the stewards of a medium-sized open economy,[19] the French novelties in industrial policy also revealed themselves to be more apparent than real. While the nationalizations were novel in their scope, they were hardly innovations. Nor were the nationalizations particularly radical. Although the first wave of nationalizations in France had occurred under the auspices of the 1936 Popular Front (e.g., French Rail, Banque de France), the next wave of public takeovers (e.g., Renault, Electricité de France) were initiated by Charles de Gaulle, whose conservative credentials were impeccable.[20] The Socialist program of nationalizations after 1981 mainly differed from the previous waves in the number of *profitable* industries taken over. Otherwise, the idea was not new.

Nor were the other elements of Socialist industrial policy a marked departure. While emphasis had been placed on French efforts to promote high-technology industries, French industrial policy had traditionally been as much concerned with the rear-guard industries as with the vanguard.[21] Steel had been the focus of government attention for over 30 years and was surreptitiously nationalized by Giscard d'Estaing in the form of government purchase of convertible bonds.[22] The automobile industry in France, where state-owned Renault accounted for the lion's share of public enterprise deficits (12.55 billion francs),[23] largely survived on small-car marketing strategies and cheap labor. The company was now manifesting the effects of its long-term neglect of capital investment.[24] Much the same was true in France's other traditional industries.

THE RECORD OF FRENCH NATIONALIZATIONS

The record of the latest French experiment in nationalization was mixed. As argued below, this variation was primarily due to the nature of the sectors nationalized rather than to the change in ownership. The total deficit of the nationalized sector continued to mount after the Socialists took office. Losses of the newly nationalized groups totaled 2.4 billion francs in 1980, 9.3 billion in 1981, and 14.2 billion in 1984.[25] The figures for the entire nationalized sector were worse: 1.9 billion francs were lost in 1980, 36.4 billion in 1984.[26]

It is hard, however, to attribute these losses to the specifics of public-sector mismanagement. Much of the deficit is attributable to industries which are declining everywhere: coal, steel, mechanical industries, heavy chemicals, and textiles. Richard Pryke's analysis of the lackluster performance of Britain's public enteprises is equally relevant to France: "It would, however, be wrong to attribute to the nationalized industries' failings simply to public ownership. Almost any collection of British industries would have shown up badly.... Many of the weaknesses which appear from British experience to be a consequence of public ownership are displayed by the same industries abroad under private ownership."[27]

However, the record of public enterprise in France also had bright spots. While François Mitterrand's claim that nationalization "saved" six major industrial groups seems hyperbolic, many nationalized companies, such as Rhone-Poulenc or Pecheney, which were in bad shape as private firms, have returned to profitability under the aegis of public ownership. (See Table 6.1.) In fact, by the end of 1985, nearly all newly nationalized sectors except steel looked good.[28] Stephen Brooks argues that nationalization did indeed permit a successful restructuring of the petrochemical industry, although often this meant simply transferring a losing operation from a weak firm to a strong firm: e.g., the transfer of Ato and Chloe from the Compagnie Française des Pétroles to Elf-Aquitaine.[29] Furthermore, confidence in the financial system was maintained by infusions of government capital into the shaky Rothschild

Table 6.1
Public Enterprise Profitability: Selected Companies

		Earnings (Losses) in Millions of U.S. Dollars		
1981		1982	1983	1984
{Private}	Company	{Nationalized}		
(48.5)	Groupe Bull	(146.0)	(67.5)	(52.8)
63.3	CGE	68.9	71.5	70.2(a)
(106.0)	Pecheney	(306.6)	(50.0)	54.0(a)
(36.2)	Rhone-Poulenc	(91.2)	10.6	215.0
48.6	Saint-Gobain	40.0	43.8	54.0
(18.2)	Thomson	(238.6)	(135.2)	(2.7)(a)
(96.9)	TOTALS(b)	(673.4)	(126.9)	337.7

Source: The Wall Street Journal, April 18, 1985, p. 22.

Notes: (a) Estimated
(b) Totals are affected by rounding decimals.

Bank (now called Banque de l'Union Européene), Banque Vernes, and Banque Worms.[30]

The nationalized firms were at first under heavy pressure from the government to maintain employment at the expense of profits, but this strategy gave way under Socialist *rigueur*. While Raymond Barre had been afraid to overtly nationalize steel because of the expected pressure on the government to maintain redundant jobs,[31] the Socialists allowed the firms' management to proceed with massive layoffs. "Modernization," the successor euphemism replacing "rigor," meant, above all, closing unprofitable plants and cutting unprofitable activities.

PÔLES DE CONVERSION

Socialist policies, much like the Socialist party itself, reflect a hodge-podge of thinking. The notion of "declining sector" or "condemned industry" was alien to the first stages of Socialist rule. Jean-Pierre Chevènement, whose star briefly rose and then fell during his tenure as minister of research and industry (although he later went on to other prestigious posts), was often associated with the remark that "there are no condemned sectors, merely outdated technologies." However, his replacement at the Rue de Grenelle by Laurent Fabius signaled the decline in subsidies to hard-pressed traditional industries.

To ease the burden, the government initiated *pôles de conversion* in areas experiencing the worst unemployment: notably, areas associated with shipbuilding, coal, and steel production. The idea was both to make these areas more attractive to prospective investors and to create employment opportunities. At first glance *pôles de conversion* looked suspiciously like right-wing "enterprise zones" in that they included substantial efforts to cut local red tape—oddly enough, by empowering the *Commissaire de la République* (formerly called the "prefect") to act as ombudsman—and considerable tax abatements.[32] However, where Thatcher and Reagan planned enterprise zones as areas of dismantled government intervention (especially minimum wage and safety regulations),[33] the Socialist project seemed the opposite: a host of new subsidies for infrastructure and retraining, premiums for job creation, and reinforced power of the central authority in the form of increased authority for the Paris-appointed *Commissaire de la République*.[34] In terms of social peace, *pôles de conversion* were at least partially successful, but a year after their inauguration no significant new investment had been generated.[35]

The lack of success of the *pôles de conversion* in economic terms could be explained by the simple fact that a year is too short a time to judge. Given the time horizons of long-term industrial investment, however, the dismal record of private-sector net capital formation in France generally may be the ultimate explanation. Investment was still at extremely low levels throughout the country. The reluctance of the private sector to deepen capital for over a decade had created a stark reality in France. In the words of *Le Monde* economics editor Bruno Dethomas, "Logically, all of France should be *pole de conversion*."[36]

POLICIES OF THE RIGHT

It was, perhaps, the nature of criticism emanating from the right that most illuminated the constraints on the Socialist government. The problem for the right was that, excepting their call for privatizing some or all of the nationalized firms, they differed very little from the policies of the Fabius government. Even their emphasis on privatization did not offer a substantive divergence from French Socialist policies.

Indicative of the implicit left-right consensus, the issues intended to mobilize mass publics during the 1985–86 legislative election campaign were not (explicitly) economic. Valery Giscard d'Estaing launched a trial balloon[37] suggesting that France needed to "Americanize" its institutions by creating a vice presidency, although he was unclear as to the specific advantages afforded by such an institution.[38] François Leotard, leader of the Republican party, emphasized the immigrant labor problem and, in a move obviously intended to take votes from the far-right National Front, promised that a conservative government would make naturalization more difficult.[39]

While the only economic program offered jointly was *liberalisme* (reduction of the state's role in the marketplace), it was clear that this meant all things to all people. Even the disparate writings of former prime minister

Barre and former labor minister Lionel Stoleru concurred that French social democracy was only mildly to be changed from the practice of Fabius' (Fabian?) Socialism.[40] While Barre argued that the only feasible employment plan was one that permitted a restoration of profitability, he was not very far from the public presentations of Fabius. In fact, it was Stoleru who dissented: "To promise full employment now just by returning to growth is a shameful political lie."[41] Even the neo-Gaullist RPR (Rassemblement pour la République [Rally for the Republic]), normally designated the furthest right of the conventional conservative parties (i.e., excluding neo-fascists), allowed for the retention of the welfare state.[42] No party or group seriously urged that monetarism be inflicted on the French Republic.[43]

Thus, left with agreement on the welfare state, vague calls for *liberalisme* which the right had never implemented when in power,[44] and a consensus that French industry needed to make profits and become more competitive, the right had only one economic policy to clearly distinguish it from the Socialists: denationalization.

The chief publicist for this alternative was the ex-chairman of Crédit Commercial de France (one of the largest banks nationalized in 1982), Jean-Maxime Leveque. Leveque mainly argued that a sale of the nationalized firms would provide the state with enough cash to reduce the budget and reduce taxes, thus making French industry more competitive, but even he notes that the problem with this project is to find buyers. France is a country where the "total capitalization of the stock market equals two-thirds that of International Business Machines."[45] Whether by reducing taxes, providing subsidies, finding investors, or nationalizing banks, ultimately the principal debate was over how best to channel funds to French industry.[46]

Ultimately, the coalition of Gaullist and Giscardian parties (the RPR and UDF [Union pour la Démocratie Française (union for French Democracy)]) respectively came to power with a two-seat majority on March 16, 1986, and were able to initiate their program. As they had promised, they passed a law (Law 86–793 of July 2, 1986) authorizing the denationalization of some 66 firms. The Conservative hit list not only included the five industrial groups and myriad banks nationalized by the Socialists, but also aimed at privatizing older public firms. Nationalized insurance companies, advertising agencies, oil companies, glass factories, television networks, and steel mills all were to go on the block, albeit to different degrees and at different times, with the entire project completed by 1991, the end of the parliamentary term. Essentially, the aim was to privatize all public-sector firms where there existed the possibility of competitive markets.[47]

Because of France's shallow capital markets, Conservatives were especially vulnerable to the charge that the privatized firms would be bought by foreigners. For this reason, as well as an ostensible interest in creating a "people's capitalism" by encouraging small investors, the Chirac government deliberately underpriced the stock of the first few firms to be privatized. To the delight of the government, investors "gobbled up the shares of the denationalized companies with a gusto usually reserved for *canard à l'orange*."[48]

This was perhaps their only economic delight, however. For after a year in power, the macro-economic statistics showed that the French economy under the Conservatives was doing no better than it had under Socialists.[49] Interest in the stock market was killed off by the October 1987 crash, and by May 1988 the Conservatives lost their majority in the National Assembly.

UNDERSTANDING THE FRENCH CONUNDRUM: THE AUTONOMY OF THE STATE

Several themes emerge from this brief examination of the French economic policy. First, the constraints exercised by the international market seem to force a convergence upon the left and right in France. Second, the debate over nationalization versus privatization may be described as, in Walter LaFeber's phrase, "two halves of the same walnut," that is, two strategies for defending capitalism.[50] These two themes have important implications for notions of democratic choice.

The first theme, emphasizing balance-of-payments considerations, suggests international constraints on the French state, no matter what the political coloration of the existing government. This is hardly a remarkable observation and, as such, fits easily into the broad band of scholarship emphasizing international interdependence.[51] States, at least medium-sized states, can no longer make policy without considering the policies of their trading partners.[52] This is not only a scholarly observation, but is also reflected in the actions of politicians. One cannot otherwise explain the annual meetings of heads of state of the advanced industrial countries.

Of course, interdependence is relative. The term itself suggests some room for maneuver, while accenting the international reverberations of each movement taken by policy makers. Moreover, some policy makers have more room for movement than others. Peter Katzenstein and John Zysman have both argued that the relatively independent French bureaucracy has been successfully able to ignore domestic opposition and pursue strategies of adaptation to the international market.[53] These authors conclude, in other words, that the French state is autonomous, and state structures make a difference.[54]

Why, then, did France reflate in 1981? In part it was a bad gamble by the Socialists. They bet that the U.S. economy would recover sooner than it actually did and, in recovering, would bring along the rest of the world with it. "All our reforms were based on an expectation of growth," commented one Socialist appointee. "Now we are flying by the seat of our pants."[55] Unfortunately, there was no other flight plan. Of course, the government was also serving a specific constituency. A Keynesian reflation was meant to reward labor and the French underclasses. However, the power of the state to serve this constituency was limited by roadblocks abroad. The balance-of-payments crisis and the danger of capital outflow was too great.

The image presented above is of a state that is buffeted and constrained by outside forces. Yet to remark that the state must depend on the international market for the success of its policies, that it lacks autonomy in this sense, verges on banality. The obstacles to policy change were both at home and abroad. Fred Block's analysis of how class relations define the structural limits on economic reform is illuminating in that it does not take international conjuncture into account. Block argues that left-wing reformist governments are ultimately constrained by the need to elicit the confidence of business. If not, they risk an investment strike, capital out-flow, and balance-of-payments difficulties that eventually require the remedy of a full-scale austerity program and retraction of the initial reform. Thus, even though France had a large public sector, 80 percent of investment had to come from the private firms, and this required the cooperation of the capitalist class.[56] If one wishes to relate this phenomenon to another body of literature, France easily fits Charles Lindblom's description of a polyarchy, and this in turn means recognition of the "privileged position of business."[57]

In short, the logic of capitalism serves as a double constraint on state autonomy. First, reforms tend to be inflationary. Non-Marxists argue that Keynesian demand stimulus is inherently inflationary: deficit spending causes "monetary illusion," because prices rise faster than wages and make it possible for businesses to rehire workers at lower real wages.[58] Marxists argue that, reforms being costly, businessmen will try to reconstitute higher profits by raising prices.[59] Either way, products become less competitive internationally and exports decline, while imports become cheaper. A balance-of-payments crisis ensues.

Second, declining profitability at home and decreasing value in the national currency discourage domestic investment and encourage capital flight. Thus, the international market exerts balance-of-payments pressure and provides a home for fleeing capital. Under these conditions, it is the private sector, reacting to the increased costs of social democratic reforms, that decides where and when capital will fly.

This helps us understand the policy convergence of left and right in France. The Socialists could not stimulate demand because of balance-of-payments considerations, and they could not raise their constituents' real wages because doing so would deter investment. Austerity became the common solution of left and right because the international market would permit no other. Nationalization, however, might have distinguished the two sides, for it would have allowed the state to control a substantial portion of the investment process. This did not occur, for reasons to be elaborated below.

The state's principal lever against an investment strike was to encourage a new investment via the nationalized firms; this would create jobs and serve labor's interest at the macro-economic level. Why did the nationalizations prove so disappointing? Why were they not an engine of growth? Was the culprit the international environment, the nature of public ownership, or something else?

Clearly, the international recession and competition from low-labor-cost countries such as Brazil and South Korea considerably reduced the size of markets for France's traditional industries. This factor alone suggests that the nature of ownership was less important than the kind of products being produced by the nationalized sector. It was also true that European private-sector companies were reluctant to enter into cooperative agreements with French high-technology firms (Thomson-CSF and Compagnie Générale Electrique) because of fear of French government interference. These fears disappeared, however, even before the privatization movement began, judging from the alacrity with which the European high-technology firms joined French public-sector firms in the "Eureka" project.[60] This change in attitude occurred when it became evident that the French government maintained arm's length relations with public firms, thus reassuring potential private-sector partners. Profitable deals would have the blessing of the state, a policy that was reinforced when the Conservatives returned to power.

This last observation, I think, provides a clue to understanding how privatization and nationalization were two halves of the same walnut. That is, arm's length relations between the state and its own industries reveal that nationalizations were not used to deter a capital strike by the French business class. Allowing the market to dictate investment decisions of the nationalized companies indicated that the state accepted the logic of capitalism and, with it, the privileged position of the private sector as the animator of economic activity. Private firms were less reluctant to deal with public-sector firms when they were assured that nationalized firms were not a Trojan horse for government interference: that is, the private sector cooperated when it could be assured that government was not interested in adversely affecting profitability. This assurance came with the Mitterand government's reiteration that it would not interfere with the day-to-day activities of the firms and that it would reimburse or subsidize the unprofitable activities of the public firms. With such caveats, the private firms could just as easily substitute for public firms. In short, the activities of nationalized companies were to be motivated by the same profit motive as private ones, with the government allowing them maximum freedom to pursue such ends.[61] This was made all the more clear by the replacement of Jean-Pierre Chevenement by Laurent Fabius as minister of industry and research. Chevenement, leader of the left-wing CERES (Center for Socialist Studies, Research and Education) group in the Socialist party had taken entirely too close an interest in the operations and strategies of nationalized firms, many of them captained by executives hired directly from the private sector. The "socialist" captains of industry rebelled, and Mitterrand decided in their favor.[62] Chevenement was relieved of his duties as industry minister.

While there was mixed thinking about how the nationalized industries should be governed, the end result was that their management was to be oriented by the dictates of the market.[63] Thus, if the profitability of the nationalized sector was to be the prime concern, the behavior of public and private firms was not only compatible, it was identical. As one public-sector executive told me, "Privatization would not change anything!"[64]

In the French case, the tendency to let the market dictate policy was reinforced by the decision to sell to private investors nonvoting shares in nationalized firms.[65] While these were seen as a way of raising money without relinquishing public control—and therefore not officially "privatizing"—the result, in fact, was to reinforce the emphasis on public enterprise profitability: for how else could one expect to attract private investors? So it is that state policy again bends to the interest of the investing classes.

To the extent that public policy decisions are increasingly left to the market, the notion of the state as an autonomous actor, let alone an instrument of social reform, becomes increasingly difficult to defend. Finally, as the market is increasingly international, the state's "dead hand of regulation"[66] reveals itself simply as the appendage of an international marionette, a limp hand controlled by market forces.

There is, then, a limit to reform in capitalist societies, but this should not lead us to conclude that domestic politics does not make a difference, nor that left and right are indistinguishable. Even in the general industrial decline of the 1980s, democracy retains at least some meaning.

The Socialists themselves felt that while the effects of nationalization were disappointing, the institutionalization of the rights of labor remained an enduring accomplishment. The *Loi Auroux* not only legimitized unions, but gave them genuine power in shop-level and company-level decision making. Thus, if the Socialists could not serve labor's interest in the immediate economic sense, they could create institutions to serve those interests in the future. This needs to be put in perspective, of course, as several authors have noted that the *Loi Auroux* merely provided French laborers with rights that were won in other countries (e.g., the United States and Sweden) over four decades earlier.[67] Indeed, French labor won new power on the shop floor, but that power did not immediately influence macro-economic policy.

CORPORATISM

Some might argue that the *Loi Auroux* had the effect of taking France in the direction of democratic corporatism, along the lines described first by Schmitter and elaborated by Katzenstein.[68] Certainly, France was no stranger to corporatism, especially during the fascist experiments of the Vichy period.[69] Compared, however, with Mussolini's Italy or with the democratic varieties found in the smaller countries of Europe, French corporatism has always been incomplete. This may have been a blessing. John Keeler has shown that even in democratic France, corporatist strategies have been aimed at improving state control.[70]

In the case of labor, however, democratic corporatism would have been an improvement, for labor has traditionally been excluded from the policy process. I use the words *would have been* intentionally, because the Auroux law was not corporatist. Corporatism assumes bargaining among peak associations, and such bargaining was not envisaged by the law. Indeed, the Socialist deemphasis of state planning, the historic mechanism for bargaining among economic sectors, reinforced the decline of corporatist solutions in France. However, the mechanisms of the law did allow labor to increase its influence in a decentralized setting, even as unions lost power at the national level.

While the Conservatives were anxious to retract such reforms once they took control of the government, it would be hard to stem the mobilizing effects the legislation triggered at the micro-economic level. If the right was interested in creating an atmosphere conducive to promoting the initiative of investors, the Socialists left a legacy of opportunities for their own constituency.

THE WORLD MARKET, CENTRALIZATION, AND DEMOCRACY

France, like other advanced industrial countries, is torn by a central quandary. Integration into the world market has provided tremendous benefits. Yet trade liberalization has had a dark side. The free movement of capital, coupled to the free movement of goods, has meant a transfer of manufacturing activities to the newly industrializing countries. The loss of jobs in the traditional sectors most sensitive to this new competition has not been compensated by a growth in high-technology sectors. Retraining workers costs money, and raising taxes reduces, at least in the short term, the competitive capacity of those (profitable) industries which must pay the bill. Nor is there any guarantee that the jobs created by high technology industries will produce the same standard of living as those in the older industries.

In addition, competition on a world scale has meant increasing firm size. Firms have merged and multinationalized to meet the demands of international competition.[71] The merger movement and industrial concentration mean that fewer and fewer individuals are responsible for making the investment decisions that shape the future, a future that seems increasingly uncertain.

All of these issues suggest a greater need for government intervention. Reliance on the market and faith in the invisible hand are acceptable only to the faithful. To solve this problem, the 1981 Socialist campaign platform recommended democratic planning. Planning would seem a logical alternative. The greater concentration of investment decision making would seem to make planning, that is, a government effort to coordinate investment decisions, an easier task. If public or private firms have a tendency to act in their own short-term interest, then it is the job of government, that is, the state, to act in the long-term interest of society by influencing the large firms' strategies and harmonizing their investments.

Unfortunately, this solution is not likely, for both technical and political reasons. On the technical side, planning disappeared in France precisely because of French integration into the international economy. As the French economy became increasingly dependent on foreign demand and increasingly tied to the movements of factors beyond the reach of even the powerful French administration, decisions made in the *Commissariat au Plan* simply became irrelevant.[72]

On the political side, planning assumes that the state can act independently of the different interests in French society, that it can balance competing groups and pursue the long-term goals of the general interest.[73] It has been the thrust of this chapter, as well as my firm belief, that the French state has not been—and cannot be—autonomous from these competing groups.

The news that the French state is not autonomous should, of course, be good news to democrats (small "d"), for it bespeaks a sensibility of the state to constituencies outside of the institutions of government. As ever, interest groups are important in understanding the actions of the state. And as E. E. Schattschneider noted almost three decades ago, the system remains flawed. "The flaw in the pluralist heaven is that the heavenly chorus sings with a strong upper-class accent."[74] It is to the Socialists' credit that they expanded the constituency of France's government to include labor and the less favored of French society.

Indeed, the impact of this change may be difficult to judge in the short term. Once in, new constituencies have a staying power that is not easily eroded. A recent study, for example, argues that American labor, traditionally weak by European standards—not unlike its French counterpart—was able to exert influence over policy long after its absolute numbers declined because of its entrenchment in recently created bureaucracies.[75] The Socialists' *Loi Auroux* suggests a similar pattern. States are not autonomous from social forces, but the capture of specific institutions may outlast the conditions that permitted capture in the first place.[76]

CONCLUSION

Even though the economic indicators marginally improved in the first quarter of 1986, democratic choice suffered. The web of international constraints and the general evolution of advanced capitalism do not bode well for those interested in maximixing democratic values and distributional reform. The French economy improved only when the Socialists ignored their mandate. "Structural unemployment" was redefined to fit sober realities, for the international division of labor had imposed its law, and the Socialists accepted that division's dictates. The 1986–88 Conservative interregnum merely solidified this acceptance. "Prosperity" would forever more be a relative term.

The conclusion of this chapter appears pessimistic. The problems of the French political economy seem overwhelming, if not intractable. Democratic choice seems almost irrelevant against the strictures of the world market and domestic entrenched privilege. Yet there is always reason for optimism. Economic incentives, for all their power, never wholly determine political outcomes. The genuine enfranchisement of more groups in the political process, however meager that new participation may first appear, means an addition of human effort, an increment in the potential to solve problems. Democracy, even at the margins, can make a difference.

NOTES

1. I would like to thank Richard Foglesong, Joel Krieger, Donna LaTorre, and Joel Wolfe for their comments on earlier drafts of this chapter.

2. *Wall Street Journal*, April 22, 1985; *Financial Times*, May 9, 1985.

3. "Bilan économique et social 1984," *Dossiers et Documents du Monde*, special edition, January 1985, p. 13; *Le Monde*, February 10, 1984, and February 5, 1985.

4. The literature on this debate is too voluminous to cite in its entirety. Representative of the Marxists are Nicos Poulantzas, *Political Power and Social Classes* (London: New Left Books, 1973), and Ralph Miliband, *The State and Capitalist Society* (London: New Left Books, 1969). Representative of the non-Marxists are Robert Gilpin, *U.S. Power and the Multinational Corporation* (New York: Basic Books, 1975), and Theodore Lowi, "American Business, Public Policy, Case-Studies, and Political Theory," *World Politics* 16 (July 1964). On the "strong state," see Peter Katzenstein, "Conclusion," in Katzenstein, ed., *Between Power and Plenty* (Madison: University of Wisconsin Press, 1978).

5. Volkmar Lauber, *The Politics of Economic Policy: France 1974–1982* (New York: Praeger, 1983), pp. 2–10.

6. Ibid., p. 15.

7. Ibid., pp. 13–15.

8. Stephen S. Cohen, James Galbraith, and John Zysman, "Rehabbing the Labryinth: The Financial System and Industrial Policy," in Stephen S. Cohen and Peter A. Gourevitch, eds., *France in the Troubled World Economy* (London: Butterworth, 1982), pp. 51ff.

9. Lauber, *Politics*, p. 45.

10. Pierre Maillet, *La Politique industrielle* (Paris: Presses Universitaires de France, 1984), pp. 99ff.

11. The minimum wage increased 15 percent by 1982, but this increment was much less than that under the 1936 Popular Front or under the Grenelle agreements of May 1968. Cf. the many contrasts with the Popular Front presented by Philippe Simonnot, *Le Grand Bluff économique des socialistes* (Paris: J. C. Lattes, 1982), chap. 2; Lauber, *Politics*, p. 69.

12. Peter A. Gourevitch, "Making Choices in France: Industrial Structure and the Politics of Industrial Policy," in Cohen and Gourevitch, *France*, p. 15.

13. The newly nationalized corporations were Rhone-Poulenc, Saint-Gobain-Pont-à-Mousson, Compagnie Générale Electrique, Pechiney-Ugine-Kuhlman, and Thompson-CSF. The steel industry was officially nationalized (Usinor and Sacilor), as were all banks with deposits over 1 billion francs. Parts of Dassault and Matra also came into public hands.

14. Alain Boublil, *Le Socialisme industriel* (Paris: Presses Universitaires de France, 1977); Lauber, *Politics*, p. 54.

15. *Financial Times*, November 24, 1981.

16. Peter A. Hall, "Socialism in One Country: Mitterrand and the Struggle to Define a New Economic Policy for France," in Philip G. Cerny and Martin A. Schain, eds., *Socialism, the State and Public Policy in France* (New York: Methuen, 1985), p. 85.

17. Simonnot, *Le Grand Bluff*, p. 31; Cohen, Galbraith, and Zysman, "Rehabbing," pp. 50ff.

18. O.C.D.E. (O.E.C.D.), *Etudes économiques 1983–84; France* (Paris: O.C.D.E., 1984), pp. 19–24, 57–59.

19. On this point, Cohen and Gourevitch's projections were absolutely correct: Stephen S. Cohen and Peter A. Gourevitch, "Postscript: The Socialists—Major Movements in a Narrow Space," in Cohen and Gourevitch, *France*, pp. 180ff.

20. On the prewar nationalizations see, for example, Maillet, *La Politique industrielle*, p. 98. On the immediate postwar nationalizations, see David Pinckney, "The French Experiment in Nationalizations: 1944–1958," in Earl Meade, ed., *Modern France: Problems of the Third and Fourth Republics* (New York: Russell and Russell, 1964).

21. See especially John Zysman, *Political Strategies for Industrial Order* (Berkeley and Los Angeles: University of California Press, 1977), and Zysman, *Governments, Markets and Growth* (Ithaca, N.Y.: Cornell University Press, 1983). Zysman also examines policy in traditional industries. For a stress on the continuity of pre- and post–1981 industrial policy, see Maillet, *La Politique industrielle*.

22. Maillet, *La Politique industrielle*, pp. 105–6; Cohen, Galbraith, and Zysman, "Rehabbing," pp. 69–72.

23. *Financial Times*, June 26, 1985.

24. Interview with a French ministerial cabinet member, Ministry of Industry, July 19, 1985.

25. *Financial Times*, June 26, 1985.

26. Ibid.

27. Richard Pryke, *The Nationalized Industries: Policies and Performance Since 1968* (Oxford: Martin Robertson, 1981), p. 265.

28. *Financial Times*, June 26, 1985; *Le Monde*, February 28, 1986.

29. Stephen Brooks, "The Mixed Ownership Corporation as an Instrument of Public Policy," paper presented at the International Political Science Association Quadrennial Meeting, Paris, France, July 15–20, 1985 (mimeographed).

30. *Financial Times*, June 26, 1985.

31. Raymond Barre, conversation with the author.

32. On enterprise zones, see the special issue of *Urban Affairs Quarterly* 18 (September 1982). On *poles de conversion*, see *Le Monde*, February 10, 1984.

33. See William W. Goldsmith, "Bringing the Third World Home: Enterprise Zones for America," in Larry Sawyers and William K. Tabb, eds., *Sunbelt/Snowbelt* (New York: Oxford University Press, 1984); originally published in *Working Papers for a New Society* (March/April 1982).

34. This, of course, contradicts the spirit of the Defferre Law of 1982, which gave more power to local government. The notion of the *commissaire de la république* as a chief local coordinator of aid is, however, remarkably similar to demands for a central ombudsman found in the American urban policy literature. Cf. Roger W. Schmenner, "Industrial Location and Urban Public Management," in Arthur P. Solomon, ed., *The Prospective City* (Cambridge, Mass.: MIT Press, 1980). On the jungle of aid to industry in France, see Jean-Pierre Robin, "La Jongle des aides à l'industrie," *La Vie Française*, October 1–7, 1984.

35. *Le Monde*, February 5, 1985.

36. Conversation with the author, July 15, 1985.

37. July 1985.

38. It was clearly motivated by concern for the upcoming institutional crisis, should the right capture a majority in Parliament and demand a conservative government to share power with the Socialist president. It is hard to see how a vice president would clarify the ambiguity of executive power under the 1958 constitution.

39. French television, July 1985.

40. Raymond Barre, *Réflexions pour demain* (Paris: Livres de Poche, 1984); Lionel Stoleru, *L'Alternance tranquille* (Paris: Flammarion, 1985); for the RPR (neo-Gaullist) point of view, see *Projet pour la France* (Paris: Flammarion, 1985). For a critique, see Denis Clerc, "Un Programme pour la Droite?" *Le Monde Diplomatique*, June 1985.

41. Quoted in Clerc, "Un Programme," p. 28.

42. Ibid. For details of the right's proposals, see *Expresse*, July 19–25, 1985; see also *Financial Times*, August 13, 1985.

43. Clerc, "Un Programme," p. 28.

44. Cohen, Galbraith, and Zysman, "Rehabbing."

45. David Marsh, "The Bid to Reverse the Tide," *Financial Times*, August 13, 1984; see also Jean-Maxime Leveque, "Réussir les denationalisations," *Le Monde*, June 25, 1985.

46. Marsh, "The Bid."

47. *Journal Officiel*, July 3, 1986. The Conservatives left open the percentage of ownership that would be privatized for each company. See David R. Cameron, "The Nationalized Industries After March," *French Politics and Society*, 14 (June 1986): 20.

48. Philip Revzin, "Capitalist Culture Takes Root in France," *Wall Street Journal*, May 11, 1987, p. 22.

49. *Le Monde*, April 25, 1987.

50. Walter LeFeber, *America, Russia and the Cold War* (New York: John Wiley and Sons, 1967), p. 37. LaFeber's reference is to NATO and the Marshall Plan as two strategies of defending the West.

51. For example, Robert Keohane and Joseph Nye, *Power and Interdependence: World Politics in Transition* (Boston: Little, Brown, 1977).

52. "Hegemonic states," of course, need not be so constrained; cf. Stephen D. Krasner, "State Power and the Structure of International Trade," *World Politics* 28 (April) 1976: 317–43.

53. Peter J. Katzenstein, "International Relations and Domestic Structures: Foreign

Economic Policies of Advanced Industrial States," *International Organization* 30 (Winter 1976) 295–336; Katzenstein, "Conclusion"; Zysman, *Political Strategies*.

54. For a recent review of this now voluminous literature, see Stephen D. Krasner, "Approaches to the State: Alternative Conceptions and Historical Dynamics," *Comparative Politics* 16 (January 1984): 223–46.

55. Interview with a French ministerial cabinet member, Ministry of Industry, July 18, 1985.

56. Fred Block, "The Ruling Class Does Not Rule," *Socialist Revolution* 33 (1977): 144ff. On the percentage of investment, see Maillet, *La Politique industrielle*, p. 99.

57. Charles Lindblom, *Politics and Markets* (New York: Basic Books, 1977), pp. 170–88.

58. This was Keynes' original formulation of his solution to replace a low employment equilibrium with full employment. See J. M. Keynes, *The General Theory of Employment, Interest, and Money* (London: Macmillan, 1936), pp. 268ff.

59. See, for example, Samuel Bowles and Herbert Gintis, "The Crisis of Liberal Democratic Capitalism: The Case of the United States," *Politics and Society*, 11 (1982): 51–93.

60. "Eureka" was the French-sponsored answer to Ronald Reagan's call for European cooperation on his "Star Wars" or Strategic Defense Initiative (SDI) satellite weapons program. After several mutations, Eureka emerged as a collection of vague programs promoting high-speed computers, lasers, and telecommunications.

61. I have elaborated on this theme in Harvey B. Feigenbaum, *The Politics of Public Enterprise: Oil and the French State* (Princeton, N.J.: Princeton University Press, 1985), viz. chap. 6.

62. This theme was repeated by a number of people who interviewed for this study.

63. Hall, "Socialism in One Country," pp. 89ff; Feigenbaum, *Politics of Public Enterprise*, p. 162.

64. Interview, July 12, 1985. The executive represented a public utility, but the same sentiments were repeated by public managers in "competitive" industries.

65. *Le Monde*, June 21, 1985; *Wall Street Journal*, April 22, 1985.

66. The term is James Q. Wilson's.

67. Mark Kesselman, "Prospects for Democratic Socialism in Advanced Capitalism: Class Struggle and Compromise in Sweden and France," *Politics and Society*, 11, (1982): 397–438; Jane Jensen and George Ross, cited in Frank L. Wilson, "The French Left in Power," *Western Political Quarterly* 38 (June 1985): 339.

68. Philippe Schmitter, "Still the Century of Corporatism?" *Review of Politics* 36 (January 1974: 85–131); Peter Katzenstein, *Small States in World Markets* (Ithaca, N.Y.: Cornell University Press, 1985). Cf. Guy Groux, "Organized Labor and Industrial Relations," paper presented at the Sixth Annual Conference of Europeanists, Washington, D.C., October 31, 1987.

69. Philippe Simonnot, *Le Pouvoir monétaire* (Paris: Seghers, 1973); Henri Rousso, "French Planning," presentation, International Studies Association Annual Meeting, April 18, 1987, Washington, D.C.

70. John T.S. Keeler, "Corporatism and French Union Hegemony: The Case of French Agricultural Syndicalism," in Suzanne D. Berger, ed., *Organizing Interests in Western Europe* (Cambridge, Eng.: Cambridge University Press, 1981). For an example of how one group was able to turn the state to its own advantage, see Ezra N. Suleiman, *Les Notaires* (Paris: Seuil, 1987).

71. On this point see Charles-Albert Michalet, "France," in Raymond Vernon, ed., *Big Business and the State: Changing Relations in Western Europe* (Cambridge, Mass.: Harvard University Press, 1974), p. 125.

72. On the decline of planning in France, see Feigenbaum, *Politics of Public Enterprise*, pp. 110ff.

73. Cf. Peter A. Hall, *Governing the Economy* (New York: Oxford University Press, 1986), Part III.

74. E. E. Schattschneider, *The Semisovereign People* (New York: Holt, Rhinehart and Winston, 1960), pp. 34–35.

75. Vernon Coleman, "Labor Power and Social Equality: Union Politics in a Changing Economy," *Political Science Quarterly* (Winter 1988), 687–705.

76. Cf. George Ross, "Nicos Poulantzas, Eurocommunism, and the Debate on the Theory of the Capitalist State," *Socialist Review* 9 (March-April 1979).

7

Industrial Adjustment in the French Steel Industry

Anthony Daley

Louis XIV would have taken pride in the ink spilled over the French state. After the mid–1960s, it served as a model of industrial policy making, especially for the "weak" British and American states. The French state has typically been characterized as having secretive and selective policy processes in which state actors choose winners and channel resources to them. This picture is problematic, however, because the same policy process has produced national losers as well as national champions. Policy tools do not guarantee successful implementation. Politics can intervene.

We will analyze industrial policy making in the French steel industry to examine the role of the French state in the process of industrial change. Thus, we need to uncover the institutional incentives available to state agencies, industry, and organized labor. We combine interest-group analysis with an investigation of policy-making linkages. Arguing against the prevailing explanations of French interest articulation, we point instead to a state-led model of industrial adjustment and a protest model of interest-group behavior.

This chapter argues that the French state has structured the overall possibilities for business and labor in coping with market decline. First, it looks closely at industrial change in the French steel industry. Market decline and state policy combined to transform the state into the only mechanism for change. Consequently, the industry became politicized, and both the unions and employers have sought state intervention for their own purposes. Second, it analyzes the inability of French labor and capital to negotiate privately the terms of industrial dislocation. As a result, French unions can employ various modes of direct action to "complement" negotiation. Third, it investigates state leverage in the labor market which has enabled it to deliver some of the key demands of organized labor. Fourth, it shows the extent to which the French state has conceded important employment guarantees without jeopardizing the adjustment model. Finally, this chapter argues that both the channels of interest representation and the policy-making linkages point to a distinctive pattern of industrial adjustment.

STATE AND STEEL

The crisis in international steel markets affected most producers in the advanced world. After the peak year of 1974, production and profits declined precipitously in response to competition from the newly industrializing countries and changing patterns of consumption. Yet, if weak demand faced all steelmakers, strategic responses have varied. The Japanese and the Germans preserved market position and employment much longer than other competitors.

The competitive difficulties of the French steel industry are long-standing. An insufficient technological base has led to low labor productivity. The low-quality iron ore from Lorraine was expensive to reduce. A focus on low-end products did not meet changing market demand. Poor production strategies resulted in low profitability in the best of times and an inability to invest quickly in new technologies, such as oxygen steelmaking in the 1960s and continuous casting in the 1970s. New strip plants at Dunkerque and Fos produce some of Europe's best and cheapest sheet, but enough unproductive plants remained open to ensure continued losses. This industry could not face the lower prices and decreased demand of the post–1974 international steel depression. Neither Usinor nor Sacilor turned a profit between 1974 and 1986. The result has been plant shutdowns, employment contractions, and losses of market share.

The French steel industry has been on the brink of bankruptcy since the mid–1960s. The state has intervened massively to restructure the financial and productive base of the industry. The frequent bailouts, however, have come with conditions. The state sought to link employment preservation with industrial restructuring. This altered the nature of interest representation and changed the terms of adjustment. In spite of continued market failure, the state has spent more on steel than on any other industry in the postwar period.

How could steel policy making fail given the extraordinary powers of the interventionist state? Such a question transcends the formal policy-making linkages and enters the realm of politics. The state has had the capacity to ensure successful investment strategies, to monitor compliance, and to discipline transgressions. However, adjustment has taken place in the steel industry with only the partial utilization of those policy tools.

The story of the French steel industry shows how market decline offers institutional actors incentives to alter patterns of power. Constant "crisis" has forced new ways of thinking old relationships. In a three-step process, the state has assumed control of the industry. Institutional arrangements have been altered, but many of the reflexes to market uncertainty remained.

Hands-Off Intervention. The French state has a long history of intervention in the steel industry. It enjoyed numerous means to influence market behavior. Still, it confined its activity to a gate-keeping function. The Ministry of Finance (MoF) used industry data in its decision making. The modernization commissions of the National Plan relied exclusively on the industry's interpretation of the market. Conflict existed over production and investment targets, but only on the basis of forecasts provided by the industry.[1] Until 1966, state funding came with few strings attached.

Two major policy decisions, however, contravened the intentions of the steel producers: price controls and the European Coal and Steel Community (ECSC). Control over steel prices constituted a costly interference in the affairs of the industry. Low-interest credits were used as compensation for the lost funds. The defeat over the ECSC was perhaps even more serious. The prospect of cooperation in these two sectors terrified the steelmakers, who knew they could not compete with the Germans. (Subsequent and persistent trade deficits with Germany proved them correct.) Still, base-point pricing eased the consequences of political supranationalism.[2] Infrastructural improvements in the steel regions also compensated for projected lost markets.

Otherwise, the state accepted the industry's view of the market and let it maintain its autonomy. Jack Hayward argues that the state was reluctant to assume responsibility for the industry because of the bureaucratic conflict between the MoF and the Ministry of Industry (MoI).[3] Adjustment issues were not as pressing during the boom of the 1950s. Growth was slow in the steel industry, but it still existed. The public optimism (the Lorraine was hailed by the industry as the new frontier) clouded policy makers' doubts.[4]

Industrial strategy was mapped out in the Chambre Syndicale de la Sidérurgie Française (CSSF—the steel industry association) and confirmed by the MoF and MoI. Membership in the CSSF was compulsory by government decree. In the 1940s, the CSSF played an important role in the allocation of raw materials. It also ran the cartels that organized French production until the ECSC came into existence. After abolition of the cartels in 1953, the CSSF continued to process most sales of steel products, so it did not need to rely on members for information. The governance of the CSSF was by election, and the Lorraine producers (of small family-owned plants) controlled the largest bloc of votes.

Collective borrowing further centralized powers within the CSSF. The Groupement des Industries Sidérurgigues (GIS) operated under the auspices of the CSSF and issued bonds guaranteed by the industry. Collective borrowing meant better terms than any individual firm could get in the bond market. This benefited the small firms disproportionately. It also led to a greater availability of privately raised credit, since the accumulated guarantees could cover any single default. The GIS board (composed of industry members) had to approve investment projects in order to secure such group funding. This gave the GIS the possibility of influencing investment plans. Once the GIS decided to issue borrowings, it needed approval from the MoF and the MoI. GIS borrowing accounted for a third of all industry investment until the mid–1960s. The CSSF also negotiated credits from the Economic and Social Development Fund (FDES) collectively for the industry.[5] Thus, the mechanisms of credit allocation brought a pyramid of authorizations that placed the CSSF in a strategic position to influence industry politics.

Although the CSSF was a coherent organizational force within the context of French employer associations, it did not intervene actively in the affairs of its members. The CSSF's hands-off policy derived partially from its leadership. Until 1963 its presidents came from the steel firms themselves. They sought carefully to build consensus within the organization. Therefore, its policies betrayed a conservatism. Until the mid–1960s, the CSSF provided collective protection from outside threats. The changing of the guard, with the election of Jacques Ferry, brought new initiatives to the CSSF.

Political Duopoly. Economic decline altered industry-state relations. By the early 1960s, the industry could not finance new investments. Aggregate productivity levels remained low by European standards. Only Usinor-Denain and Sollac (both built with Marshall Plan funds) and Usinor-Dunkerque (finished in 1963) were competitive, and they produced a similar range of products—wide-band strip. The smaller plants in the Lorraine that made construction-grade steel operated at a loss and remained afloat with state monies.

The CSSF negotiated a comprehensive plan with the MoF and MoI to relieve pressure on the beleaguered companies. The *Convention état-Sidérurgie*, signed in July 1966, took a comprehensive approach to the competitive difficulties of French steel. The range of measures was impressive—lower freight rates, competitive coke prices, 2.7 billion francs in FDES credits. For the first time, a "contract" bound both the industry and individual firms: management had to negotiate with the state over *their* production and investment priorities.

The *Convention* shifted the balance of power between business and the state. The MoF conditioned the plan with a "reform of the industry."[6] Yet, state actors were divided over appropriate policies. The Pompidou government excluded nationalization and what it called *dirigisme*. It realized, however, that failure to make any significant move could permit financial bankruptcies and force overt public control.

The state plan originated in the offices of the CSSF. Its final version constituted a brilliant piece of political negotiation. It responded to state concerns (a policy of mergers) while trying to guard the maximum amount of freedom for its members (voluntary compliance). Ferry may have been playing a balancing act within the CSSF: certain Lorraine producers suspected him of trying to consolidate the industry into a giant "French Steel Company." The severity of the financial problem nixed the idea of voluntarism for even the MoI. The final document conceded more power to the state, but it also placed the CSSF in a kingpin position between its members and the state.

The agreement operated at two levels: industry-wide and firm-based. Previous steel policy had worked at these levels but through different intermediaries. General policy was formulated in the steel modernization commission and ad hoc refinements for individual firms were worked out with the *Trésor*. The *Convention*, however, was negotiated between a small group of people, including Ferry and representatives from the MoI, MoF, and Planning Commission. The CSSF mediated firm-level commitments. Ferry reinforced the already strong position of the CSSF.

Industrial concentration also strengthened the position of the CSSF. The firms were run by managers, not the old guard. The Wendel-Sidélor merger in 1968 removed the steel oligarch François de Wendel from the daily operations of the firm. Usinor's purchase of Lorraine-Escaut removed another independent power base from the Lorraine. The modernism of these new industrial leaders fit in snugly with the orientations of state actors. Ferry, in particular, was a dynamic man leading an industry known for its cautious, conservative style. He argued publicly that state-led adjustment was necessary to modernize French industry. (He even split with the peak employers' association, the Conseil National du Patronat Français, over this issue.) He argued that the "contractualism" of the *Convention* (bordering on corporatist bargaining networks) should be extended to their industries.[7]

The mediating role of the CSSF depended on a willingness to recognize, and take advantage of, the distribution of power in the steel system. Ferry conceded a loss of industry autonomy in relations with labor in exchange for comprehensive relief. The state forced the industry to negotiate with the unions the terms of labor rationalization, which would result in 15,000 job reductions. It set the minimum standards by which the industry could negotiate; layoffs would not take place. The owners had to negotiate a social plan with the unions, and successful negotiations constituted a precondition for implementation. The CSSF assumed the responsibility of keeping the unions informed of the industry's compliance.[8]

By the late 1960s the industry needed to produce at coastal sites to reduce costs and take advantage of economies of scale. The politics surrounding a possible new plant spotlighted the power sharing between the CSSF and the state. Ferry accepted the political criteria of the siting.[9] (This project carried considerable prestige for the government.) He worked with Wendel-Sidélor to negotiate FDES credits with a reluctant MoF, which hoped the project could be financed out of internal savings. Ferry was aided by the MoI arguments that massive financing was needed both to build the plant and to continue rationalizing production in the Lorraine. By 1972, the cost overruns at Fos-sur-Mer forced a further infusion of aid. He helped to mobilize governmental support to allay the suspicions of the banking community over the weak financial position of Wendel-Sidélor.[10] He mediated between Wendel-Sidélor and Usinor to bring the latter into the project as co-investor. Usinor in turn insisted that Ferry head the subsidiary! The commitment of the MoF proved so extraordinary that, in 1973 alone, it contributed 150 percent of its FDES budget to the Fos project.

Depression in world steel markets after 1974 changed the foundation of the duopoly. The massive and well-publicized aid in both 1966 and 1971–73 brought the industry itself under considerable public scrutiny. The crash of the steel market coincided with the onset of mass unemployment. Prime Minister Jacques Chirac forbade employment reductions as part of his government's countercyclical economic policy. In return, the MoF disbursed 1.5 billion francs in FDES loans so that the steel firms could meet interest payments and engage in countercyclical investment. The crisis was so severe that these public funds were used only for operating expenses.

The period between 1966 and 1976 brought increasing state oversight of the industry. However, Ferry provided the optic through which state actors intervened. The state financed investments, but it lacked control over the final use of those funds. Implementation was left to the individual firms, with the CSSF playing a mediating role. Some projects received state funding but were never undertaken. Moreover, while the state sought to reduce the workforce, the firms continued hiring new workers, especially between 1968 and 1974, thereby negating possible productivity gains. Intervention had not yet closed the gap between policy tools and implementation.

Statism. By 1977 continued market decline instilled sufficient frustration in state actors with the policy-making process. Mounting losses forced a strategic reevaluation. Ferry tried negotiating more FDES credits in 1976 to prepare the industry for the boom in steel markets that would surely follow! An interministerial committee (from the MoF, MoI, and Ministry of Labor) saw this as "irresponsible."[11] Instead, the committee sought more public control. As a condition for another 1.3 billion francs in FDES credits, the government demanded in March 1977 that Usinor and Sacilor deposit 100 million francs of stock with a state financial intermediary. Again, a condition for aid was the successful negotiation of a social plan with the unions to reduce the workforce by 17,000. Finally, the holding companies for Usinor and Sacilor had to integrate forward their operations. Their subsidiaries assumed control to secure additional funding.

This latter requirement constituted a major overhaul of business-state relations. The holding companies had carefully sought to separate their profitable holdings from steel. The government decreed four months later that the holding companies be brought directly under the control of that committee. This new supervision entailed access to all company information. It dashed the industry's autonomy, which had been carefully protected by the CSSF.

In retrospect, the 1977 aid package seems provisional. The money was targeted to "reorganize production." Instead, it helped service interest payments. The new institutional arrangement left intact the notion that the key to success was investment funding. The control committee could affect neither the firms' financial deterioration nor the market. State aid was predicated on a recovery of steel demand in 1977. Unfortunately, product demand and prices continued to decline. By 1978 debt constituted over 100 percent of sales.

After the right unexpectedly confirmed its majority in the March 1978 legislative elections, Prime Minister Raymond Barre shook up the industry a second time to rescue it from bankruptcy. The state ruptured completely the power of the companies: it took de facto control of the industry. The debt carried by the companies was exchanged for a limited form of equity, so-called participatory loans. These could be repurchased by the companies if they started to make money. However, they were so large (9.4 billion francs owed to commercial banks, 9 billion to the state, and 14 billion to the GIS) that repayment remained a convenient fiction for the political right, which sought to avoid calling this move a nationalization. Debt service dropped from 15 percent of sales to 3–6 percent, the European average. Another 20,000 job cuts, whose terms had to be negotiated with the unions, would increase productivity.

To carry through these radical measures, the government formulated policy entirely outside channels, thereby divorcing itself from the CSSF. It excluded Ferry from the substantive negotiations, consulting him only in his capacity as head of the GIS. The presidents of Sacilor and Usinor were never consulted. The MoF assembled the industry's major creditors and negotiated the financial measures. The MoI formulated the accompanying industrial measures. The state then removed the heads of Usinor and Sacilor and installed its own choices. It also forced the resignation of Ferry from the presidency of the CSSF. The latter was relegated to outsider status—simple statistical work combined with advice to policy makers.

The Socialists formally nationalized Usinor and Sacilor in 1982. They revived the industry's productivism. The 1982 steel plan consequently adopted for investment purposes the most optimistic production level of the three envisioned in a report commissioned on the industry. The Socialists increased the downstream diversification necessary to integrate steel production with other metalworking activities. They also pursued reindustrialization measures in the steel regions more successfully than their predecessors. Nonetheless, the new government remained reluctant to pare down the industry in line with the new terms of international competition.

Nationalization did not eliminate politics from steel policy making. Instead, bureaucratic conflict would determine the future of the industry. The 1984 restructuring plan evidenced the conflicts between the MoF and MoI. The former sought to maintain capacity, while the latter wanted to limit the state's liability. The MoF won this conflict but had to pay the costs of covering existing deficits and easing another 20,000 workers out of the industry. Moreover, nationalization did not immediately envision a merger. The intitial competition for resources from state coffers complicated the task of state-led adjustment. Streamlining investments became a difficult political task. Only in 1987 did a newly-elected right government merge the two companies in order to prevent a deterioration of corporate in-fighting.

By the late 1980s, the French steel industry could finally announce profits. Productivity levels are among the highest in the world. Its technology is competitive. Six major bailouts between 1966 and 1984 have belatedly brought profitability. After 14 years of continuous losses, Usinor-Sacilor turned out its first profit in 1988, but the industry has lost half its workforce, its optimism, and its motor role in regional development.

State control raised the stakes for policy making. The promise of future profitability provided for future embarrassment when the market did not perform as expected. It provided a focus for worker anxiety over the future of the steel regions. Steel absorbed the lion's share of state subsidies to all public firms between 1981 and 1986. Both left and right governments have paid generous benefits to labor to purchase the necessary job reductions. By the mid–1980s, early retirement was at 50, and retraining programs promised new skills and a guaranteed job upon completion.

THE POLITICS OF LABOR

The close business-state relations in France typically exclude organized labor. Adjustment in the steel industry was no different. Yet, employment was guaranteed until 1977, and the social measures have been generous. How do we explain this paradox? Unless we can prove benevolence from either the state or the employers, then we need to look at labor politics. Labor exclusion has not meant lack of influence. Rather, labor's voice has encouraged an activist state role.

Political conflict divides French labor. Less than 20 percent of the working class is organized. At least four different unions exist in most industrial sectors: the Conféderation Générale du Travail (CST), the Conféderation Française Démocratique du Travail (CFDT), the Force Ouvrière (FO), and the Conféderation Française des Travailleurs Chrétiens (CFTC).[12] Thus, at least five confederations compete for the same workers, who seem reluctant to join unions in the first place. Until the 1960s the CGT was dominant in most industrial sectors, although its history had been sprinkled with division and secession.

The CGT's close ties with the French Communist party (PCF) structured labor politics for most of the postwar period. As an oppositional force, excluded from governing between 1947 and 1981, the PCF has provided strident critiques of French capitalism and state-led modernization. Its articulation of working-class positions has sharpened the expression of class conflict among French workers. The CGT engaged in an "oppositional unionism" which contests the legitimacy of the adjustment model.

The representative functions of French unions further complicate labor politics. French workers vote regularly in shop-floor elections for works councils, shop stewards, arbitrators' councils, and social security administration boards. Thus, at least four major rounds of elections take place on a regular basis, with the major confederational unions regularly garnering 80 percent of the vote.

Representation combines with a logic of irresponsibility to produce a pattern of industrial relations that can best be called "controlled anarchy." Unions have no legal requirement for discipline. A work stoppage can take place on a moment's notice without violating the labor contract. The majority of such actions last under a day, but such disruption holds considerable symbolic value. Mobilization may be difficult to sustain because of the structural poverty of French unions, but local communities and the left parties frequently offer material aid to striking workers. Such unconstrained labor-market behavior has important consequences for competitive unionism. Union agents tackle issues they might otherwise neglect because they are constantly up for reelection. In France perhaps more than elsewhere, constant agitation finds expression on the shop floor. Class consciousness is not restricted by negotiated rules.

The steel industry's geographic concentration has compounded the effects of unconstrained behavior. Until the construction of Fos, 90 percent of crude steel was produced in the Lorraine and the Nord, with over 50 percent in the Lorraine alone. Steel has played a critical part in the local economies of these areas. In towns such as Longwy or Denain, 80 percent of the economy is tied directly to steel employment. Thus, any form of industrial adjustment will have important consequences for these localities.

The history of social relations in the steel basins has also left a legacy of bitter shop-floor relations. Rural industrialization led to employer paternalism in an effort to attract skilled workers. (The companies owned the housing, schools, and stores, even paying the clergy.) Paternalism also sought strict employer control. Until the 1960s, management refused to share power with the unions and actively repressed organizational efforts. The CGT articulated the consequent class anger.

Employer strategy also discouraged the institutionalization of collective bargaining. Until the *Convention*, industry-wide bargaining focused primarily on minimum wage rates for individual job categories. A number of agreements were signed, but they had little impact on real wages, which were set unilaterally by individual plants. In the absence of negotiating structures, the social component of industrial change hinged on union mobilization.

The three weeks of strikes in the Lorraine in April 1967 showed the potential for social explosion in the steel regions.[13] The strikes did not result from union calls for action. Rather, rationalization in the iron mines brought sporadic local walkouts. Because the iron miners were blocking shipments, the steel owners threatened layoffs. Given the climate of uncertainty over the future of steel—the *Convention* had been announced in July 1966—steelworkers struck as ore stocks dwindled and before they could be laid off. The entire Lorraine steel industry was paralyzed within a week. The strikes became town affairs. Housewives came out en masse to demonstrate their solidarity. Local politicians and the clergy took part in the demonstrations and denounced the plans to reduce employment.

While no direct evidence links the social accord with the strikes, the indirect evidence is convincing. Only after the strike did the negotiations mandated by the *Convention* become serious. The agreement between the National Employment Fund and the industry to finance transfers and to pay for early retirement came in June. The social accord was signed the next month.

The lack of collective discipline in steel industrial relations was most evident in the 1978–79 period. After the announcement of job reductions in September 1978, acts of social violence rocked the Lorraine and the Nord, and even reached Paris. These actions were as varied as they were dramatic. FO militants occupied the Bank of France. CFDT militants invaded regional television offices in Metz and broadcast appeals for solidarity. The CGT occupied police headquarters. Turnpikes were barricaded. The town of Longwy was blockaded. These actions were seldom conceived through regular decision-making processes in the union locals, although the latter usually claimed responsibility to head off individual prosecutions.

These spontaneous actions publicized the effects of state-led adjustment: for six months the national press covered steel almost on a daily basis. The participants reasoned that union-led demonstrations would not suffice to reverse the job reductions or rally popular support. Most actions targeted private property or state symbols. Personal injuries tended to come from confrontations with the police. Consequently, the perpetrators did not alienate public opinion. The cross-class opposition to the redundancies constituted an important element in the 1978–79 struggles. Local merchants shut their doors in protest. Shopkeepers in Longwy and Denain acted together to close down their towns. Public servants used vacation time to join marches. The clergy joined the demonstrations and spoke out from the pulpit.

While the central unions supported their members, they remained uneasy about the violence. The CFDT expelled a local in Dunkerque and disciplined the Longwy section for what it called "leftist" actions.[14] The CGT pirate radio station Lorraine Couer d'Acier mobilized broad segments of the population—

even Gaullists and Trotskyites received air time. It also lost its union flavor, at least according to union officials, and was closed after the mobilization died down.[15] Thus, the unions exerted some social control if only to maintain the integrity of their organizations.

The evolution of union strategy dovetailed with attempts to reassert centralized control. Important factions of both the CGT and the CFDT grew dissatisfied with the returns of oppositional unionism. In the steel industry, oppositional positions were "hard" positions. The intent was to stretch management as far as it would go on wages while simultaneously making a statement about class exploitation in the demand itself. Yet, employment bargaining seemed to require a different strategy. The electoral failure of the political left in March 1978 and the severity of the 1978 steel plan induced both unions to experiment with a new type of labor-market strategy: "counterproposals" would show alternative ways of facing competition. What the unions term a "proposition-force" strategy sought to "extend the scope of collective bargaining to include industrial decision-making."[16] The attempt to impose a coherent vision for the steel industry meant the centralization of demands. The change in union strategy foundered on both the resistance of the state to alter its plans and the resistance from union members whose oppositional tactics came almost as a reflex.

By the 1980s local mobilization proved more difficult to achieve. The plans of 1977 and 1978 had already decreased employment. Relations between the CGT and the CFDT turned bitter after the left's failure in 1978. Attempts at centralized control led to a demobilization of local initiative. After the left unexpectedly reached power in 1981, the unions felt torn between their political loyalties and their labor-market responsibilities. The cutbacks announced by the Socialists in 1984 constituted a *coup de grâce*. The turbulence over the previous 20 years had produced a shell-shocked generation. Sporadic guerilla actions took place, but mostly there has been a mixture of resignation and disillusion. Still, a pattern of institutional interaction was in place. The state intervened to quell potential class violence.

INDUSTRIAL POLICY AND SOCIAL COMMITMENTS

The French state plays a dominant role in industrial relations, as it does in the process of industrial adjustment. It maintains an active role in shaping the pattern of industrial bargaining. It influences wage negotiations through a minimum wage tied to both the cost of living and macro productivity increases. Industry-wide minimum wage rates are linked in turn to the minimum wage. Legislation on the framework of bargaining has determined who can bargain and over what. Legislation and governmental decrees on social policies—such as paid vacations, sick pay, working time, retirement pay—influence the content of collective bargaining. The state, through its special powers, can extend privately negotiated agreements to an entire region, an industry, or all wage-earners. It can also force social partners to negotiate by threatening state action if bargaining does not take place or succeed. The French state thus guarantees the success of social bargaining. "If there is a 'web of rules' about industrial relations in France," writes George Ross, "then it has been predominantly spun by the state."[17]

The key issue for organized labor since 1974 has been employment, and the state has the means to alter the substance as well as the process of bargaining. It can mobilize monies to pay for early retirement, transfer costs, or training measures for displaced workers.[18] (A disproportionate share of the financing of these funds, however, comes from workers themselves through payroll contributions.) Over 100 different subsidy programs exist to create incentives for the business community to create new jobs.[19] A large public sector facilitates the state's ability to manipulate labor markets.

The most frequently used instrument for financing the costs of industrial restructuring has been the National Employment Fund (Fonds National de l'Emploi—FNE). Under the administrative auspices of the Ministry of Labor, it has evolved from a facilitator of labor-market equilibrium in the 1960s to the French equivalent of an active (albeit ad hoc) labor-market fund in the 1980s. Funded to the level of 20 billion francs in 1984, it represents a major instrument for intervention in the labor market. The government can use it as seed money or as a major financier of preretirements, training programs, supplemental unemployment benefits, and reductions in working time.[20] For the most part, its use is invoked during collective bargaining negotiations when the social partners reach a "contract" with the FNE over the methods and financing of agreements. Intervention can take place at the level of the industry or the plant.[21] Consequently, state officials maintain a handhold on the outcomes of collective bargaining.

The dominant role of the state in industrial relations has had two effects. First, state actors tend to be suspicious of privately negotiated agreements which might contravene public policy. Second, perhaps because of this suspicion, social actors look first to the state to solve their problems. The French state wields the key resources to facilitate bargaining.

In spite of apparent state capacity, attempts to coordinate labor policy with industrial policy have mostly failed. The linkage of labor and industrial policy has consistently hinged on the issue of union participation. Public-sector incomes policy broke down in the 1960s in the face of unified hostility from the CGT and CFDT. The state's attempt after May 1968 to institutionalize the labor market failed because the unions rejected limitations on their right to strike and because a large part of the business community remained deeply hostile to the entrenchment of union power on the shop floor (in spite of the reforms after May 1968). The Auroux Laws, passed by the Socialists in the early 1980s, promised to regularize collective bargaining at the plant level while offering workers new rights of expression. They have been moderately successful, but the employers have transformed the promised openness on the shop floor into ways to circumvent dialogue with the unions. Inclusion of trade unions in the routine of collective bargaining would have required a state less sure of itself, different shop-floor relations, and a labor movement with a different historical legacy.

We argued above that the state politicized the steel industry by its very intervention. Public pronouncements of future success only nourished future disappointment when results were not obtained. Both unions and local notables talked constantly of "promises not kept." Union publications have been replete with denunciations of industry bailouts, measures taken on the "backs of workers." Such business-state collaboration only fueled the arguments of the CGT and CFDT for nationalization. Only the FO has refrained from engaging in such class rhetoric, and its reward for such moderation has been declining electoral shares. This politicization confirmed to the unions that they too needed state backing. The innovative measures to ease labor adjustment came through state-managed programs. The unions reasoned that the only way to obtain guarantees was to appeal directly to the government. State intervention entailed political responsibilities.

Labor's political appeals assumed two forms. First, union representatives made direct contacts with ministers or their *cabinets* in order to alter the content of the decisions. These governmental contacts increased as the steel problem became national. Second, the symbolic actions taken by workers sought to mobilize public opinion in favor of the threatened regions. By the mid–1960s these actions constituted electoral blackmail.

As industrial policy in steel became politicized, electoral fortunes seemed to ride on its success. This was as true for the right as for the left. After the 1965 presidential election, the electoral difference between the two sides of a polarized political community narrowed considerably, and public outcry caused by industrial dislocation could decide critical seats in the National Assembly. The political calendar after the mid–1960s dictated that a test of electoral strength would take place almost on an annual basis.[22] Calming social tensions was at least partially motivated by electoral concerns. The 1978 plan was apparently delayed several critical months until after the legislative elections, a contest most observers thought would be close.[23] The announcement of the 1977 plan fell conveniently after the municipal elections of that year. The Socialists delayed their 1984 restructuring plan until after the 1983 municipal elections.

State investments in the success of industrial policy and the electoral concerns of various political regimes combined to reinforce for the unions the logic of state-led adjustment. Consequently, union action took the form of a state focus that was sharper than that historically characteristic of the French labor movement. Not only did mobilization target the political regime, but negotiating strategies depended on state intervention.

The failure to link industrial and labor policies meant that the latter became ad hoc attempts to appease the unions over the terms of industrial change.

In the steel industry, this has brought numerous measures to reduce workforces by whatever means possible: by buying off workers (lump-sum "departure" bonuses), by retiring them early, and by shifting them into different occupations. Institutional uncertainty in industrial relations increased the stakes for the interventionist state. The amount necessary to buy social calm was uncertain in advance. By the late 1970s, however, the CGT and CFDT sought the unthinkable: input into industrial policy as a precondition for social bargaining. They were rebuffed. Still, the social costs of adjustment would consist of whatever was necessary to buy social peace.

SOCIAL INTERVENTION AND STEEL POLITICS

The organizational logic of selective industrial policy in France almost demands that unions be removed from the policy-making process. The state claimed to have long-term interests while portraying the unions as lacking qualified personnel and seeking short-term benefits.[24] This justification grew weaker by the 1970s. The unions' proposition-force strategy brought trained economists into union decision making. Likewise, the argument about short-term political horizons seemed to characterize the political regime as well.

Because the process of industrial policy involves active *discrimination* among firms and sectors of the economy, institutions committed to equality would seem to participate with great difficulty. Such discrimination would threaten the class basis of French unionism by pitting unions against each other, and the confederations do not have sufficient standing to arbitrate. Union involvement remained a moot point in any case: given managerial ideologies and the technocratic disdain of state actors for union representatives, such union participation has never really been considered.

Before the proposition-force unionism of the 1970s, unions did not actively seek such decision-making status. Fear of incorporation into the policy process dominated the thinking of oppositional unionism. This union refusal to "co-manage" created a "culture of the social" which has been difficult to displace. This culture entailed the focus on "quantitative" issues—wages and benefits—to the exclusion of the industrial context that permitted such remuneration.[25] After 1978, both the CGT and the CFDT sought changes in investment plans to save employment. Yet, important factions within both unions reminded their organizations that their task was not to govern. This conflict was resolved initially by the nature of union demands. The explicit connection between the "social" and the "industrial" was grounded solidly in job preservation. For the CGT that meant maintaining the steel industry at whatever cost. The CFDT was willing to negotiate job creation. To maintain these jobs or create alternative ones, the unions borrowed the industrial optimism of state actors.

Proposition-force unionism broke down in the early 1980s under the weight of inter- and intra-union rivalry. The incentives built into competitive unionism favored carving out niches that were easily identifiable and intellectually convenient. Both the newfound "oppositionism" of the CGT and the CFDT's focus on collective bargaining reinforced social over industrial bargaining. Old reflexes meshed well with state-led adjustment.

Until the mid–1970s, neither the state nor the steel industry solicited union involvement, except to quell industrial unrest. Afterwards, a larger dialogue took place with governmental officials. Yet, contact did not imply influence. These audiences seemed designed to inform the unions of decisions already made. By this late stage, the financial drain on the companies was so severe that policy makers were handicapped in their options, whatever their initial inclination. The norms of the steel system favored the infusion of investment funds into the industry. They did not favor participation.

The marginalization of the trade unions was not absolute, however. The massive employment dislocation necessitated some role for labor. Consequently, the unions have been shoved into a plethora of consultative roles. Union participants have sat on boards that executed the various social measures. They sit on the regional industrialization committees. They advise the prefects on departmental employment issues. They advise the subsidiaries set up by Usinor and Sacilor to find jobs for displaced workers.

The *Convention* initiated these consultative positions. It required regular consultations with the unions over the success of the social measures. These developed into little more than glorified sessions of the sectoral commissions of the Plan. Ferry kept the debate entirely within the social realm, informing the unions of decisions already taken by the state and the industry.[26] After the expiration of the *Convention*, the CSSF remained in the position of deflecting attention from industry decision making.

Nationalization perpetuated this outsider status of labor in industrial policy making. Although union representatives sat on company boards after 1982—positions that meant important access to information—they did not participate in investment or employment decision making. This had the paradoxical effect of tying worker representatives at least formally to policies with which they disagreed.

The relative marginalization of union participation in decision making created an explosive situation. Consultative bodies did not compensate for the absence of institutionalized powers. However, such responsibility was not possible given the legacy of conflict between labor and management. Competitive unionism aggravated the effects of marginalization; unions bickered among themselves over the distribution of social benefits. Market deterioration and policy reflexes defined the terrain of decision making: the industry and the state formulated industrial policy, while the unions were relegated to executing social policies decided from above.

Within this context, the French state assumed the paternalistic role formerly held by the employers. It guaranteed employment from 1966 until 1977. When such guarantees became impossible in the face of industry losses, it assured the orderly exit of workers with increasingly lucrative measures. Like the employers' policies of an earlier period, however, the neo-paternalistic state refused the devolution of responsibilities to the unions. Industrial policy remained the prerogative of state actors.

The consultative role neither stemmed decentralized militancy nor offered unions real powers. The absence of union responsibility weakened federational authority in relation to the rank-and-file. Negotiations in Paris secured a few delays in plant closures. Centralized bargaining only brought the array of measures to ease workers out of the industry. These were important feats in their own right, but they did not meet the aspirations of either the CGT or the CFDT. Most important, they did not protect the integrity of the worker communities.

Weakening the federation has meant the resurgence of initiative at the base, although high overall unemployment rates in the political economy dampened mobilization energies by the mid–1980s. In the absence of coordination within and between unions, the violence that accompanied the 1978–79 and 1984 restructurings became peripheral to the adjustment model. State social intervention assumed the fire-fighting role of buying social peace. Alternative employment, pre-retirement, and training have been guaranteed by the French state as the necessary price to maintain social order. This has set important precedents for other industries. (The MoI was offering workers 200,000 francs in 1986 to leave the shipyards.) Yet, these measures also brought union marginalization. State-led adjustment remained intact.

CONCLUSION

The relationship between interest-group behavior and state policy making is necessarily close knit. The state in capitalist society needs to rely on social actors to respond to its initiatives. Likewise, those actors probe various state agencies to reinforce their own capacities. This institutional interaction is even more critical in industrial policy making, for competitive markets require constant innovation.

Yet, scholarship has tended to devolve into two separate literatures. The literature on interest groups emphasizes the interaction of groups with one another and with the state. Conceptualizations until the early 1970s tended to stress group resources. Pluralism, both as an analysis of interaction and as a prescription for organization, argues that political power cannot be centralized. A later generation argued that pluralism is only one form of interest-group interaction: groups can be defined and delimited by state power. Thus, corporatism describes a pattern of interaction in which interest organization is limited, membership is compulsory, and the state selects and approves those groups with whom it will carry on a privileged relationship.[27] A number of "neos" exist for both categories, and important definitional controversies exist, but the fundamental difference between pluralism and corporatism rests in the degree of group autonomy: in pluralism it is much higher than in corporatism.

The literature on industrial policy stresses the institutional linkages which permit actors to pursue their goals. Here discussion tends to focus on the goals of economic growth, employment, and response to international competition. Policy makers focus on coordinating the behavior of economic actors whose interests may diverge considerably. The task is to create the institutional mechanisms to achieve the desired goals.

Thus, interest-group theory looks to the procedure of the policy process itself, while the industrial-policy analyses speak to the substance of policy. This bifurcation in the literatures distorts the political reality of industrial change: substance and processes interact to alter politically the terms of competition. It is accentuated in the French case because of the importance of the French state in altering market behavior.

Ironically, the French word *corporatisme* typically connotes group egotism, exclusion of outsiders, and a group withdrawal in defense of previous gains and vested interests.[28] Its antonym is the general interest, represented by the state and public authority. Behavior, of course, departs considerably from this linguistic dichotomy.[29] Private parties rarely sacrifice their own "sectional" interests, yet the pursuit of such interests by a rival is not always considered legitimate. The result is an ambiguity of conduct in which the public and private spheres are confused.

Pluralism fails to describe interest aggregation in the French political system because of its strong state. Competition for resources may exist among voluntary groups which are free from state control, but such competition may be meaningless when the state has policy tools insufficient to act on its own. Corporatism remains weak because of the rarity of peak-level agreements. Organized labor is excluded from policy making on a formal level. It articulates demands through forms of protest outside the ordinary political process.

Yet, the whole is not always the sum of its parts. Sectoral-level corporatism—what Alan Cawson refers to as "meso-corporatism"—constitutes a category of interest representation that gets at consensual politics at lower levels of the political economy.[30] As such, it is still characterized by a political exchange between interest associations and the state in order to reduce political conflict, but it takes place at the level of industry rather than at the macro political economy.

The steel story is important because of the corporatizing elements that combine with the fundamentally statist character of adjustment. Corporatist bargaining networks typically involve cooperation in both the formulation and implementation of public policy. While the steel industry association participated in the formulation of policy, its role in implementing it varied because of the lack of a will to enforce policy. The steel unions participated in some of the execution of social measures, but they were uninvolved in the formulation of industry-wide policy.

Business-state relations during the period before the *Plan de Sauvetage* had the appearance of bipartite meso-corporatism. The formal machinery necessary for corporatist bargaining certainly existed in the postwar period. The CSSF enjoyed a monopoly of representation, and it mediated relations between firms and the state. It also generated the consensus to reduce conflict between the industry and the state. The political exchange consisted of a mutual "power dependence": the state relied on the industry for information, while the industry relied on the state for funding.

Yet, the asymmetry of power made bargaining unstable. The state held the policy tools necessary to resolve market crisis and to alter unilaterally the political exchange. The CSSF saw itself as extracting concessions. It did not seek to enforce discipline among its members. Whether the market or member self-interests prevented the execution of policy is a moot point. Rather, the CSSF saw itself as the industry mouthpiece, reconciling divergent interests, but *not* enforcing decisions made in negotiations. Finally, in attempts to diffuse class conflict resulting from bipartite cooperation, the state imposed its will on the industry.

The tripartite boards, however, did not involve labor participation in the formulation of public policy. The attempt at inclusion—proposition-force unionism—encountered both the opposition of industry and state actors and the historical legacy of union behavior. Instead, the participation of labor was restricted to the execution of social policies decided from above.

Sectoral-level interest representation in the steel industry looks more like a modified pressure or "sponsored" pluralism.[31] A statist model, however, captures better the nature of steel politics, for institutions of both labor and capital constantly appealed to the state for its intervention. The state crystallized the political power necessary for the virtual survival of labor and capital. While CSSF played a major role in mediating the interests of its members, it depended on state policy. It recognized its subordination and, especially under Ferry, adroitly played politics. Only in the 1970s did the state actually exercise its logical role in terms of industrial policy. Still, in social policy, it set the standard for the employers. Since labor has been excluded from the instances of the state, the logical corollary would be a protest model of interest representation.

The task here is not simply to categorize. The corporatist literature has been justly criticized for its purely heuristic intentions. Rather, we are interested in the distribution of political power. The French steel story has shown the extent to which the market is important for the formation and duration of patterns of interest intermediation. The model that evolved in response to market failure contained a strong but vulnerable state and an increasingly subservient CSSF. Along with the larger state role came direct and strategic pressure from labor on public policy. The more the state became involved in industry politics, the more it was susceptible to societal pressure. The French model of interest representation centralizes political power and fractionalizes societal interests.

NOTES

1. Andrew Shonfield describes how the industry circumvented the disagreements of the planners over the targets of the Fourth Plan by rallying support in the government (presumably via the *Trésor*). See *Modern Capitalism: The Changing Balance of Public and Private Power* (London: Oxford University Press, 1965), p. 139.

2. Base-point pricing enabled steel firms in the European Community to set regional prices which could not legally be undercut by competitors. The result was a cartelization of the European market which reduced import penetration.

3. Jack Hayward, *The State and the Market Economy: Industrial Patriotism and Economic Intervention in France* (Sussex: Harvester, 1986), p. 74.

4. For the optimism on the Lorraine, see Anthony Daley, "Labor and Industrial Change: The Politics of Steel in France," Ph.D. dissertation, University of California, Berkeley, 1988, chap. 4.

5. The Fonds du Développement Economique et Social is a fund controlled by the MoF for subsidizing investment in infrastructure and manufacturing.

6. Giscard d'Estaing, who was Finance Minister in 1965, put this condition in writing. See Jean G. Padioleau, *Quand la France s'enferre: La politique sidérurgique de la France depuis 1945* (Paris: P.U.F., 1981), p. 52.

7. Hayward, pp. 79–80.

8. Provisions that deal with labor displacement occupy almost half of the text of the *Convention*.

9. Sidney Tarrow, "Regional Policy, Ideology, and Peripheral Defense: The Case of Fos-sur-Mer," in *Territorial Politics in Industrial Nations*, ed. Sidney Tarrow, Peter J. Katzenstein, and Luigi Graziano (New York: Praeger, 1978).

10. Padioleau, pp. 121–28, 188–211.

11. See Daley, chap. 8.

12. In other sectors besides steel, "independent" unions play a role in bargaining with employers. Although it did not affect politics in the steel industry, another union broke off from the CGT after the war. The Fédération de l'Education Nationale remains the largest French teacher's union.

13. These strikes have been called the "May '68 of Lorraine."

14. The union reorganizations can be followed in the CFDT-FGM archives. See file "Sidérurgie 1978/1979, Marche sur Paris, Longwy, Denain." Conversations with Longwy CFDT militants indicated an incomprehension in Paris of the demobilizing effects of the negotiations.

15. David Charrasse with Randolphe Di Sabatino and Denis Pierron, *Lorraine Coeur d'Acier* (Paris: Maspero, 1981).

16. Jean-Pierre Huiban, "The Industrial Conterproposal as an Element of Trade Union Strategy," in *The French Workers' Movement: Economic Crisis and Political*

Change, ed. Mark Kesselman with Guy Groux (London: George Allen and Unwin, 1984), p. 234.

17. George Ross, "The Perils of Politics: French Unions and the Crisis of the 1970s," in Peter Lange, George Ross, and Maurizio Vannicelli, *Unions, Change and Crisis: French and Italian Union Strategy and the Political Economy, 1945–1980* (Boston: George Allen and Unwin, 1982), p. 71.

18. See Pierre Laroque, ed., *Les institutions sociales de la France* (Paris: La Documentation Française, 1980).

19. Hayward, p. 134.

20. See Jean-Yves Hocquet, "Les conventions du Fonds national de l'emploi," *Droit social*, September-October 1985, pp. 651–57.

21. See Gérard Couturier, "Le plan social: Aspects juridiques," *Droit social*, September-October 1985, pp. 643–50.

22. Presidential elections took place in 1965, 1969, 1974, 1981, and 1988. Legislative elections were held in 1967, 1968, 1973, 1978, 1981, 1986, and 1988. Municipal elections occurred in 1965, 1971, 1977, and 1983.

23. According to Diana Green, "When a number of prominent bankers (from the BNP, the Banque de Paris et Pays Bas and Société Générale) made representations to the Ministry of Finance about the industry's insolvency, they were told to go away until after 19 March!" See *Managing Industrial Change? French Policies to Promote Industrial Adjustment* (London: HMSO, 1981), p. 28n.

24. See John H. McArthur and Bruce R. Scott, *Industrial Planning in France* (Boston: Harvard University School of Business Administration, 1969), p. 418.

25. See Philippe Zarifian, "La culture syndicale face à la nécessité de propositions industrielles: Défis, mouvements, portée," *Critiques in l'économie politique* 23–24 (April-September 1983): 263–84.

26. For union frustration with the process of consultation in the 1960s and early 1970s, see CFDT-FGM archives, boxes "Sidérurgie Plan Professionnel (Point de vue national 1965–1967)" and "Sidérurgie CEDA."

27. See Philippe C. Schmitter, "Still the Century of Corporatism?" in *Trends Toward Corporatist Intermediation*, ed. Philippe C. Schmitter and Gerhard Lehmbruch (Beverly Hills: Sage, 1979). Although this article was originally written in 1974, it remains the classic statement differentiating these terms.

28. See Dénis Segrestin, *Le phénomène corporatiste: Essai sur l'avenir des systèmes professionels fermés en France* (Paris: Fayard, 1985).

29. See Andrew Cox and Jack Hayward, "The Inapplicability of the Corporatist Model in Britain and France: The Case of Labor," *International Political Science Review* (1983): 217–40.

30. Alan Cawson, "Varieties of Corporatism: The Importance of the Meso-level of Interest Intermediation," in *Organized Interests and the State: Studies in Meso-corporatism* (Beverly Hills: Sage, 1985), pp. 1–21.

31. See Michael M. Atkinson and William D. Coleman, "Corporatism and Industrial Policy," in Cawson, *Organized Interests*, pp. 22–44.

8

Deindustrialization, Economic Performance, and Industrial Policy: British and American Theories Applied to Italy

Anthony C. Masi

Until fairly recently there were only two sides to the debate over postindustrial society, one technocratic and the other technophobic.[1] Both of these perspectives are based on "what-if" extrapolations of alleged trends, with very little attention to careful empirical analysis. Now, there is a third, more concrete, "what-is-happening" type of analysis of economic activities and their implications which challenges both notions of postindustrialism. For lack of a more appropriate term, it has been labeled "deindustrialization." While the former two perspectives on the future tend to emphasize dynamic industrialism as the central factor affecting changes, the most recent contribution is guided by an increasing body of evidence that, while still controversial, seems to indicate that the transformation that is occurring is neither the one forecast by wishful thinkers nor that of worrisome alarmists. In short, rather than witnessing the emergence of the "service economy" based on increased industrial productivity (analogous to the transformation from agriculture to industry), there appears to be a marked process of industrial decline, particularly in the United Kingdom and the United States.

Proponents of this "deindustrialization" thesis argue that these trends undermine the very foundations of advanced capitalist society as we have come to know it. They advocate governmental policies to combat what they see as increasing and noncyclical economic stagnation in the advanced industrial democracies. Critics of these arguments have tended to ignore the implications of social institutional arrangements for this problem, arguing instead that government should do less, not more, and that the trends are probably cylical, not structural, in origin and therefore in cure. Some even claim that there is nothing wrong with a white-collar service society, even if it is not based on an internationally competitive industrial base.

Apart from the research on England and the United States, however, few other national economies have been studied in detail using concepts from the literature on deindustrialization. In part this is because of statistical trends which seem to indicate that this process surfaced first in Britain and America. Japan, of course, has been used as a reference point for good economic performance in this literature, particularly in the part dealing with industrial policy. Another reason for the lack of in-depth case studies of deindustrialization is the very different research agendas of experts studying other advanced industrial democracies, which have had somewhat different experiences with industrial decline.[2] I contribute to remedying this deficiency here by applying the concepts and operational measures derived from the Anglo-American literature on deindustrialization to the case of Italy. In addition, reference is made to some significant Italian writings on the topic to demonstrate how Italian social scientists and policy makers are interpreting trends in their country and what differences they see between their situation and that of England and the United States on the one hand and Japan on the other.

To anticipate somewhat the conclusions of this chapter, on the whole no uniform and unambiguous interpretation of the statistical evidence is possible. The interpretation of empirical results depends, to some extent, on the critical reading that one gives to the literatures on deindustrialization, economic performance, and industrial policy. Yet detailed statistical analyses, even the purely descriptive analysis presented here, call into question whether deindustrialization per se is a generalizable feature of advanced democratic societies. While this may be valid for the overall situation, specific empirical indicators of deindustrialization definitely manifest themselves in Italy, if not as secular trends then at least as conjunctural features of industrial decline. In short, much more data and debate are necessary before a final theoretical and empirical synthesis will be possible.

There are five parts to this analysis. First, I summarize and operationalize, with several critical comments, the main deindustrialization arguments, paying special attention to three issues: trends in industrial employment and output, government spending and finance, and the composition of international trade for selected manufactured goods. Second, I confront these indicators with the Italian statistics. Unfortunately, the same types of data are not always available, and what is available is not always comparable or adequate. Third, I address the nature of state industrial strategies in the Italian case, focusing separately and then jointly on the role of government-controlled enterprises (called the state participation sector in Italy) and small- to medium-sized entrepreneurial firms in Italian trade and overall industrial performance. Fourth, I explore regional trends in Italian industrial structure and investment to uncover possible parallels between the shift of economic activity from the "Rustbelt" to the "Sunbelt" in the United States and what is happening to the "industrial triangle" (Milan, Turin, Genova) and the "Mezzogiorno" (the South and Islands) of Italy. Finally, I speculate on the political and social implications of the statistical evidence and trends and their institutional context.

WHAT IS DEINDUSTRIALIZATION?

In a series of essays on the British case, the main themes of the deindustrialization arguments were formalized for the first time. The problem can be summarized as follows: There are sharp, persistent, and apparently noncyclical declines in manufacturing employment *and* in manufacturing output in the most advanced industrial democracies, as measured by a variety of sources; these declines are accompanied by a similar loss of world market shares for industrial goods; and there is a noticeable, and seemingly irreversible, penetration of foreign manufactured goods into the domestic market.[3] The discussion of the American case saw capital flight or, less polemically, capital mobility—primarily but not exclusively that of multinational corporations closing plants in one area and opening them in another, sometimes in the same country and sometimes abroad—added to the battery indicators of deindustrialization.[4]

While there is general agreement about the variables used to characterize deindustrialization, no uniformly acceptable set of explanations has emerged to satisfactorily account for them.[5] Rising public/collective consumption is often cited as having "squeezed out" or "crowded out" private investment and initiative. A variety of authors have placed the blame squarely on the loss of competitive power due to a variety of institutional, sociopolitical, and economic forces. Declining rates of productivity increase is a favorite theme and probably represents the key variable in understanding what, in fact, is happening.[6] Policy proposals to combat deindustrialization often implicitly contain yet other potential causes: unfair trade practices that must be met with import restrictions, governmental regulation of the marketplace that must be replaced by salubrious supply-side interventions, investments that must be redirected to allow for the reindustrialization of the economy, or active industrial policies that must be pursued to protect losers and pick winners.[7] Underlying much of this debate is the belief that manufacturing really matters to the economic well-being of advanced industrial democracies.[8]

The literature on deindustrialization has focused on five indicators of deindustrialization (these are sometimes also used as explanations) as that concept has been developed and evolved in British and American sources.[9] Deindustrialization theory predicts that:

1. the share of manufacturing in national output should decline;
2. manufacturing employment, relatively and in absolute numbers, should decrease;
3. budget deficits and the presence of the state in the capital and labor markets should have a negative influence on private manufacturing investments;
4. changing patterns of international trade structure and balance of payments deficits marked by a "ratchet effect" in the level of imports for specific sectors of the national domestic market should be evident in the economies of the advanced democracies;
5. the advanced economies should be rationalizing toward smaller more capital-intensive units of production, decentralizing production functions and locating them away from traditional areas of industrial production, and organizing these activities in a flexible manner.

EMPIRICAL EVIDENCE ON DEINDUSTRIALIZATION IN ITALY

To assess these hypotheses, Italian statistical materials, together with data aggregated for the seven largest industrial democracies, are presented below. These data are principally drawn from materials published by the Organization for Economic Cooperation and Development (OECD), the Italian Central Institute of Statistics (ISTAT), and the United Nations (UN).

To avoid the pitfall of dealing with a potentially cyclical phenomenon, this chapter focuses on approximately 25 years of employment and output statistics for Italy and the other six largest advanced industrial democracies (the United States, the United Kingdom, France, Japan, Canada, and West Germany, which together with Italy are referred to as OECD–7), supplemented where appropriate and available with secondary analyses of already published data. Trade statistics are presented, where possible, with information on the composition of imports and exports by sector or technological group, again over a relatively long period. Governmental involvement in the economy is also addressed qualitatively. In addition, some qualitative evidence on private business strategies in Italy is also discussed.

Industrial Output and Employment

Italy's economic performance, as measured by the percent change in real gross domestic product (annual averages), has been consistent with that of the other six largest industrial democracies (see above) since around 1970. Italy in the 1950s and the early 1960s was, of course, supposed to have experienced an "economic miracle" insofar as its growth rates in real gross domestic product were in the order of 8 percent annually.[10]

The strikes of the "hot autumn of 1969" and the first OPEC oil price hike of 1973, however, seem to have disrupted patterns in Italy, so that it is slightly out of phase with the rest of the OECD–7. Italy has also tended to have higher upturns and lower downturns. In any case, Italy averaged annual growth rates of 3.8 percent compared to an average of 3.4 percent for the OECD–7 during the 15 year period from 1967 to 1981.[11]

The share of manufacturing in the creation of Italian gross domestic product during the period under consideration has been slightly higher than elsewhere in the OECD–7. For 1968, 1976, and 1981, manufacturing contributed 27.8, 31.7, and 29.1 percent of Italy's gross domestic product, respectively. In the same years, the OECD–7's figures were 29.1, 26.9, and 25.2 percent. Manufacturing's share of GDP has, however, shown a tendency to decline since the end of the 1970s.[12] Agriculture in 1981 contributed 5.9 percent of gross domestic product in Italy compared to 3.0 percent for the OECD–7, demonstrating that it continued to be more important in the Italian economy than in the OECD–7 as a whole. In fact, Italy still employed 14.2 percent of its labor force in agriculture in 1981. On the other hand, the service sector was less important in Italy during the period under consideration (50.1 percent value added to gross domestic product compared to 58.4 percent for the OECD–7), but these activities have clearly tended to increase in importance.[13]

Here it is necessary to return to one of the criticisms of the deindustrialization literature noted above, i.e., the percentage share of industry in the formation of GDP, by itself, should not be taken as evidence of deindustrialization. Italian agricultural production increased during the period of industrialization that followed World War II. Similarly, total industrial production has also increased. Consequently, just because the latter has fallen as a share of gross domestic product therefore does not mean that Italy is undergoing deindustrialization. In fact, overall manufacturing production increased in real terms over the entire 1967–81 period. Thus, with regard to the first deindustrialization indicator—the purported decline of industrial manufacturing—it is simply too early to tell. Notwithstanding the downturn in industrial and manufacturing output as *shares* of Italian gross domestic product, it is unclear whether the observed pattern is cyclical or secular. It is likewise unclear whether the decline reflects or may lead to falling living standards.

Labor Market Patterns and Productivity

Manufacturing employment began to decline as a share of the civilian labor force in the OECD–7 toward the end of the 1960s, while continuing to rise in Italy until 1975. Figure 8.1 illustrates that for the period from 1968 to 1976 Italy's pattern diverged sharply from the rest of the advanced industrial countries. Since 1976, however, the declines in Italy and in the OECD–7 have been equally acute, even though Italy has maintained a higher percentage of its

Figure 8.1
Manufacturing Employment as a Percentage of Civilian Employment, 1968–81

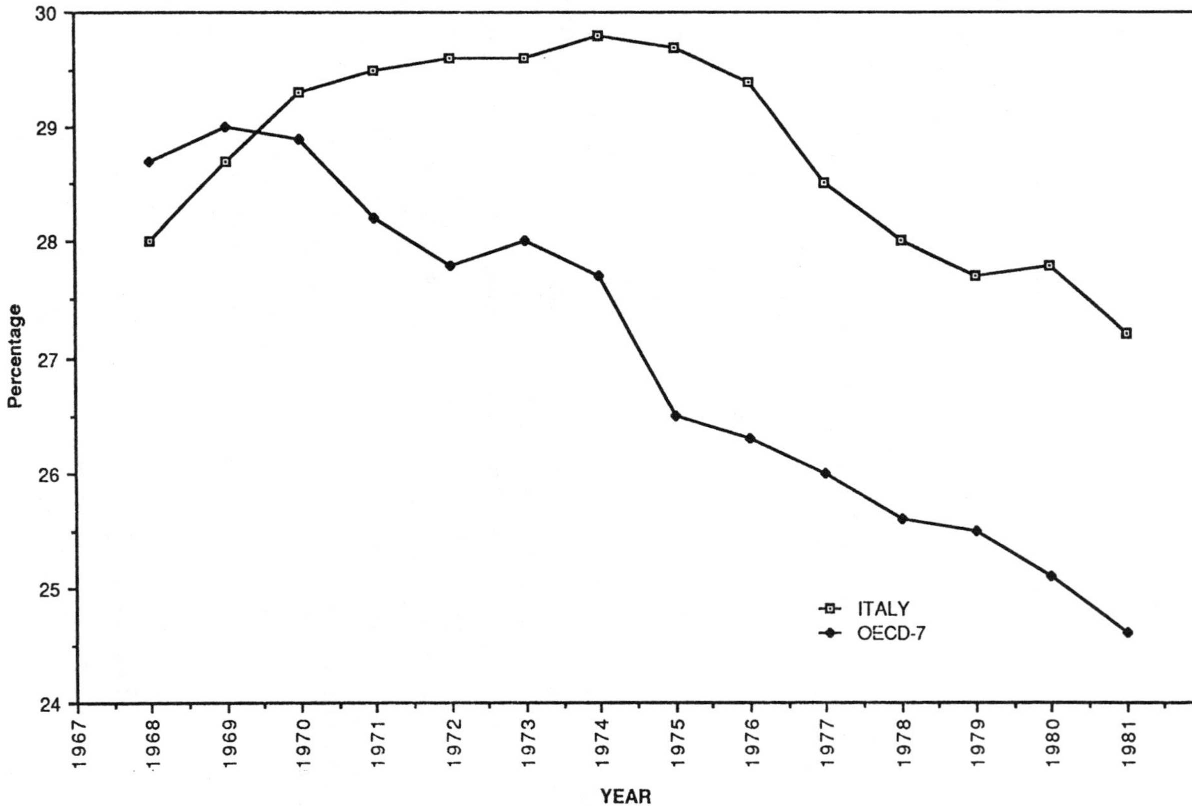

labor force in manufacturing than the average for the other countries. In 1960, Italy employed 25.1 percent of its labor force in the manufacturing sector compared to an OECD–7 average of 27.4 percent. Over the 1968–81 period, however, Italy's average for that sector was slightly higher than for the OECD–7 (28.8 percent compared to 27.0 percent).

As a component of the labor force, government employment (i.e., public administration, excluding nationalized industries) was historically higher in the OECD–7 than in Italy. It leveled off for all the advanced industrial democracies by the mid–1970s but has continued to rise in Italy. A crossover occurred in 1977; since then the Italian government has employed a slightly larger share of the nation's civilian labor force than does its major international partners. In 1981, Italy had 15.2 percent of the labor force in government service compared to 14.7 percent for the OECD–7.[14]

Overall unemployment rates in Italy have been higher than elsewhere in the OECD–7, and the composition of Italy's unemployment has changed over time as it has elsewhere. At the beginning of this decade, the nation had nearly 2.5 million unemployed individuals, approximately half of whom were searching for their first job. According to data from Italy's ISTAT, the principal problem for Italy remains these first-job seekers, mostly youth. For example, Italy's overall unemployment rate for the first quarter of 1987 was 15.7 percent, compared to an unweighted OECD–7 average of 9.3 percent. However, youth unemployment rates in Italy ran at approximately double the OECD–7 figures for the first half of the 1980s. In fact, one could say that official youth unemployment in Italy is nothing short of tragic. While the 1986 OECD projection for the seven largest industrial democracies was for a youth unemployment rate of 15 percent, that figure for Italy was 35.8 percent.[15]

Yet the relationship between output and employment in manufacturing in deindustrialization arguments hinges not only on the level of employment in this sector, but also on productivity growth differentials. Italy's patterns of real value added and unit labor costs over the period from 1967 to 1981 were a little above and a little below average, respectively, when compared to the figures for other advanced industrial democracies. Over that time span, increases in real value added in manufacturing in Italy averaged 4.5 percent compared to 3.7 percent for the OECD–7. Real wage increases in Italy, however, over the same period averaged 12.5 percent, but only 7.3 percent for the entire OECD–7.[16] From 1970 to 1982, Italy was about average among the big four European economies in hourly productivity in manufacturing, with a 4.4 percent rate of increase.[17] The deindustrialization thesis emphasizes productivity decreases in attempting to account for the industrial decline observed in the United States and Britain.

Another factor related to the productivity issue is increasing real wages. In Figure 8.2 the structure of Italy's wage-indexation scheme (*la scala mobile*) is clearly evident. Despite the rather substantial variations in the rate of increase, Italian manufacturing wages have increased faster than the OECD–

Figure 8.2
Percentage Changes in Real Wages in Manufacturing, 1967–81

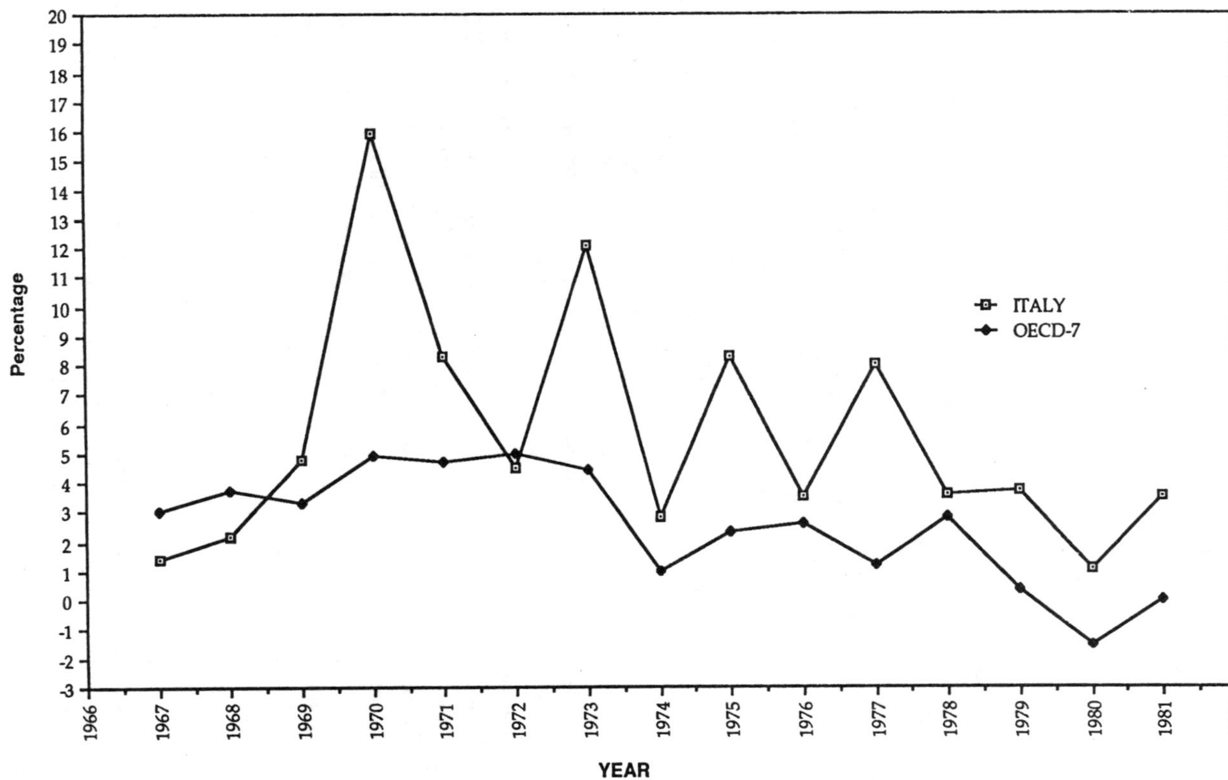

7 average. One sees that there has been a shift in the shares of income going to labor over time. As noted above, several commentators attribute deindustrialization in the United States to sluggish productivity growth.[18] Italy has escaped slow productivity growth, despite substantial real wage increases. It seems to have become more competitive and thus better able to increase production and living standards, negating the cheap-wage explanations for why some countries have outperformed the United States in the international marketplace. At least part of the explanation for Italy's relative success is found in the country's institutions and social structures, to which I return below.

Consequently, on the basis of the net decline in overall industrial employment that cannot be accounted for by Italy's massive productivity gains, the country shows some signs of the deindustrialization experienced by Britain and the United States. Yet Italy's productivity performance was certainly much better than Britain's over the 1968–82 period. Therefore, judgment must again be reserved about whether Italy fits the hypothesized deindustrialization pattern until a longer time-series of relevant data with which to document such declines becomes available.

Public Consumption and Fixed Capital Formation

British writings on deindustrialization often argue that private investment and initiatives are being "squeezed out" by the increasing share of government expenditures and an increasing role of the state in capital investments.[19] Figure 8.3 illustrates how the percentage shares of gross domestic product expenditures owing to the public sector and gross fixed capital formation are related in the Italian case. While gross fixed capital formation appears to be cyclical in the 18 to 24 percent range, the public expenditures have clearly tended to rise. Public consumption in Italy has moved from a cyclical pattern in the 12 to 15 percent range to a level of over 20 percent. The crossover in 1982 needs to be investigated further as more data become available. If one looks at government outlays as a percentage of gross domestic product, Italy is above the average for the seven most industrialized nations and seems to be pulling away. Using OECD figures, Italy's public deficit represented 12.5 percent of its gross domestic product for 1986, while the unweighted OECD–7 average for that year was 4.3 percent (2.9 percent if Italy is excluded).[20] Along these same lines, net lending by the government is very high in Italy. Government outlays as a percentage of gross domestic product and net lending by the government are also serious problems for Italy.[21] For example, while the ratio of the budget deficit to net private savings in Italy has grown from 69.4 to 87.1 percent in the 1975–86 period, the comparable increase for the OECD–7 was only from 42.5 to 45.0 percent. Further, the ratio of government debt to gross domestic product for the same period went from

Figure 8.3
Percentage Shares of Public Consumption and Capital Formation in Italian GDP

59.9 to 107.4 percent for Italy, but from 20.7 to 34.9 percent for the other large industrialized countries.

Two aspects of how government spending might affect deindustrialization should be noted. First, some government spending may actually stimulate the economy, so analysis should be conducted with disaggregated statistics on government shares. For example, government transfers to households should be distinguished from those to businesses. Second, regional economic differences in Italy (discussed below) and the central government's attempts to reduce them may account for some of Italy's peculiarity in this regard. In short, government spending patterns do not necessarily indicate a "crowding-out" effect, but they may nevertheless be associated with deindustrialization. The crowding-out thesis asserts that government deficits raise interest rates, harm the investment climate, and therefore hinder productivity growth. Yet much governmental activity is redistributive in nature and may stimulate the domestic market. Further, while Italy's tax rates are considerably higher than those of the United States, one must remember that stock market profits are not taxed in Italy.

Trade Patterns

Italy's economy, like those of the other advanced capitalist democracies, is becoming more internationalized. Imports and exports have risen more or less steadily over the period under consideration, climbing from just over 14 percent of gross domestic product to nearly 28 percent.[22] The ratio of exports to imports for Italy tended to be cyclical over the 1959–85 period. Italy did not show the general pattern of overwhelming trade imbalances associated with deindustrialization in the United States and Britain. However, it did not show a clear winning pattern either.[23]

Table 8.1 and Table 8.2 demonstrate that Italy's export trade is moving away from high technology toward standardized products, and that Italy is different than other industrial countries in this regard. A major part of the deindustrialization thesis is that nations are moving away from mature products and technologies (i.e., those that have standardized production engineering) in order to remain competitive. For example, R. V. Ayres has argued that international competition first focuses on performance/quality, then market share, and finally on price. Because the less developed countries become good sites for standardized production, Italy's specialization in such markets, even if at the high value-added end, subjects it to price competition from the less developed countries.[24]

Italy has enjoyed success in steel and clothing-related industries. In fact, from 1961 to 1983 the textiles, clothing, and footwear sectors increased their exports from just under 6 percent to nearly 12 percent. And in the 1970s, Italy surpassed France and the United Kingdom to become Europe's second largest producer of crude steel after West Germany.[25] These commodities

Table 8.1
Italy's Share in Total Imports of Industrial Countries (in Value Terms)

	Years	
	1970-72	1978-80
Total Manufactured Goods	7.8	8.1
High Technology Products	4.9	4.1
Intermediate Technology Products	7.2	6.9
Standard Products	10.3	12.9

Source: OECD Economic Surveys, Italy, December 1982, footnote 34, reporting data on foreign trade from the Bank of Italy, Annual Reports.

involve trade competition with the Third World in both capital-intensive and labor-intensive production. For clothing, Italy is at the high value-added end of the market; for steel, its principal export markets have been specialized large-diameter welded pipe and basic steel. The situation for the first appears favorable, and for the second unfavorable.[26]

It is difficult to interpret these trade patterns in terms of the deindustrialization thesis. On the one hand, as shown in Table 8.1, Italy actually increased its share of total imports of the industrial countries (in value terms) during the 1970s. It looks like Italy was winning and, given the way the figures were computed, someone else was losing. On the other hand, Table 8.2 illustrates that the composition of Italian trade seems far from favorable. Steel and textiles, clothing and shoes, even at the high end of their respective markets, are likely to be unstable, to lack much serious growth potential, and to not generate much employment. In fact, the United Nations' "Economic Survey of Europe in 1980" reported that Italian manufacturing employment in textiles, clothing, shoes, and furniture fell by approximately 80,000 workers (to 1.3 million workers) between 1968 and 1978.

Regional Differences in Italy

A significant rebuttal of the deindustrialization thesis for the United States is that, while certain regions suffered gross manufacturing job losses, others

Table 8.2
Comparison of Specialization Indices in Trade in High-Technology Products, Italy, European Community, Japan, and the United States, 1963–81[(a)(b)]

	Year			
	1963	1970	1978	1981
Country/Region				
Italy	0.83	0.87	0.65	0.60
European Community	1.01	0.94	0.88	0.87
Japan	0.72	1.07	1.27	1.37
United States	1.27	1.18	1.27	1.19

Source: Adapted from Commission of the European Community, European Economy, March 1983, Number 15, Table IV, p. 126.

Notes: (a) The specialization index is calculated as follows:

$$\frac{x(i)(j)/\text{Sum } x(j)}{X(i)\ /\ \text{Sum } X}$$

where x(i)(j) = exports of product (j) by country (i);
Sum x(j) = total world exports of product (j);
X(i) = total exports of manufactures by country (i);
Sum X = total world exports of manufactures.

(b) Figures are expressed in relation to the OECD average index of specialization recalculated to 1.00.

and the country as a whole experienced net gains. In Italy, the economic disparity between the Center-North and South-Islands (Mezzogiorno) is still noticeable, despite legislative efforts to correct the situation since World War II. In 1951, the ratios of gross domestic product per capita and gross domestic product per labor force participant between Northern Italy and the Mezzogiorno were 52.3 to 62.4. By 1979, these values had increased slightly to 57.0 and 71.7.[27]

Table 8.3 provides baseline data on output and employment in the North and South of Italy in 1951 and 1978–79. With regard to output, agriculture remains more important in the Mezzogiorno, and government accounts for

Table 8.3
The Regional Structure of Output and Employment in Italy, 1951 and 1978–79 (Expressed as Percentages)

	Output(a)			
	1951		1978–79	
	North	South	North	South
Sector				
Agriculture	19.3	34.0	6.0	13.0
Industry	36.2	17.8	36.1	20.6
Construction	4.5	5.9	6.4	9.6
Private Services	31.6	29.5	40.1	38.3
Government(b)	9.3	12.8	11.6	18.4
TOTAL	100.0	100.0	100.0	100.0
	Employment			
Agriculture	37.6	56.6	9.0	25.2
Industry	28.3	14.6	33.2	17.4
Construction	5.6	5.5	7.1	11.3
Private Services	22.6	17.3	34.3	28.1
Government	5.7	5.8	16.3	17.7
TOTAL	100.0	100.0	100.0	100.0

Source: Adapted from OECD Economic Surveys, Italy, June 1981, Table 14, p. 38.

Notes: (a) Share in GDP at factor cost, current prices.
(b) Including all non-market services from 1970 onwards.

nearly one-fifth of the 1978 total, compared to approximately one-tenth in the North. Industry's contribution has remained at just over one-third for the North for the starting and ending points. In the South, however, it has increased slightly, from about 18 percent to almost 21 percent. With regard to employment, the government's share is three times larger in the South than

Table 8.4
Regional Structure of Gross Fixed Investments in Italy, 1963 and 1979 (Percentages, Current Prices)

	Year			
	1963		1979	
	North	South	North	South
Sector				
Agriculture	6.6	13.6	5.5	12.4
Industry	35.5	33.6	32.3	20.0
Private Services	52.2	45.1	55.3	54.4
Government(a)	6.0	7.7	6.8	13.2
TOTAL	100.0	100.0	100.0	100.0

Source: Adapted from OECD Economic Surveys, Italy, June 1981, Table 17, p. 42.

Note: (a) Including all non-market services from 1970 onwards.

in the North. Comparatively, government employment appears much more productive in the North than in the South.

From the late 1970s to early 1980s, the unemployment gap between North and South widened, with Southern levels nearly double those of the North. In 1978, the Center-North of Italy had an unemployment rate of 6.0 percent, compared to the Mezzogiorno's 10.0 percent rate. The comparable figures for 1982 were 7.3 percent and 13.0 percent, respectively.[28]

While possibly subject to cyclical variation requiring a full time-series to detect, industrial investments in the South accounted for a larger share of total fixed capital investments in the early 1960s than they did in the late 1970s. Table 8.4 illustrates this discrepancy between the North and South. Yet government investment in the South nearly doubled, while remaining static in the North.[29] In the 1957–63 period, state-participation firms in the North accounted for only 13.4 percent of fixed investments in industry but were responsible for fully 36.6 percent of such investments in the Mezzogiorno. For 1974–79, the percentages were 13.0 in the North and 23.6 in the South. The highest contribution of state firms to industrial investments in the Mezzogiorno was 45.9 percent in the 1971–73 period, when such investments in the North represented only 15 percent.[30] This continuing large variation between the two regions indicates that Italy has a problem that may be unique among the advanced industrial democracies.

QUALITATIVE ASSESSMENTS OF BUSINESS PRACTICES

The deindustrialization thesis addresses not only the quantitative indicators of economic trends, but also attempts to account for these trends by identifying causal factors. In many ways these discussions are the most interesting part of the deindustrialization literature. While this chapter does not review that literature, three issues need to be discussed. The first concerns labor market rigidities, the second entrepreneurship, and the third general industrial strategies for dealing with decline.

Labor Market Rigidities and Location Strategies

Barry Bluestone and Bennett Harrison have written that gross job losses in the manufacturing belt (Northeast and North Central regions) of the United States represent the best single indicator for deindustrialization.[31] Further, these job losses have created severe economic disruption for the areas affected. The principal rationale for this capital mobility (flight) is the apparent desire to escape the labor market rigidities associated with doing business in older, established industrial areas. Given the massive regional differences in Italy, it is interesting to ask whether a similar pattern may be emerging in that country.

The extensive programs for industrializing the South, which commenced in the early 1950s, represent one avenue for relocating capital in Italy. A second source for redistributing industrial capital and manufacturing employment is the more recent expansion of private concerns from the North to the Mezzogiorno.[32]

I have elsewhere argued that the legislation mandating that the state-participation sector invest fixed percentages in the Mezzogiorno was not the principal reason for the location of new productive enterprises there.[33] Rather, there were sound economic reasons for most, if not all, of the large capital-intensive enterprises which the state sector placed in the South. Further, they did not intend to develop the South, or even the areas immediately surrounding these enterprises with such investments.

Investments by state-participation firms in the South expanded much faster than they did in the North, although the bulk of such investments are still located in the North. From the mid–1950s to the mid–1970s, the Mezzogiorno's share of these investments was roughly three times that in the North. In the 1974–79 period, however, the South's share of new industrial investments from government-controlled enterprise dropped to only twice that of the North. Yet, the North still has about two-thirds of total government-controlled enterprise employment and industrial investments.[34]

Private enterprises such as Fiat and Pirelli, which have located facilities in the South recently, seem to have been motivated, however, by concerns associated with labor market rigidities in the Northern industrial triangle. Expansion in the South enabled these firms to decentralize production and introduce new technologies and production techniques. There were, of course, credit and financial incentives for such location decisions. Interestingly, the laws creating these incentives existed prior to 1969–70, yet were not utilized until the situation in the mid–1970s made it economically attractive to "escape" to the South.[35] However, the very different frameworks for labor relations legislation in Italy compared to the United States certainly play a role in limiting this type of response.

Flexible Specialization

Another aspect of deindustrialization is the maturing of products and technologies. Michael Piore and Charles Sabel suggest that the practices of some Italian entrepreneurs and cooperatives, most notably "flexible specialization," tied to craft and small-batch production, are potentially a way around the problem of maintaining international competitiveness.[36]

This analysis raises more questions than it answers, however. In Italy, as elsewhere, flexible specialization seems to be linked to very specific subsectors of the economy and very limited regions of the country. In addition, as noted below, a large portion of the sector they consider central to flexible specialization in Central Italy—namely, textiles, clothing, and footwear—is heavily subsidized by the government, particularly that component oriented to the export market.

E. Kurzweil argues that Italian entrepreneurs are a "rear-guard of progress" because they have reacted to rather than stimulated the country's economic climate. She, along with others, also indicates, however, that Italy has historically had many more small entrepreneurs than the other advanced industrial democracies.[37]

Strategies for Declining Industries

K. R. Harrigan analyzes the factors that influence firms' strategies in declining industries. Many of what she sees as positive approaches are found in Italian business, private and public.[38] For example, prolonged industry-wide excess capacity, as in the steel industry, certainly represents a problem for Italy. There seems little hope for reestablishing previous high levels of production and market share. Rationalizing this sector has meant not only decreasing employment, but also modernizing production techniques and revising operating practices and process engineering. But government-controlled steel producers in the South have also developed products to compete in specialized markets (large-diameter welded tubes for pipelines), and private producers in the North specialize in concrete reenforcing bars for the construction industry. Both markets are considerably more favorable than that for crude steel. In addition, private producers in textiles, clothing, and footwear have developed strategies for staying on top of their markets, although at the expense of lost jobs. In short, the Italian economy seems to possess the "flexible specialization" to evolve with demand, modernize techniques, and remain competitive.

INDUSTRIAL STRATEGY IN ITALIAN INDUSTRIAL DEVELOPMENT

State-Participation Firms: A Reassessment

In the post-World War II period, the cornerstone of attempts by government-controlled enterprises to stimulate economic development was, until the 1980s, the steel industry. The major accomplishment of these efforts was the location of Europe's largest integrated steel facility in the South at Taranto. This vaulted Italy into second place among European producers, enhancing Italy's market shares of a declining world market. Italy thus succeeded where the French (with Fos-sur-Mer and Dunkerque) failed. There were two reasons for this success: they built a plant of the right size for the time (10.5 million metric ton capacity), and they specialized in large-diameter welded pipe. When this facility began to mature—during a period of excess worldwide capacity—the Italians turned to the Japanese for assistance. A consultation was organized with Nippon Steel, which focused on production techniques, maintenance, and inventory-quality control, and which helped to guarantee productivity increases.[39]

While the steel facility at Taranto contributed to Italy's overall economic development in the postwar period, the stimulus effect in the Mezzogiorno is more ambigous. Its location there was never really intended to develop the South or, for that matter, even the local Taranto economy. Yet its incredible dimensions, as well as the need to keep it a viable economic enterprise, have given the Taranto integrated steel works a special character among state-participation firms located in the South.

Table 8.5 provides data on employment and output in 1980 by firm size and region of Italy, together with changes over the 1972–80 period. These findings provide some evidence for a deindustrialization process, as defined by Bluestone and Harrison, involving a net transfer of manufacturing capacity, employment, and output from one region to another. Overall, manufacturing employment fell by 4.2 percent in this period. Yet it grew by 3.4 percent in the South while declining by 6.8 percent in the North. This indicates gross loss in the older industrial areas and some net gains in the Mezzogiorno.[40]

Table 8.5
Value Added and Employment in Manufacturing by Size of Firm and Geographical Region of Italy, 1980 and Changes 1972–80 (Expressed as Percentage Shares of Total)

	Value Added	Employment	Cumulative Employment Change	Changes in Annual Average Wages
Firm Size:				
20-99 Employees	22.7	24.3	-15.0	20.4
100-999 Employees	42.0	39.7	n.a.	n.a.
1000+ Employees	35.3	36.0	- 0.2	16.2
Total	100.0	100.0	- 4.2	17.9(a)
Area of the Country:				
Centre-North	86.8	85.7	- 6.8	17.3
Mezzogiorno	13.2	14.3	3.4	17.3
Total	100.0	100.0	- 4.2	17.3(a)

Source: Adapted from OECD Economic Surveys, Italy, December, 1982, Table 10; values for middle-sized firms calculated (where possible) from the given values.

Note: (a) The total percentage changes for wages by firm size (17.9) refers to 1972-1980, while that for area of the country (17.3) refers to 1972-1979, thus accounting for the discrepancy.

Entrepreneurship, Flexible Specialization, and Subsidies

Table 8.5 shows that small firms lost nearly 15 percent of their employment levels between 1972 and 1980.[41] These smaller firms tend to be in the more traditional areas of Italian manufacturing, namely, textiles, clothing, and footwear. Interestingly, this is one of the sectors Piore and Sabel enthusiastically proclaim as flexibly productive. In order to resolve this apparent contradiction, these employment figures need to be placed in the larger perspective of state transfers to manufacturing industry.

G. Carone identifies five major sources of public transfers: the budget, regional expenditures, the "fiscalization" of social burdens, the wage integration fund (*la cassa integrazione guadagni*), and tax exemptions. He estimates that in the 1970s these transfers amounted to an average of 1.1 million lire per employee in the manufacturing sector (about $1,000 U.S. dollars at current exchange rates). Total transfers over the period 1973–80 equalled 45.3 percent of gross fixed assets, which was also equivalent to 9.6 percent of total social security expenditures.[42]

Within this framework, those firms oriented toward the export market received between 30 and 54 percent of all subsidized budget credit. Carone further calculates that of total credit available to textiles, clothing, and footwear, the subsidized proportions in the 1973–80 period ranged between two-thirds and four-fifths. In addition, the textile, clothing, and footwear sectors were among the most frequent users of the wage integration fund, with between 3.1 and 5.8 percent of their labor/hours affected. It is important to note, however, that the Central Italian regions enjoyed the lowest level of subsidized credit, at 23.3 percent (compared to 27.3 percent for all of Italy and 44.3 percent for the South). Consequently, judgment about the dynamism of flexible specialization in those sectors and areas of Italy must be reserved for more disaggregated analyses.[43]

Craft-based, small-scale, specialized firms seem to be more characteristic of successful developments all over the Italian peninsula. Their specialization does not keep them from being able to change rapidly and meet customer demand.

Plant-Closing Legislation

Another important aspect of Italian industrial policies concerns workers' rights. The main focus of such policies has been to protect the jobs of existing employees. Where layoffs do occur, policies are oriented to assist redundant workers in getting new training and finding new jobs.[44] Many American authors have argued for precisely such measures to buffer the transitional periods for Rustbelt workers in the United States.[45]

By adopting measures to avoid outright dismissals or to limit their extent, Italy has taken steps to limit many "effects" attributed to deindustrialization. The most important is creating a *cassa integrazione guadagni* (wage-integration fund) which guarantees a relatively high proportion of earnings to workers in sectors undergoing restructuring or located in severely depressed areas. Other measures include reduced work time, early retirements (which place additional burdens on social security payments), recruitment freezes, and internal transfers.[46]

From the perspective of management the legislation is demanding, requiring as it does advanced notification, compensation for loss of employment, and the suspension (rather than interruption) of the employment relationship (meaning that redundant workers are the first to be rehired). The relationship of these measures to deindustrialization and other industrial policies deserves closer attention.

CONCLUSIONS

Some General Criticisms of Deindustrialization

The concepts and operational definitions used here to define and empirically study the application of the British and American theory of deindustrialization to the case of Italy raise several problems. In brief, the potential criticisms are (1) that deindustrialization is a statistical artifact, (2) that it is a cyclical, not a structural, phenomenon, (3) that it cannot be properly identified without reference to institutional structures, and (4) that some part of the observed trends associated with deindustrialization are simply due to unfair trading practices in the international marketplace.

It may be that deindustrialization is a statistical artifact due to the reclassification of firms, activities, and therefore jobs from the industrial to the service sector during a process of economic restructuring, or due to increasing use of subcontracting to service firms, or due to a significant portion of manufacturing activities being transferred to the underground economy.[47] There is some evidence of these phenomena in the Italian case. Consequently, rather than deindustrialization per se, it might be more appropriate to speak of structural changes occurring in Italy's industrial base.[48]

Deindustrialization may be a tempest in a teapot. It may simply be a cyclical occurrence which manifests itself in the most open economies in the international system during periods of instability in international exchange rates. The symptoms which have been identified with deindustrialization may also appear when competitive advantages are changing rapidly. Further, the "paradox" of trade structures in terms of capital-intensive and knowledge-intensive goods offers an alternative hypothesis.[49] In fact, Italy has had some recent difficulty in exports which appears directly correlated with the falling value of the U.S. dollar in relation to the Italian lira.

Deindustrialization may not be generalizable to all advanced industrialized democracies, and in particular not to Italy, since institutional arrangements and government policies specific to individual countries affect its development. In other words, industrial policy affects how industrial decline is experienced. Italy has had, and continues to have, active industrial policies, both in terms of its large state-sponsored sector and in terms of its policies favoring exports and underdeveloped regions.

The nongeneralizability of deindustrialization may be because several countries do not compete fairly in international trade (having artifically low value on currency, export tax credits, internal nontariff trade barriers, etc.). Recent U.S. court actions against European steel producers and administrative threats against Japanese microchip manufacturers illustrate the sentiment, although without proving the case.

Yet it is precisely for these reasons that Italy represents an excellent test case of the deindustrialization thesis. It is a country with considerable experience—and some success—in developing and carrying out industrial policies. It has been undergoing regional decentralization of production, in part through the large state-participation sector. Government involvement in business practices is much more widespread than in the United States. Finally, recent developments in the Italian economy—the reappearance of inflation, an export slowdown, growing unemployment, continued government deficits, and large estimates of the amount of underground economic activity—all raise questions that must be addressed by the proponents of the deindustrialization thesis.

Research Directions and Some Speculations on the Future

This chapter illustrates that the Italian economy's performance over the last 25 years or so significantly differs from the patterns found in the two countries most closely identified with the deindustrialization hypothesis, namely, Britain and the United States. Italy's pattern of development is also sharply different from that of the successful European economies of France and West Germany. Nor has Italy modeled itself after Japan. Notwithstanding some severe economic problems, one might characterize recent Italian industrial development as "a success in spite of itself." The Italy of the 1970s and 1980s is certainly not the Italy of the "economic miracle" of the 1950s and early 1960s. But its institutional structures and economic performance, which are closely linked, have forged an interesting and, from the perspective of other advanced industrial democracies, anomalous case for analysis.

Italy has combined aspects of "indicative planning" and efforts to create a favorable "business climate" (read: subsidies) for small and medium entrepreneurial firms with the largest state-held sector of any advanced industrial democracy. It has also provided a context for labor that favors those still employed (via subsidies, plant-closing legislation, etc.) while maintaining unacceptably high levels of youth unemployment. One very important question, however, remains. How long can the government pursue strategies that create budget deficits and long-term debt? By studying the development of Italian industrial structure over the last 25 years, paying careful attention to its institutional structure and economic decision-making processes, much can be learned not only about its relative successes (and failures), but also about the difficulties faced by other advanced industrial countries.

To assess more completely how the deindustrialization thesis applies to the Italian case, the analysis must proceed with disaggregated data, examining different sectors within industry and manufacturing in different regions and subregions. Qualitative and quantitative aspects of Italian industrial policies must be more carefully analyzed in relation to government debt, unofficial labor market practices (*lavoro nero*), and demographic patterns. Further work must also be done on research and development expenditures in different sectors. The boom of the tertiary sector in Italy, as elsewhere, may bring new problems of inefficiency, inflation, and fiscal evasion. The president of Italy's ISTAT, commenting on new figures regarding the underreporting of Italy's gross domestic product, stated; "If this is postindustrialism, we are not doing a very good job of it!"[50]

NOTES

1. This chapter was written while I had a sabbatic leave fellowship and a research grant from the Social Sciences and Humanities Research Council of Canada and was a guest in the Sezione di Sociologia, Facoltà di Giurisprudenza, Università di Bari, Italy. I would like to thank Michael Smith, Joel Wolfe, and especially Richard Foglesong for their comments. Unfortunately, not all of their useful suggestions have been incorporated into the present text. An earlier draft of this chapter appeared as a Working Paper in a series edited by the Department of Sociology, McGill University.

2. Alternatively, one could see this as a statement that there is no deindustrialization other than in the United Kingdom and the United States. However, to do so would be to make a judgment before seeing the evidence.

3. F. Blackaby, ed. *De-industrialization* (London: Heinemann, 1979). The countries from which the manufacturing imports originate are important for the deindustrialization thesis. If they come from other advanced countries, then deindustrialization cannot be a generalizable phenomenon.

4. B. Bluestone and B. Harrison, *The Deindustrialization of America: Plant Closings, Community Abandonment, and the Dismantling of Basic Industry* (New York: Basic Books, 1982).

5. For an excellent summary of the basic theoretical and empirical arguments, see A. Picchieri, ed., *Il declino industriale: Il contributo delle scienze sociali alla diagnosi e alla definizione di strategie di risposta* (Turin: Rosenberg and Sellier, 1986).

6. For example, see C. Johnson, "The Moral Equivalent of Defeat," *Atlantic Monthly,* December 1985.

7. A partial list of such policy proposals can be found in the following: A. Etzioni, "Industrial Incentives," *New York Times,* December 16, 1983; R. McGahey, "Industrial Policy's Problem," *New York Times,* July 6, 1984; R. Reich, "The Next American Frontier," *Atlantic*, March and April, 1983; and D. M. Gordon, "Do We Need to Be No. 1?" *Atlantic Monthly*, April, 1986.

8. See S. S. Cohen and J. Zysman, "The Myth of a Post-industrial Economy," *Technology Review,* February/March 1987.

9. These empirical indicators are derived from Blackaby, *De-industrialization*, Bluestone and Harrison, *Deindustrialization of America*, R. Z. Lawrence, "Is Trade Deindustrializing America? A Medium Term Perspective," *Brookings Papers on Economic Activity* 1 (1983); and R. D. Norton, "Industrial Policy and American Renewal," *Journal of Economic Literature* 24 (March 1986).

10. See K. Allen and A. Stevenson, *An Introduction to the Italian Economy* (New York: Harper and Row, 1975), and J. Hennesy, ed., *Economic "Miracles"* (London: Andre Deutsch, 1964).

11. These figures are calculated from data reported in the OECD *Economic Surveys, Italy*, for the years 1960 through 1985, and from information contained in the OECD

volumes on *Main Economic Indicators: Historical Statistics 1964–1983* and *Economic Outlook: Historical Statistics 1960–1981.*

12. The latest figures, reported by Italy's Central Institute of Statistics (ISTAT), are given and discussed below.

13. In a series of interviews and press conferences held after ISTAT released data on the underestimation of Italy's gross domestic product, Professor Guido Rey, the institute's president, indicated that these figures are indeed worrisome since the rapid growth of the tertiary sector in Italy, in his view, is not related directly to increases in industrial productivity. He believes that Italy must still increase its industrial base and complete its "industrial cycle."

14. Efficiency in public service is a completely different question and deserves systematic attention. Unfortunately, this is not the place for such an analysis.

15. Youth refers to the age group 14–24 in Italy, 16–24 in the United States and the United Kingdom, and 15–24 in Canada, France, Germany, and Japan. The OECD data were based on household surveys in Italy, Japan, Canada, France, and the United States, and on household surveys and registration information for Germany and the United Kingdom. The forecast reported in the text was adapted from *OECD Economic Outlook,* No. 38, Table 14, p. 30, December 1985. Other figures are from "Le cifre dei sette," *La Repubblica,* June 5, 1987, Supplement, p. 6, which reported the OECD as the source.

16. The relationship between labor costs and standards of living should also be considered in detail. This aspect of deindustrialization has been mentioned only briefly in the literature (see Pichierri, *Il declino*). There are two versions. One argues that deindustrialization must, in the long run, lead to decreasing real wages and declining living standards. The other maintains that deindustrialization may occur without necessarily reducing either one.

17. OECD, *Economic Surveys, Italy,* May 1984, p. 52, n. 16.

18. Johnson, "Moral Equivalent."

19. See Blackaby, *De-industrialization.*

20. These data were reported in *La Repubblica,* June 5, 1987, supplement. In addition, over the entire period reported by the OECD ("Historical Statistics"), Italy has had a higher percentage of its gross domestic product tied up in direct government outlays or in budget deficits. See below for some contradictory interpretations of these aggregate statistics.

21. OECD, *Economic Outlook,* No. 38, December 1985, Table 3.

22. Even the United States, which, given the size of its domestic market, has the lowest ratio of imports-exports to gross domestic product, has experienced this trend, albeit at a lower level.

23. Of course, a winning pattern is not needed to falsify the deindustrialization thesis. Cyclical variations would suffice.

24. R. V. Ayres, *The Next Industrial Revolution: Reviving Industry Through Innovation* (Cambridge, Mass.: Ballinger, 1984). He also points out that less developed areas can become competitive in standardized production processes that are capital-intensive as well as in those that are labor-intensive.

25. Figures for textiles, clothing, and footwear are from OECD (1960–1985, "'Historical Statistics"), and those for the steel industry were reported by the United Nations, *The Steel Market In 1977* (New York: United Nations, 1978), Table 1.

26. For the implications of being at the high value-added end of markets, see

Lawrence, "Is Trade Deindustrializing America?" On the potential of flexible specialization in Italian textile manufacturing, see M. Piore and C. Sabel, *The Second Industrial Divide: Possibilities for Prosperity* (New York: Basic Books, 1984). On restructuring in Italian steel, see A. C. Masi, "Nuova Italsider and the Steel Crisis: Problems, Innovations, and Prospects," in Y. Meny and V. Wright, eds., *The Politics of Steel: Western Europe and the Steel Industry in the Crisis Years, 1974–1984* (New York: De Gruyter, 1987).

27. These figures are in current prices and were adapted from *OECD Economic Surveys, Italy*, Table 16, p. 42, June 1981.

28. Data adapted from *OECD Economic Surveys, Italy*, March 1980, December 1982, and May 1984.

29. This seems to be different than the situation in the U.S. Sunbelt regions, where government incentives have not been that significant a factor in location decisions.

30. The data in this paragraph were taken from *OECD Economic Surveys, Italy*, Table 15, p. 40, June 1981. The share of steel and chemical investments in total government-controlled enterprise industrial development (cumulative over time) for the period 1960–70 was 45.5 percent in the North and 53.1 percent in the South, and for the period 1971–79, 35.4 percent for the North and 67.8 percent for the South.

31. Bluestone and Harrison, *Deindustrialization of America*. They also note that areas of new industrialization have borne a heavy burden in terms of economic readjustments.

32. A. Amatucci, "La nuova legge per il Mezzogiorno," *Mezzogiorno d'Europa* 6 (October-December 1986); M. Leccisotti, E. Pace, and M. Sica, "Incentivi al Mezzogiorno: Nuova legislazione e convenienza ad investire," *Mezzogiorno d'Europa* 6 (October-December 1986).

33. A. C. Masi, "The Relationship Between National Industrial Strategy and Regional Economic Development: Some Lessons from the Case of Nuova Italsider-Taranto," *Journal of Regional Policy/Mezzogiorno d'Europa* 8 (January/March 1988).

34. A. Giannola, "I dati dello sviluppo economico nel decennio, 1965–1974," *Economia Pubblica* 2–3 (1976); L. Giusso, "IRI e Mezzogiorno," *Mezzogiorno d'Europa* 6 (October-December 1986).

35. A. Amin, "Industrial Restructuring, State Intervention and Regional Growth: The Example of Alfa Sud in Southern Italy," *Geographical Papers*, No. 77, Department of Georgraphy, University of Reading, England, 1983.

36. Piore and Sabel, *Second Industrial Divide*.

37. E. Kurzweil, *Italian Entrepreneurs: Rearguard of Progress* (New York: Praeger, 1983); A. Amin, S. Johnson, and D. Storey, "Le piccole imprese e il processo di sviluppo economico," *Mezzogiorno d'Europa* 6 (October-December 1986); M. Messori, "Sistemi di imprese e sviluppo meridionale: Un confronto fra due aree industriali," *Stato e Mercato* 18 (December 1986).

38. K. R. Harrigan, *Strategies for Declining Business* (Lexington, Mass.: Lexington Books, 1980); see also Masi, "Nuova Italsider," for coping strategies which the Japanese suggested to public-sector Italian steel.

39. Masi, "Nuova Italsider"; Masi, "Relationship."

40. At the same time, there were no differences in average annual wage increases between the North and South. Without the absolute numbers, however, it is difficult to interpret this finding. One possible explanation is that in the North employment was traded off for higher wages.

41. Large firms also lost workers (−0.2 percent). No data were provided on the

situation for middle-sized firms, and without the base numbers no recalculation was possible.

42. G. Carone, "State Transfers to Industry," *Mezzogiorno d'Europa* 4 (January/March 1984).

43. Ibid.; Messori, "Sistemi di imprese."

44. T. Treu, "Italy," in E. Yemin, ed. *Workforce Reductions in Undertaking: Policies and Measures for the Protection of Redundant Workers in Seven Industrialised Market Economy Countries* (Geneva: International Labour Office, 1982).

45. M. F. Sheehan, "Plant Closings and the Community: The Instrumental Value of Public Enterprise in Countering Corporate Flight," *American Journal of Economics and Sociology* 44 (October 1985); R. J. Lustig, "The Politics of Shutdown: Community, Property, Corporatism," *Journal of Economic Issues* 1 (March 1985); B. Harrison, "The International Movement for Prenotification of Plant Closures," *Industrial Relations* 23 (Fall 1984); J. Fallows, "America's Changing Economic Landscape," *Atlantic*, March 1985.

46. Treu, "Italy."

47. Norton, "Industrial Policy"; L. Pasinetti, ed., *Mutamenti strutturali del sistema produttivo: Integrazione tra industria e settore terziario* (Bologna: Il Mulino, 1986); G. Tassinari, *Le trasformazioni dell'industria italiana negli anni settanta: Analisi dei risultati censuari* (Bologna: Editrice CLUEB, 1984); B. R. Scott, "Can Industry Survive the Welfare State?" *Harvard Business Review,* September-October 1982.

48. ISTAT (*La Repubblica,* April 10, 1987, supplement) recently released data which have a bearing on these aspects of the deindustrialization thesis. First, they indicated the extent of underestimation of Italy's gross domestic product (nearly 15 percent for the year 1982). Second, they reported that the textile, clothing, and footwear sectors emerged from the study with a somewhat less strong image than was previously reported. Third, the so-called services to productive firms were shown to represent close to a million workers, many of whom before restructuring and reconversion efforts would have been classified as industrial employees. See also Tassinari, *Le trasformazioni,* and Pasinetti, *Mutamenti strutturali.*

49. Lawrence, "Is Trade Deindustrializing America?"

50. *La Repubblica,* April 10, 1987, supplement, p. 3.

9

Democracy and Economic Adjustment: A Comparative Analysis of Political Change

Joel D. Wolfe

How have governmental strategies for economic adjustment affected democracy in advanced industrial societies?[1] This important question remains largely unexplored. In recent years there has been an explosion of literature on corporatism and privatization—the main responses to the challenges of intensified competitiveness and real or potential economic decline among the advanced states. Yet, the consequences of these adjustment strategies for the theory and practice of democracy have been largely neglected. Only Alan Cawson,[2] Philippe Schmitter,[3] and Victor Magagna[4] have discussed the connection between democratic theory and corporatism. There has, moreover, been no systematic attempt either to conceptualize corporatism and privatization as forms of democracy or to understand their relationships to pluralism.

As the preceding chapters have demonstrated, different adjustment strategies have led to the incorporation of some private interests, eventuated in some states in a retraction of state intervention, and facilitated some groups in blocking the imposition of possible losses. Corporatism, though the most widely discussed, is thus only one pattern of adjustment to emerge in the 1980s. The chapters by Christopher Allen and Jeremiah Riemer and by Kathleen Thelen document aspects of this strategy of adjustment in West Germany.

Privatization, broadly construed to include all forms of control through property and market relations, is also a strategy being applied extensively. My chapter on privatization in Britain and Richard Foglesong's study of the choice of U.S. industrial policy examine a strategy that has become a worldwide phenomenon, being practiced, for example, in other industrial states like France, Austria, West Germany, Spain, and Japan, in newly industrialized nations like Singapore, and in developing states like Mexico, Turkey, and Bangladesh. Even Communist states like China and the Soviet Union are now introducing some market incentives. And the continued importance of pluralist forms of interest representation in influencing policy is evident in Harvey Feigenbaum's study of French economic and industrial policy, Tony Daley's analysis of adjustment in the French steel industry, and Anthony Masi's assessment of deindustrialization in Italy.

The need to move beyond separate discussions of privatization by economists and of corporatism by political scientists and to establish their relationships to pluralism is apparent. John Goldthorpe identifies corporatism (the concertation of state, unions, and employers) and dualism (the segmentation of actors, as in labor markets) as divergent institutional tendencies in capitalist democracies, posing issues about their nature and consequences.[5] Moreover, recent debates about the meaning of "privatization," "corporatism," and "pluralism" indicate the need for a clarification of concepts. Privatization can refer to disposing of a nation's public assets, deregulating markets, or applying profit-making standards to public-sector decision making—practices sometimes misinterpreted as signs of a return to a nineteenth-century laissez-faire economy and nightwatchman state. Corporatism, on the other hand, can denote a type of political economy that differs from capitalism or socialism, a system of policy formation, or a mode of associational problem solving assisted by state collaboration.[6] And for some, corporatism is similar to pluralism.[7]

This chapter develops a comparative analysis of different forms of democracy and identifies their characteristic patterns as responses to the problem of economic adjustment. The first section proposes a framework of analysis which views models of adjustment as exemplifying particular types of democratic power relations. From this perspective, economic adjustment strategies seek to counteract losses of state power and economic competitiveness. The second section analyzes the power relations found in the three types of democracy discussed in the preceding chapters—pluralism, corporatism, and privatization. To clarify further the meaning of these concepts, the discussion refines the initial typology by developing a comparative analysis of power relations within each. The third section then develops propositions to explain the changes within and between these types of democracy, and a final section demonstrates their utility.

THE ANALYSIS OF POWER AND MODELS OF DEMOCRACY

An examination of how adjustment strategies affect democracy must show how those strategies embody different power relations and have different consequences. To do this, this chapter advances an analysis of power influenced by the holistic pragmatism of Thomas Kuhn's description of scientific revolutions[8] and Sheldon Wolin's application of Kuhn's theses to political theory and political life.[9] According to Wolin, society consists of an ensemble of practices and beliefs which defines its identity, organizes its action, and enforces certain types of conduct. A pragmatist analysis makes possible a nonfunctionalist analysis of political change by focusing on consequences. As a result, what matters for systems of power is the capacity to make a difference when confronted with challenges. This "power to work" involves the adaptation of novelty to the system (through routine decision making and reform) or, alternatively, the system to novelty (through system transformation).

The pragmatist's focus on success in meeting challenges posed by the system's environment provides a test of the viablity of a system's power relations and emphasizes human agency, involving actors in defining and coordinating the realization of their values as the key to system reform and transformation. As actors formulate and pursue goals, they judge which factors affect their capacity for control and therefore need to be changed. In thus defining and coping with their environment, they apply, amend, or transform the patterns of control and coordination that comprise systems of collective action among constituent groups. Most often, like the puzzle solvers of normal science, leaders do this by drawing upon the resources of the ongoing ensemble of beliefs and attitudes defining political life to assimilate routine demands or new challenges requiring reform—for example, by introducing measures that counter deflationary trends. Less frequently, like anomalous cases that foster extraordinary science, the political environment proves resistant to the governing formula, resulting in uncertainty and instability and compelling authorities to restructure society's internal power relations in order to meet challenges. For instance, the dismantling of the state's direct role in the economy through selling public assets, deregulation, and contracting out exemplifies just this type of reorganization of the state–interest-group complex, aimed at facilitating macro-economic policies and the restoration of public authority.

Democracy thus becomes a matter of how different patterns of collective praxis (policy making) within institutionally complex representative systems produce different consequences. This involves changing relations of control and coordination as organizations seek to realize collective ends and maintain system integrity. Different patterns of coordination and control among relatively independent groups involve different power relations and result in different types of policy.[10] From this perspective, institutional procedures like elections and institutional structures like the market or bureaucracy represent conduits through which individuals and groups pursue their chosen ends, producing different types of power relations and distinctive types of public policies. Since political action is purposive, flexible, and conditional, types of democracy can be distinguished by the way that relatively autonomous groups and individuals engage in the collective control and coordination of policy making.

To distinguish how various patterns of collective control and coordination within institutions have different consequences involves examining how the basic elements of systems of effective power—values, initiatives, and modes of control—are shaped in response to environmental challenges. Values define goals, activate autonomy by mobilizing lines of interest and influence among actors, and guide the use of modes of control, thereby shaping power relations and limiting the choice of policy responses to specific problems. Thus, the policies through which decision makers resolve challenges either reinforce the reigning value-type, pattern of intiative, and mode of control or evoke changes in the relationship among these basic elements.

Elements of Power in Democratic Systems

To analyze how the patterning of associated activity results in different power relations involves examining (1) how values motivate and guide action, (2) how the source of initiative reflects group or state autonomy, and (3) how the mode of control distributes the capacity for decision making and implementation. These elements can be used to identify the various ways in which democratic beliefs and practices can be adjusted to meet economic challenges.

First, values establish the imperatives for action found within a cultural system. They act as guides, maps, or templates for action in the same way that Kuhn's concept of the paradigm identifies how a scientific cultural system defines a scientific community and its research problems and projects.[11] Evolving historically as solutions to particular problems, cultural systems reflect the different interests of various actors, by giving meaning and imposing order. The adjustment models in the advanced democracies are concerned mainly with instrumental values, reflecting the means-ends rationality of capitalism and a legal-rational bureaucratic order.[12] While drawing upon sentiments of nationalism, the modern democratic state is essentially an institutional complex based on instrumental values exemplified in various versions of liberalism and socialism. Ideological diversity nonetheless flourishes because conflicts between relatively autonomous institutions within the whole and between the state and private capital (since the state does not originate capitalist power or directly control it) generate fresh problems requiring political solution.[13]

Second, the source of values both illuminates the relative autonomy of individuals, associations, and state actors and reveals the pressures for system change. In judging the autonomy of an individual or group, one must determine whether its interests are internally originated or imposed from without. Liberal democratic theory presupposes an internal generation of interests.[14] This sociological-centered perspective reflects a view that the ability to formulate and articulate claims serving one's real interests indicates autonomy, whereas the inability to do so shows the lack of it.[15] Unfortunately, distinguishing between objective (real) and subjective interests raises difficult analytical problems: subjective or overt interests may not always express real interests, and interpretations of both subjective and objective interests evolve as living standards, mobility chances, and other life experiences shift.

In comparison, when states formulate and strive for ends that do not simply reflect the interests of groups, classes or individuals, the source of initiative is external to these groups and state-centered. The state may seek to shape interest groups' internal political processes or their relationships to the state itself. Such state-centered initiatives pose questions about the sources of state action and state capacities, concerns common to both recent neo-Weberian discussions[16] and neo-Marxist analyses of the state.[17] In each, the identification of the state as the locus of initiative and an institution capable of imposing its interests on society signal a decisive break with sociological-centered analyses.

More important, the source of interest initiative (internal or state-centered) illuminates the nature of system change. Since routine decision making confirms the efficacy and demonstrates the stability of a particular system of effective power, the following analysis focuses on whether change entails adjustment within a pattern of power (social integration) or a shift to another pattern (system integration). So long as the guiding imperatives of the dominant values and interests enable decision makers to assimilate demands and solve problems, reforming the ongoing system of effective power produces order and stability. Interest demands consistent with accepted practices, whether originating from an elite or from group members, can be assimilated by policies that enhance authority, as illustrated by the development of the Keynesian welfare state promoting full employment.

Conversely, whenever the environment produces challenges which cannot be assimilated, there will be increasing disorder and ineffectiveness associated with the loss of authority, similar to Kuhn's description of periods of extraordinary science. To regain control, authorities must institute a more effective means of collective decision making. This "structural accommodation" not only requires an exercise of power by relatively autonomous leaders capable of reorganizing the character of demands in relation to performance capacities but depends on a change in the hegemonic ideology. For example, structural adjustment policies like corporatist incomes policies of the 1970s or privatization in the 1980s arose when political elites responded to ideological shifts that emerged when the system failed to cope with increasing conflict and disorder arising from the problem of economic decline. In short, whether the imperative for change arises from a need for different forms of group access and benefits or from a need to limit demand on the system determines whether interest groups or the state will be likely to exercise autonomy.

The third element of a system of effective power is the mode of control and coordination. This involves descision-making mechanisms which determine the way leaders and members engage in policy making and implementation. Modes of control and coordination reveal choices about the means of achieving ends and depend on their pattern of historical development, the type of values motivating and guiding action, and the imperatives for social and system integration. Significantly, modes of control and coordination are the practices that realize ideological imperatives about the criteria for decision making, transforming motive and belief into reward or punishment.

Modes of control fit into three analytic (though not necessarily exhaustive) categories: authority based on legal-rational, remunerative, and normative foundations; compacts entailing reciprocal exchanges based on the conditional fulfillment of material and moral obligations; and markets involving commodity-based exchanges. The authority mode gives rise to formal organizations and voluntary groups which are operated by officeholders invested with legitimate power (sometimes affording substantial independence) through formal procedures of selection and decision making. The compact mode, seen in some incomes policies, involves shared norms that result in contingent or exchange relationships between representatives and their members, subjecting officeholders and members to mutual obligations. Unlike the legal-rational authority of elected representatives (though it may coexist with them), the compact mode entails mandates that link grants of support for delegates to the concrete results of officials' actions. The market mode identifies exchanges in which the mutual adjustment of self-interest occurs on the basis of "market resources" like property and skills. Market modes exchange labor skills and energies for money, which in turn is used to purchase goods and services provided by business enterprises, giving rise to an unending pursuit of opportunities for exchange which inevitably fosters ever larger systems of mutual coordination and commodity-based control.[18]

Power Relations, Associational Action, and Types of Democracy

These three elements—the type of value, its source, and the mode of control and coordination—define patterns of collective action and, when combined, produce a typology of the ways in which democratic power relations can adapt to economic, social, and political challenges. (See Table 9.1)

This typology identifies and provides a basis for systematically analyzing the major types of democratic power relations in industrial democracies. It demonstrates each type's conceptual distinctiveness by specifying the motive

Table 9.1
Types of Democratic Power Relations

Values Orienting Action	Source of Values	Modes of Control		
		Authority	Contract	Market
Instrumental	External	Corporatism (1)	Consensus (2)	Privatized (3)
Instrumental	Internal	Pluralist (4)	Procedural (5)	Consumer (6)

or justification for action, the source of initiative, and the manner in which power is exercised. These six different types of power relations represent distinctive *patterns of collective control and coordination* that make possible particular types of policies.

A brief description of each of the six major types of democracy defined by the typology will provide a useful overview. Of the distinctive patterns of collective control and coordination which the typology defines, pluralist democracy encompasses the reigning models of elitist democracy and polyarchy, and corporatist and privatized democracy are of growing empirical and theoretical significance. Consequently, these types will be analyzed in greater detail in the next section.

First, corporatist, consensus, and privatized democracy constitute types of representation shaped by social and state control. *Corporatist democracy* relies on a combination of state initiative and associative processes that combine representation with social control to promote instrumental ends like economic growth and political stability. Moreover, corporatist democracy gains its capacity for interest intermediation and concerted policy formation from its basis of formal legal-rational or associational mechanisms for aggregating support and demands, even though actual policy decisions, including the decision to incorporate particular associations, involve bargaining among elected representatives in the context of a social consensus.[19] The central properties characterizing the patterning of collective control and coordination are inclusiveness, concertation, and enlistment.

Next, *consensus democracy* entails intermediation based on a bargained exchange involving negotiation and agreement between autonomous organizations, movements, or communities in order to establish a consensus on the distribution of power as a precondition for commitment to a formula of governance. The British Labor government's "social contract" with the trade unions during the 1970s and the consociational arrangements[20] involving bargains between linguistic groups that underlie constitutional agreements in Belgium and the Netherlands illustrate this type. These examples demonstrate that it is the procedure for working out a constitutional or social compact rather than the exchange of public status (authority) in policy making that distinguishes consensus from corporatist democracy. What characterizes this pattern of collective control and coordination, then, is compact-making or community-building.

Privatized democracy, finally, utilizes market relationships rather than interest intermediation to attain the goals of social control and state regulation of interest articulation. As the sale of British Telecom and the deregulation of the telecommunications industry in Britain, the United States, and the Netherlands illustrate, the use of property ownership and market discipline, instituted and regulated by the state, shifts power away from workers and unions toward management. The patterning of power relations in privatized democracy exemplifies preclusive, segmentary, and exclusive properties.

Second, pluralist, procedural, and consumer democracy comprise forms of interest representation. In contrast to corporatist, consensus, or privatized democracy, these three types describe relationships between the state and interest groups that arise in the absence of social and state control. As a result, interest representation shapes group pressures and policy formation. Within a formal (legal-rational) system of government, *pluralist democracy* involves multiple, voluntary, and competing groups (business, labor, agriculture, etc.) exerting direct pressure on policy makers or indirect pressure through an electoral process in which politicians appeal for and create the support of voters. These are power relations characterized by group-level voicing, claiming, or advocacy. Thus, pluralist democracy encompassing the notion of democracy articulated in the works of Joseph Schumpeter,[21] S. M. Lipset,[22] and Robert Dahl,[23] in which contenders for office appeal to group interests in an electoral contest or in which public policy emerges from the balance of contending interests.[24] Finally, procedural and consumer democracy constitute types fashioned by utilitarian or libertarian principles. *Procedural democracy* is a concept that denotes a pattern of representation based on the aggregation of individual preferences in accordance with predetermined or contracted decision rules, a concept of democracy found in the work of rational choice theorists[25] and utilitarians but having roots in the work of Jeremy Bentham and James Mill. Its pattern of collective control or coordination consists in translating individual preferences into group preferences. *Consumer democracy* is a decision-making mechanism that centers on individual subjective preferences, but it posits that political interests can best be satisfied by extending the mutual adjustment processes of the market to the political sphere, thereby permitting the expression of citizen in addition to consumer sovereignty. Expressed in the work of Milton Friedman[26] and Robert Nozick,[27] this type of democracy is modeled on the ideal of pure market exchange, backed by a minimalist state. Its organizing property is, to use Albert Hirschman's words, exiting (or dealing) rather than voice.[28]

POWER, POLICY, AND SUBTYPES OF DEMOCRACY

Having defined these six types of democracy, we now examine the variations in the power relations within the three main types discussed in the preceding chapters of this book: pluralist democracy (Feigenbaum, Daley, Masi), corporatist democracy (Allen and Riemer, Thelen), and privatized democracy (Foglesong, Wolfe). Moreover, each chapter portrays these strategies as incomplete, fluid, and mixed, as in the Thatcher governments' effort to sell off nationalized industries without also introducing greater competition or in the private-sector initiatives for development supported by the West German state governments. The essays thus support the notion that democracy involves a variety of power relations, distinguished by the way actors in representative institutions choose to control and coordinate their policy making in response to the different kinds of challenges they confront.

To link subtypes of the major forms of democracy with possible patterns of policy requires refining the basic categories of the above analysis. The bases of collective action (instrumental values and interests) can be distinguished according to their scope—broad or narrow. This identifies whether interests activate lines of influence which involve large-scale connections (for example, between classes) or limited, relatively independent relations (for example, among individuals involved in market exchanges). Similarly, the modes of control and coordination can be subdivided between those which are unified (centralized) and those which are dispersed (disaggregated) among many participants. The result is a series of subtypes of pluralist, corporatist, and privatized democracy elaborating their power relations and concomitant policy types. Each typology does this by further specifying or subcategorizing patterns of collective control and coordination and their policy consequences.

Pluralist Democracy

Pluralist democracy (see Table 9.2), first, identifies patterns of voluntary interest-group advocacy, typified by varieties of pluralism and incorporating those policy arenas and power structures developed by Theodore Lowi,[29] Rober Salisbury,[30] and B. Guy Peters.[31] The "system-claiming" power relation names a pattern of control and coordination in which the motivating interests of a group-based movement are instrumental values broad in scope and represented by a unified authority. These types of relations comprise zero-sum games in which one broadly based grouping (a working-class movement)

Table 9.2
Subtypes of Pluralist Democracy

Power Relations

Values Orienting Action	Internal Sources of Values	Modes of Control	
		Unified	Dispersed
Instrumental	Broad	System Claiming	Process Claiming
Instrumental	Narrow	Function Claiming	Resource Claiming

Policy Types

Values Orienting Action	Internal Sources of Values	Modes of Control	
		Unified	Dispersed
Instrumental	Broad	Collectivizing	Self-administering
Instrumental	Narrow	Regulative	Pork Barrel

cannot be advantaged without another (a capitalist class) being disadvantaged. Such power relations correspond to "collectivizing" policies, as illustrated by the redistribution of wealth between classes manifest in the collectivist policies of the Keynesian welfare state.[32] The "resource-claiming" power relation involves specific claims being made by dispersed actors and leads to a disaggregation of benefits and sources of support. This power relation corresponds to policies variously characterized as pork-barrel, distributive,[33] or classical-liberal.[34] Next, the "process-claiming" power relation identifies a pattern of control characterized by a fragmented system of representation which enables intensely committed and broadly organized coalitions of groups to mobilize support for fulfilling their own intersts. Because this configuration of support and interest weakens public officeholders, groups are permitted to regulate themselves. It is this power relation subtype that engenders policies of "self-administration," policies which have been asso-

Table 9.3
Subtypes of Corporatist Democracy

Power Relations

Values Orienting Action	Internal Sources of Values	Modes of Control	
		Unified	Dispersed
Instrumental	Broad	System Enlisting	Collaboration Enlisting
Instrumental	Narrow	Function Enlisting	Resource Enlisting

Policy Types

Values Orienting Action	Internal Sources of Values	Modes of Control	
		Unified	Dispersed
Instrumental	Broad	Tripartism	Ameliorative
Instrumental	Narrow	Promotional	Incorporative

ciated in recent works of democratic theory with the dilemma of democracy,[35] pluralist stagnation,[36] and the democratic distemper.[37] Finally, the "function-claiming" power relation involves a unified governmental agency facing numerous claimants, a pattern found in governmental regulation of a particular sector of the economy.[38] The zero-sum context and the extensive participation of interested parties generate group coalitions that exert pressure upon government officials. "Regulative" policies exemplify this power relation.

Corporatist Democracy

Turning next to *corporatist democracy* (see Table 9.3), the further refinement of patterns of concertation, inclusiveness, and enlisting helps to comprehend and clarify recent distinctions in the corporatist literature between macro-, meso-, and micro-corporatism. A "system enlisting" power relation, involving a unified pattern of representative control and policy issues wide in scope, denotes a subcategory of power that captures what have been considered the general features of the corporatist concept—policy concertation and interest intermediation—applied to whole political systems. The insights gained from this concept have been substantial, particularly regarding the problems of governability,[39] employment levels,[40] and labor union unrest.[41] Moreover, the system-enlisting power relation underlies policies of "tripartism," involving efforts evidenced most clearly in Austria and Sweden to engage the state, capital, and labor in negotiated pacts which transcend potentially destructive class conflict and yield positive-sum benefits for the whole system.

Yet, as Cawson argues,[42] whole-system concepts like *Modell Osterreich*[43] are unlikely to be replicated in other political systems, given current historical conditions. Recent corporatist studies have consequently focused on meso-corporatism, that is, collaborative adjustment at levels below that of the whole system. The formulation of the concept of private-interest government by Schmitter and Streeck emphasizes the importance of associational activity for meso-level developments,[44] by highlighting the licensing or legitimizing of private interests in the service of public ends as an indirect means of state control. Of relevance to meso-corporatism, our framework distinguishes two types of power relations and their consequent policy patterns, corresponding to what Cawson calls sectoral and transsectoral corporatism.[45] These types need not involve tripartite consultation and negotiation among the state, capital, and labor; rather, they require only that an association possess a monopoly of representation and membership control, factors which facilitate incorporation into a formal system of interest-group intermediation.

A "collaboration-enlisting" power relation relies on the ability of multiple-interest associations to collaborate with state authorities on issues of wide scope where there is a consensus among participants, as in the case of the British Manpower Services Commission.[46] This power relation encompasses a broad range of participants and produces policies of coordinated problem solving or "amelioration." Unlike the pluralist subtype of self-administration (in which interests capture weak and fragmented representative authority), what is significant about this subtype is the state's ability to gain acquiescence to its initiatives from a variety of associations, some of which hold otherwise conflicting interests.

A power relation of "function enlisting," on the other hand, involves a pattern of associational action in which a state agency or private firm initiates a collaborative and state-supported effort in one sector, without any coordination between associations from other sectors. This entails indirect rather than authoritative control of a firm's behavior, as well as coordination with unions and suppliers. Function enlisting thus captures instances of "promotional" policy, such as when state agencies pick winners and losers by providing incentives for private interests to participate in public goals. This is illustrated by examples from recent French industrial policy in which economic benefits are awarded by the state in exchange for a firm's pursuit of investment or employment targets,[47] or by the British government's attempts to motivate private investment where it would not otherwise occur through government-run projects such as the English Industrial Estates or through special incentive programs in depressed areas or regions such as the Urban Development Corporation scheme.[48] Interestingly, what this framework defines as a function-enlisting power relation and a corresponding promotional policy, Cawson identifies as micro-corporatism (since it centers on the firm) and Young as a form of privatization (since it involves private-sector initiative).

Finally, the notion of "resource enlisting" conceptualizes a pattern of collective control and coordination establishing the bases within a firm or association for interest intermediation. A resource-enlisting power relation corresponds to "incorporative" policies at the associational base, utilizing narrow issues and many participants at various levels and types of authority. These strategies involve the design of representational forms in order to enhance the hierarchy's capacity for social control. For example, by increasing the bureaucratization of unions at the workplace, a union leadership can reduce the rank-and-file's ability to exert autonomy.[49] Similarly, management can increase participatory mechanisms, introduce job security, and promote company unionism in order to co-opt the workforce.[50] The resource-enlisting power relation and its corresponding incorporative policies interact with corporatism at higher levels, since they help establish the social control upon which higher-level institutions depend for interest intermediation and the making of concrete initiatives.

Privatized Democracy

By arguing that privatization and other elements of the neoliberal program represent a governing strategy comparable in status to pluralist and corporatist forms, this framework advances the neoliberal formula beyond economists' and ideologues' arguments for achieving economic efficiency. Moreover, while privatization refers to a shift from the public to the private sector,[51] it constitutes the core of the neoliberal effort to restructure democratic power relations. Labeled *Privatized democracy* (see Table 9.4), this strategy combines instrumental interests, state initiative and regulation, and the market control and coordination mechanism. The concept of privatized democracy identifies a preclusive (of public status and collaboration) pattern of collective allocation and coordination, which makes possible a particular cluster of policies. Our framework yields four subtypes of privatized democracy and four corresponding types of policies.

The "system-preclusive" subtype designates the creation of market partic-

Table 9.4
Subtypes of Privatized Democracy

Power Relations

Values Orienting Action	Internal Sources of Values	Modes of Control: Unified	Modes of Control: Dispersed
Instrumental	Broad	System Preclusive	Collaboration Preclusive
Instrumental	Narrow	Function Preclusive	Resource Preclusive

Policy Types

Values Orienting Action	Internal Sources of Values	Modes of Control: Unified	Modes of Control: Dispersed
Instrumental	Broad	Denationalization	Liberalization
Instrumental	Narrow	Contracting Out	Charging

ipants or private property-holders as the pattern of control and coordination, the conditions for which are introduced and maintained by state authorities. The aim is to establish profit-making and ownership responsibility as the criteria shaping a firm's or association's internal and external relations. System-preclusive power relations, applied to a whole firm and shaping managerial decisions and labor's bargaining position, encompass "denationalization," policies that transfer public industries to the private sector through asset sales. Recent examples include the sale of British Gas in Britain, Conrail in the United States, and Paribas in France. In these and other cases, private ownership compels managements to make profits. The key element of this subtype, then, is private ownership, which functions as a mechanism for achieving internal authority and compels an unending search for profits through investment and rationalization.

A second subtype of a preclusive patterning of collective action, the "collaboration-preclusive" power relation, focuses on the relationships between firms or between other agents marketing commodities. This category identifies the use of market competition as the disciplining force between economic and associational actors in specific sectors of the economy. Many economists writing about privatization have argued that competition is the key to consumer benefits, such as lower prices, since it drives producers to contend for market shares. As they compete for the product market, firms are forced to undergo internal rationalization, weakening internal "interest groups" like trade unions. The collaboration-preclusive power relation corresponds to policies of "liberalization," which can be seen at work in the deregulation of Britain's long-distance bus industry. This has forced down coach fares and compelled its competitor, British Rail, to lower prices and cut costs. One result has been to weaken labor's power in both industries.

The third subtype is the "function-preclusive" power relation. In this the public authority or public-sector enterprise is under pressure to reduce costs and break the collective power of public-sector workers by contracting particular services to private businesses which offer their services at cost-saving prices. While the decision maker is a unified provider, the pressure to rationalize, cut costs, or reduce the power of internal interest groups leads to policies of disaggregating, spinning off, or "contracting out" particular functions. The result is that public-sector organizations or firms use cost-reduction standards to pick "winners and losers" by choosing private over public-sector providers. In Britain, the policy of contracting out is illustrated by subcontracting among local governments and the National Health Service. Picking private-sector over public-sector service providers can evoke controversy, as shown by the conflict over this area of Thatcher's privatization program.

The fourth subtype of privatized collective action, the "resource-preclusive" power relation, centers on internal control through the shifting of costs from public sources to private consumers. The issues are narrow and multiple; the decision makers are many, often individual consumers; and the market acts to structure coordination and allocation. Public institutions, participating in competitive markets or under fiscal constraints, find it imperative to adopt new, private-sector sources of income and to apply business accounting practices. This subtype identifies the use of market discipline to control internal decision making in organizations. Thus, the resource-preclusive power relation is associated with the policy of "charging." Examples include increasing charges for drug prescriptions or museum entrance fees, because of reduced subsidies and the introduction of business accounting practices in public agencies. All of these examples involve a strategy of relying on charging or cost-accounting rather than government grants and subsidies to generate and allocate resources in the service of public ends.

Thus, by further specifying variations in the value basis of collective action and the sources of initiative in the initial analysis, a comparative analysis of power relations and concomitant policies within three important empirical types of democratic power relations can be advanced. In so doing, the analysis has been able to elucidate key distinctions between types of public policy found in the pluralist literature, shed light on recent distinctions developed by students of corporatism, and formulate a parallel analysis for the subcategories of privatized democracy.

DEMOCRACY, ADJUSTMENT STRATEGIES, AND ENVIRONMENTAL CHANGE

To complete this analysis of the politics of economic adjustment, hypotheses about shifts in systemic practices can now be presented. A final section briefly illustrates the utility of the overall analysis for recent instances of democratic reform and transformation.

In general, types of system change depend on how associational activities stimulate the shaping of initiatives, values, and modes of control. The need for social integration arises when associations initiate calls for new forms of representation and benefits that involve modifying the scope (broad or narrow) of interests and/or the concentration (unified or dispersed) of their modes of decision making. This occurs within a type of democracy. The need for system integration arises when there is a loss of system control. State action to reestablish control produces changes in the locus of initiative and the mode of decision making that redefine the type of democracy.

In examining shifts within or between types, a first consideration is the success of a system of power relations in coping with the challenges presented by the environment. As argued above, the system's efficacy depends on its capacity to assimilate environmental challenges that reinforce internal power relations by reproducing expected policy solutions. Conflict about distributive outputs can result in shifts between subtypes of power relations and particular policy manifestations, as in the case of the shift from the pork-barrel politics of the nineteenth century in the United States to the Keynesian welfare state after 1945. A system crisis, conversely, fosters the need to accommodate change by altering the system's power structure so as to reestablish its capacity for exercising order and control. Transforming power relations in order to make possible policies that resolve problems of system integration (through the reestablishment of authority by contraining the level of demand in relation to support) involves system-level shifts in the locus of initiative, which establishes state control of representation and the mode of control and coordination. Such shifts in the source of initiative (from group representation to state control) and modes of control (from unrestrained association to authority-guided or market-disciplined association) result in different types of democracy, as evident in the emergence of corporatist and privatized democracy.

Having located the source of initiative for change within or between systems of democratic power relations in problems of social and system integration, we turn to the issue of motivation and prescription for action. This leads to an examination of the character of ideology in periods of ineffectivenss and uncertainty, since it is periods of crisis that have generated major ideological reformulations, and periods of normalcy that have permitted the assimilation of emergent challenges through the reigning practices. Moreover, since ideological shifts and revisions prescribe changes in who should act, who should benefit, and what mechanism of control is most appropriate, they redefine the "facts" of democratic praxis. The Keynesian interventionist state proved a successful adaptation of the liberal capitalist "paradigm" after World War II because it solved the problems of the underutilization of resources and led to full employment, thereby not only rewarding millions of working people but enhancing overall control and coordination of the political system. In response to the failure of Keynesian-inspired policies in the late 1960s and the 1970s, academics, politicians, and media commentators began looking for alternative philosophies that would revitalize authority and restore system stability. A second hypothesis, then, is that social- and system-integration crises foster a proliferation of political doctrines which purport to prescribe acceptable patterns of power and policy and which vie for the status of the dominant public philosophy.

The different ways in which particular political visions formulate, prescribe, and justify collective goals, the locus of initiative, and the mode by which decisions are made and implemented signify differences within and between types of democracy. For each type of democracy, a change in scope of values (broad or narrow) and/or in the concentration of the mode of control (unified or dispersed) arising from associational pressures for changes in policy consequences results in shifts within that type. A third (reformist) hypothesis, then, is that group pressures and elite responses can redefine the scope of issues and/or the concentration of policy making, calling into play different patterns of power relations and policies. For example, after World War II in Britain and the United States calls from trade unions and other groups for full employment and welfare provisions interacted with electoral opportunities and the ambitions of parties and politicians to foster full employment and welfare policies that shifted the distribution of national resources between classes.

System-integration crises, however, impact on factors that define the system itself, leading to changes between types of democratic practice. For instance, in the 1970s and early 1980s, there was an apparent need in many advanced democracies to limit the demands of interest groups which had overloaded post–World War II pluralist democracy. Since political control depends on the relationship between the way support or legitimacy is created and aggregated in relation to the demands made, officeholders can choose between a mode that either distances themselves and the authority structure from group pressures (illustrated by Thatcher in Britain) or enlists the support and obligations of associations (illustrated by Austria and Sweden). A fourth (system crisis) hypothesis is that in order to transform the power relations which produce only policy failures and delegitimation,[52] authorities expand public-authority (corporatist democracy) or market (privatized democracy) modes of control and coordination. These strategies enhance legitimate power by restraining group demands, thereby reducing the state's own obligation to respond to pressure. Specifically, privatized democracy relies on impersonal property relations and market exchanges to depoliticize the state and disorganize group and class solidarities, whereas corporatist democracy rationalizes interest-group demands by increasing their organizational obligations to support the system. From this perspective, privatized democracy emerges as a response to a crisis of governance, not economic inefficiency, as economists suggest. Both corporatist and privatized democracies, then, entail the use of modes of control to displace disintegrative pressures on authority and recoup legitimate control, whereas a return to pluralist democracy would entail a freeing of associational activity.

EXPLAINING PATTERNS OF DEMOCRACY

The utility of these hypotheses can be illustrated by explaining recent trends toward divergent patterns of democracy. The dominance of the pluralist model during the post–World War II heyday of "embedded liberalism" provided a context in which theorists had projected a convergence in power relations in the advanced states.[53] Yet, from the perspective of the mid–1980s, this optimism has given way to recognition of the growing diversity of power relations within and between nations.

The first hypothesis in the previous section helps to understand the causes of diverging power relations. In focusing on a power relation's efficacy in meeting challenges, this hypothesis prompts us to examine the sources of interest-group power in the advanced democracies in the late 1960s and 1970s to explain why that power became disruptive. Centering on the success of a system in interacting with its environment, the hypothesis suggests that it was not the growth of interest-group power alone which was the root cause of economic decline, fiscal burdens, and a weakened state; rather, this group power evolved in accordance with the post–World War II managed economy paradigm and in the context of a world political economy which facilitated it—but with which it subsequently came into conflict. When the advanced industrial states faced an increasingly competitive environment, the collectivist pluralism of the managed economy proved unable to adapt.

The inability of the Keynesian interventionist state formula to meet the recent economic challenges (though it has been more successful in the smaller corporatist states in northern Europe) results from both international and domestic factors. First, the advanced industrial states have faced an increasingly conflictual and competitive international economy. This reflects the breakup of the post–World War II economic hegemony of the United States, changes in supply conditions, and emergent ineffectiveness of demand management techniques that have coincided with a growth of mercantilism, economic regionalism, and sectoral protectionism.[54] These have all made the international economy less open and more discriminatory for major industrial countries and have enhanced the influence of the international economy on domestic power relations. In this book, Harvey Feigenbaum's chapter underscores the importance of the international political economy in shaping the economic policy convergence of recent French governments.

Second, by the late 1960s and 1970s internal political developments made the Western industrial states' successful responses to international challenges problematic. The Keynesian collectivist state had enhanced the power of rank-and-file labor. Full employment gave greater bargaining power to the shop floor, limiting the ability of union officials to restrain wage pressures when they were so inclined. The growth of unionization in most industrial states reinforced this rank-and-file power. Where corporatism was not successful, union power created inflexibility. And as Tony Daley's study of adjustment in the French steel industry shows, state intervention can magnify union influence by politicizing industrial conflicts. Moreover, the Keynesian welfare state created new pressure groups by fostering organization among the "policy-takers" and by providing incentives to organize among those who were overlooked by the growing panoply of welfare services. The result was a complex interaction of multiple interests that produced ineffective government.[55] As Anthony Masi demonstrates in his chapter, despite Italy's overall economic success, interventionist measures backing industry and programs safeguarding workers have corresponded with inflation, large budget deficits, and rising unemployment.

As our second hypothesis suggests, these tensions led to a loss of confidence in the collectivist social democratic or Keynesian political vision. This eventuated in a vigorous ideological debate in which those on the right offered a politics of neoliberalism, while those on the left became embroiled in ideological battles or moved to adopt their own version of austerity. These efforts have attempted to reformulate the basis of state authority and power in order to resolve what was widely perceived as disorder and decay. This can be seen in Britain in the rise of monetarism and privatization on the right and "siege" socialism and social partnership on the left.

Finally, the choice of a mode of control compatible with system-processing needs must take account of the motives for collective behavior, as well as the system imperatives compelling state authorities to act. The choice of either corporatist or privatized democracy as a response to economic and political challenges results first from the level of disorder which makes leadership action necessary and second from the capacity of authority or market modes to enhance authority. Since corporatist democracy depends on the elaboration of instrumental rationality through a high level of organizational development, it presupposes agreement on decision-making procedures, extensive organization, and a consensus on the instrumental-oriented goals of capitalist wealth-creation typical of the Scandinavian countries, West Germany, Austria, and Switzerland. Where such motivational and organizational preconditions are weak or absent as a result of cultural diversity, ideological predispositions, or historical patterns of organization among capital and labor, privatized democracy (as typified in the British and American instances) appears to be a more likely strategy, since it involves instrumental rationality being played out through individual choices in market processes of mutual adjustment.

While corporatism can facilitate flexible responses to international competitiveness,[56] the chapters in this book add a complementary conclusion: that the pressures for a restructuring of internal power relations can also be met by privatization strategies. Richard Foglesong argues that capitalists find in privatization a strategy that facilitates their adjustment to economic challenges, despite the costs such adjustment entails for workers, consumers, or the dispossessed; and I argue in my earlier chapter that the Thatcher privatization program restructures group power and promotes economic adjustment.

Interestingly, the preclusive and disaggregative (though system integrative) tendencies evidenced in privatization are also apparent in the emergence of meso-corporatism and employers' demands for more flexible use of labor in corporatist systems. In their chapter on West German economic adjustment, Christopher Allen and Jeremiah Riemer show that conditions of austerity favor meso-corporatism rather than the macro-corporatism attempted in more prosperous times.[57] And Kathleen Thelen's study of the German metalworkers' negotiations for working-time reduction reveals how employers are countering with demands for flexible working time in order to facilitate adjustment to competitive economic conditions.

CONCLUSION

This chapter offers a characterization of and explanation for how economic adjustment strategies affect democratic praxis. The analysis starts from the premise that different types of democracy result from the consequences they have for dealing with different kinds of problems. Success in different contexts requires different power relations or patterns of collective policy making. The resulting analysis moves beyond theorizations of pluralism and corporatism as distinct, unrelated models of politics in advanced states. Rather, this perspective conceptualizes the variation in democratic power relations in a comparative framework that establishes the relationships among types of democracy and the conditions for shifts within and between them.

Such a perspective moves toward integrating various existing analyses of adjustment strategies. By identifying pluralist and corporatist approaches as characteristic types of democratic theory, the analysis clarifies their conceptualization by placing them in a comprehensive comparative framework. Further, by identifying variation within each major type of democracy, the framework incorporates the institutionalist finding that shifting balances of collective policy making are expressed in institutional practices that produce different types of policy. By recognizing that the changing environment of democratic power relations can foster anomalous consequences that eventuate in an alternative strategy of collective adjustment, the analysis acknowledges the importance of changing production systems as one important type of influence on democratic practices.

By clarifying particular types of democracy, this analysis should ultimately contribute to greater collective self-consciousness about which types of democratic practices are possible and which are found most acceptable. Each type identified can be critically evaluated by examining the promises of its ideological or motivational basis as well as the consequences of its praxis for particular groups and individuals.[58] While this framework is thus not an exhaustive typology of democracy, the distinctions between transformative forms of democratic praxis which combine social control with associational representation, on the one hand, and reformist practices which feature various forms of representation, on the other, provide criteria for judging which systems are more favorable to individual or group motives and autonomy.

Ultimately, the proposed framework offers an alternative vision of politics in the advanced capitalist states. By focusing on how power relations in complex systems depend on the consequences that the patterns of collective policy making produce, this framework emphasizes not only the organizational complexity of modern politics but its purposive, interest-based, and adaptive character. And by focusing on the dynamic relationship among organizational complexity, ideological guidance, and environmental challenge, the analysis portrays modern democratic political systems as both determined and determining, consisting of shifting and conditional mixes of types of democracy.

NOTES

1. I am very grateful to Christopher S. Allen, Gerard Braunthal, Richard Foglesong, David Resnick, and Philippe Schmitter for their helpful comments on earlier versions of this chapter.

2. Alan Cawson, "Functional Representation and Democratic Politics: Towards a Corporatist Democracy?" in Graeme Duncan, ed., *Democratic Theory and Practice* (Cambridge, Eng.: Cambridge University Press, 1983), pp. 173–84; Alan Cawson, *Corporatism and Political Theory* (Oxford: Basil Blackwell, 1986), chap. 7.

3. Philippe C. Schmitter, "Democratic Theory and Neo-corporatist Practice," *Social Research* 50 (Winter 1983): 885–928.

4. Victor V. Magagna, "Representing Efficiency: Corporatism and Democratic Theory," *Review of Politics* 50 (Summer 1988): 420–44.

5. John H. Goldthorpe, "The End of Convergence: Corporatist and Dualist Ten-

dencies in Modern Western Societies," in John H. Goldthorpe, ed., *Order and Conflict in Contemporary Capitalism* (Oxford: Clarendon Press, 1984), pp. 315–43. Also see Alice Brown and Desmond S. King, "Economic Change and Labour Market Policy: Corporatist and Dualist Tendencies in Britain and Sweden," *West European Politics* 11 (July 1988): 75–91.

6. Cawson, *Corporatism and Political Theory,* chap. 2; Wolfgang Streeck and Philippe C. Schmitter, "Community, Market, State—And Associations? The Prospective Contribution of Interest Governance to Social Order," in Wolfgang Streeck and Philippe C. Schmitter, eds., *Private Interest Government: Beyond Market and State* (London: Sage, 1985), pp. 1–29.

7. Ross Martin, "Pluralism and the New Corporatism," *Political Studies* (March 1983): 68–102.

8. Thomas S. Kuhn, *The Structure of Scientific Revolutions,* 2nd ed. (Chicago: University of Chicago Press, 1970).

9. Sheldon Wolin, "Paradigms and Political Theories," in P. King and B. C. Parekh, eds., *Politics and Experience: Essays Presented to Michael Oakeshott* (Cambridge, Eng.: Cambridge University Press, 1968), pp. 125–52.

10. Joel D. Wolfe, "Corporatism and Union Democracy: The British Miners and Incomes Policy, 1973–74," *Comparative Politics* 17 (July 1985): 421–36; Joel D. Wolfe, "Class Formation and Democracy: The Decline of Working-Class Power in Britain," *West European Politics* 9 (July 1986): 343–61. For an application of this theme to theories of participatory democracy, see Joel D. Wolfe, "Varieties of Participatory Democracy and Democratic Theory," *Political Science Reviewer* 16 (Fall 1986): 1–38.

11. See Clifford Geertz, "Ideology as a Cultural System," in *The Interpretation of Cultures: Selected Essays* (New York: Basic Books, 1973), pp. 193–233.

12. Weber defines instrumentally rational action as involving expectations "used as 'conditions' or 'means' for the attainment of the actor's own rationally pursued and calculated ends." For further discussion of the instrumental-value orientation and its relation to economic action and legal-rational authority, see Max Weber, *Economy and Society,* 2 vols., ed. G. Roth and C. Wittich (Berkeley and Los Angeles: University of California Press, 1978), 1:24–26, 85–86, 217–26.

13. Gianfranco Poggi, *The Development of the Modern State: A Sociological Introduction* (Stanford: Stanford University Press, 1978), pp. 94–95.

14. Hanna Pitkin, *The Concept of Representation* (Berkeley and Los Angeles: University of California Press, 1967).

15. Steven Lukes, *Power: A Radical Analysis* (London: Macmillan, 1974).

16. Peter Evans, D. Rueschemeyer, and T. Skocpol, eds., *Bringing the State Back In* (Cambridge, Eng.: Cambridge University Press, 1985).

17. Ralph Miliband, *Marxism and Politics* (New York: Oxford University Press, 1977); Claus Offe, "The Attribution of Public Status to Interest Groups: Observations on the West German Case," in Suzanne Berger, ed., *Organizing Interests in Western Europe: Pluralism, Corporatism and the Transformation of Politics* (Cambridge, Eng.: Cambridge University Press, 1981), pp. 123–58.

18. Charles Lindblom, *Politics and Markets: The World's Political-Economic Systems* (New York: Basic Books, 1977), pp. 37, 39.

19. Alan Cawson, "Varieties of Corporatism: The Importance of the Meso-level of Interest Intermediation," in *Organized Interests and the State: Studies in Meso-corporatism* (London: Sage, 1985), p. 8.

20. Arendt Lijphart, "Typologies of Democratic Systems," *Comparative Political Studies* 1 (April 1968): 3–33.

21. Joseph Schumpeter, *Capitalism, Socialism, and Democracy,* 3rd ed. (New York: Harper and Row, 1962).

22. S. M. Lipset, J. S. Coleman, and Martin Trow, *Union Democracy: The Internal Politics of the International Typographical Union* (New York: Free Press, 1956).

23. Robert A. Dahl, *Who Governs?* (New Haven: Yale University Press, 1961).

24. Important works in the interest-group tradition of pluralism include David Truman, *The Governmental Process* (New York: Alfred A. Knopf, 1951); Grant McConnell, *Private Power and American Democracy* (New York: Alfred A. Knopf, 1967); and Theodore Lowi, *The End of Liberalism,* 2nd ed. (New York: W. W. Norton, 1979).

25. Kenneth Arrow, *Social Choice and Individual Values,* 2nd ed. (New York: Wiley, 1963).

26. Milton Friedman, *Capitalism and Freedom* (Chicago: University of Chicago Press, 1962).

27. Robert Nozick, *Anarchy, State, and Utopia* (New York: Basic Books, 1974).

28. See Albert O. Hirschman, *Exit, Voice, and Loyalty* (Cambridge, Mass.: Harvard University Press, 1970).

29. Theodore Lowi, "American Business, Public Policy, Case-Studies, and Political Theory," *World Politics* 16 (July 1964): 677–715; Theodore Lowi, "Four Systems of Policy, Politics, and Choice," *Public Administration Review* 33 (July-August 1972): 298–310.

30. Robert Salisbury, "The Analysis of Public Policy: A Search of Theories and Roles," in A. Ranney, ed., *Political Science and Public Policy* (Chicago: Markham, 1968), pp. 151–75; Robert Salisbury and John Heinz, "A Theory of Policy Analysis and Some Preliminary Applications," in I. Sharkansky, ed., *Policy Analysis in Political Science* (Chicago: Markham, 1970), pp. 39–60.

31. B. Guy Peters et al., "Types of Democratic Systems and Types of Public Policy," *Comparative Politics* 9 (April 1977): 327–55.

32. Ibid., p. 333.

33. Lowi, "American Business," pp. 692–95.

34. Samuel H. Beer, *British Politics in the Collectivist Age* (New York: Random House, 1969), pp. 34–39.

35. Robert A. Dahl, *Dilemmas of Pluralist Democracy* (New Haven, Conn.: Yale Univ. Press, 1982).

36. Samuel H. Beer, *Britain Against Itself* (New York: W. W. Norton, 1982).

37. Samuel P. Huntington, "The United States," in M. Crozier, S. P. Huntington, and J. Watanuki, *The Crisis of Democracy* (New York: New York University Press, 1975).

38. Lowi, "American Business," p. 695.

39. Philippe C. Schmitter, "Interest Intermediation and Regime Governability in Contemporary Western Europe and North America," in Berger, *Organizing Interests,* pp. 285–327; Claus Offe, "The Attribution of Public Status to Interests Groups," in Berger, *Organizing Interests,* pp. 123–58.

40. Manfred Schmidt, "Does Corporatism Matter? Economic Crisis, Politics and Rates of Unemployment in Capitalist Democracies in the 1970s," in Gerhard Lehmbruch and Philippe Schmitter, eds., *Patterns of Corporatist Policy-Making* (Beverly Hills: Sage, 1982), pp. 237–58.

41. Leo Panitch, "The Development of Corporatism in Liberal Democracies," *Comparative Political Studies* 10 (April 1977): 61–90; Leo Panitch, "Trade Unions and the

Capitalist State," *New Left Review* 125 (January-February 1981): 21–44; Colin Crouch, "Corporatism in Industrial Relations: A Formal Model," in Wyn Grant, ed., *The Political Economy of Corporatism* (London: Macmillan, 1985), pp. 63–88.

42. Cawson, "Varieties of Corporatism," pp. 10–11.

43. Bernd Marin, "Austria—The Paradigm Case of Liberal Corporatism?" in Grant, *Political Economy of Corporatism,* pp. 89–125; Peter Katzenstein, *Corporatism and Change: Austria, Switzerland, and the Politics of Industry* (Ithaca, N.Y.: Cornell University Press, 1984).

44. Philippe C. Schmitter, "Neo-corporatism and the State," in Grant, *Political Economy of Corporatism,* pp. 32–62; Streeck and Schmitter, "Community, Market, State—And Associations?," pp. 1–29.

45. Cawson, "Varieties of Corporatism," pp. 12–13.

46. Sarah Vickerstaff, "Industrial Training in Britain: The Dilemmas of a Neo-corporatist Policy," in Cawson, *Organized Interests and the State,* pp. 45–64.

47. Cawson, *Corporatism and Political Theory,* p. 120.

48. Stephen Young, "The Nature of Privatisation in Britain, 1979–85," *West European Politics* 9 (April 1986): 235–52.

49. Richard Hyman, "British Trade Unionism in the 70's," *Studies in Political Economy* 1, Pt. 4 (1979): 93–112; Michael Terry, "Shop Steward Development and Managerial Strategies," in G. S. Bain, ed., *Industrial Relations in Britain* (Oxford: Basil Blackwell, 1983), pp. 67–91.

50. Ronald Dore, *British Factory-Japanese Factory: The Origins of National Diversity in Industrial Relations* (Berkeley and Los Angeles: University of California Press, 1973); Kevin Bonnett, "Corporatism and Thatcherism: Is There Life After Death?" in Cawson, *Organized Interests and the State,* pp. 85–105.

51. Young, "Nature of Privatisation," p. 236.

52. See Jurgen Habermas, *Legitimation Crisis* (Boston: Beacon Press, 1975), Part II.

53. Goldthorpe, "End of Convergence."

54. Robert Gilpin, *The Political Economy of International Relations* (Princeton, N.J.: Princeton University Press, 1987), pp. 343–60, 394–406. Also see Robert Keohane, "The World Political Economy and the Crisis of Embedded Liberalism," in Goldthorpe, *Order and Conflict in Contemporary Capitalism,* pp. 15–38.

55. See Beer, *Britain Against Itself,* and Mancur Olson, *The Rise and Decline of Nations: Economic Growth, Stagflation, and Social Rigidities* (New Haven: Yale University Press, 1982).

56. Peter J. Katzenstein, *Small States in World Markets* (Ithaca, N.Y.: Cornell University Press, 1985); Stephen Krasner, "State Power and the Structure of International Trade," *World Politics* 28 (April 1976): 317–43.

57. Also see Cawson, "Varieties of Corporatism," p. 14.

58. See Wolfe, "Varieties of Participatory Democracy."

Selected Bibliography

Adams, William James, and Christian Stoffaes, eds. *French Industrial Policy.* Washington, D.C.: Brookings, 1986.

Allen, Christopher S. "Corporatism and Regional Economic Policies in the Federal Republic of Germany: The 'Meso' Politics of Industrial Adjustment." *Publius*, in press.

———. "Trade Unions, Worker Participation, and Flexibility: Linking the Micro to the Macro." *Comparative Politics*, 1987.

———. "The Underdevelopment of Keynesianism in the Federal Republic of Germany." In P. A. Hall, ed., *The Political Power of Economic Ideas: Keynesianism Across Nations.* Princeton, N.J.: Princeton University Press, 1989.

Allen, Christopher S., and Harvey Rishikof. "Tale Thrice Told: A Review of Industrial Policy Proposals." *Journal of Policy Analysis and Management* 4 (Winter 1985): 234–49.

Archibugi, Franco, Jacques Delors, and Stuart Holland. "Planning for Development." In Stuart Holland, ed., *Beyond Capitalist Planning.* New York: St. Martin's Press, 1978.

Arrow, Kenneth. "Innovation in Large and Small Firms." In Joshua Ronen, ed., *Entrepreneurship.* Lexington, Mass.: Lexington Books, 1983, pp. 15–29.

Ayres, R. V. *The Next Industrial Revolution: Reviving Industry Through Innovation.* Cambridge, Mass.: Ballinger, 1984.

Beer, Samuel H. *British Politics in the Collectivist Age.* New York: Random House, 1969.

———. *Britain Against Itself: The Political Contradictions of Collectivism.* New York: W. W. Norton, 1982.

Beesley, Michael, and Stephen Littlechild. "Privatization: Principles, Problems, and Priorities." *Lloyds Bank Review* 149 (July 1983): 1–20.

Berger, Suzanne. "The Traditional Sector in France and Italy." In S. Berger and M. J. Piore, *Dualism and Discontinuity in Industrial Societies.* Cambridge, Eng.: Cambridge University Press, 1980.

———. ed. *Organizing Interests in Western Europe: Pluralism, Corporatism, and the Transformation of Politics.*, New York: Cambridge University Press, 1981.

Blackaby, Frank, ed. *De-industrialization.* London: Heinemann, 1979.

Bluestone, Barry, and Bennett Harrison. *The Deindustrialization of America: Plant Closings, Community Abandonment, and the Dismantling of Basic Industry.* New York: Basic Books, 1982.

Bowles, Samuel, and Herbert Gintis. "The Crisis of Liberal Democratic Capitalism: The Case of the United States." *Politics and Society* 11 (1982): 51–93.

Brittan, Samuel. "The Politics and Economics of Privatisation." *Political Quarterly* 55 (April-June 1984): 109–28.

Brown, Alice, and Desmond S. King "Economic Change and Labour Market Policy: Corporatist and Dualist Tendencies in Britain and Sweden." *West European Politics* 11 (July 1988): 75–91.

Butler, Stuart. "The Enterprise Zone as an Urban Frontier." *Journal of Community Action* 1 (September-October 1981): 20–28.

Cameron, David. "Social Democracy, Corporatism, Labour Quiescence, and the Representation of Economic Interest in Advanced Capitalist Society." In John H. Goldthorpe, ed., *Order and Conflict in Contemporary Capitalism: Studies in the Political Economy of Western European Nations.* Oxford: Clarendon Press, 1984, pp. 143–78.

———. "The Nationalized Industries After March." *French Politics and Society* 14 (June 1986).

Cawson, Alan. "Functional Representation and Democratic Politics: Towards a Corporatist Democracy?" In Graeme Duncan, ed., *Democratic Theory and Practice.* Cambridge, Eng.: Cambridge University Press, 1983, pp. 173–84.

———. *Corporatism and Political Theory.* Oxford: Basil Blackwell, 1986.

———. ed. *Organized Interests and the State: Studies in Meso-corporatism.* London: Sage, 1985.

Cohen, Joshua, and Joel Rogers. *On Democracy: Toward a Transformation of American Society.* New York: Penguin, 1983.

Cohen, Stephen S. *Modern Capitalist Planning.* Berkeley and Los Angeles: University of California Press, 1977.

Cohen, Stephen S., and Peter A. Gourevitch, eds. *France in the Troubled World Economy.* London: Butterworth, 1982.

Cohen, Stephen S., and John Zysman. *Manufacturing Matters: The Myth of the Post-industrial Society.* New York: Basic Books, 1987.

Cox, Andrew, and Jack Hayward. "The Inapplicability of the Corporatist Model in Britain and France: The Case of Labor." *International Political Science Review* 4 (1983): 217–40.

Crouch, Colin. "Pluralism and the New Corporatism: A Rejoinder." *Political Studies* 31 (September 1983): 452–60.

Dahl, Robert. *Dilemmas of Pluralist Democracy: Autonomy vs. Control.* New Haven: Yale University Press, 1982.

Domhoff, G. William. *The Powers That Be.* New York: Vintage, 1978.

Dunleavy, Patrick. "Explaining the Privatization Boom: Public Choice Versus Radical Approaches." *Public Administration* 64 (Spring 1986): 13–34.

Esping-Anderson, Gøsta. *Politics Against Markets.* Princeton, N.J.: Princeton University Press, 1985.

Esser, Josef. "State, Business and Trade Unions After the 'Political Wende.'" *West European Politics* 9 (April 1986): 198–214.

Evans, Peter, D. Rueschemeyer, and T. Skocpol, eds. *Bringing the State Back In.* Cambridge, Eng.: Cambridge University Press, 1985.

Feigenbaum, Harvey B. "Public Enterprise in Comparative Perspective." *Comparative Politics* 15 (October 1982): 101–22.

———. *The Politics of Public Enterprise: Oil and the French State.* Princeton, N.J.: Princeton University Press, 1985.

Foglesong, Richard. "Business Against the Welfare State." *Challenge* 26 (November-December 1983): 38–45.

Friedman, Milton. *Capitalism and Freedom.* Chicago: University of Chicago Press, 1962.

Gilpin, Robert. *The Political Economy of International Relations.* Princeton, N.J.: Princeton University Press, 1987.

Golden, Miriam. "Interest Representation, Party Systems, and the State: Italy in Comparative Perspective." *Comparative Politics* 18 (April 1986): 279–302.

Goldsmith, William W. "Bringing the Third World Home: Enterprise Zones for America." In Larry Sawyers and William K. Tabb, eds., *Sunbelt/Snowbelt.* New York: Oxford University Press, 1984.

Goldthorpe, John H., ed. *Order and Conflict in Contemporary Capitalism: Studies in the Political Economy of Western European Nations.* New York: Oxford University Press, 1984.

Gourevitch, Peter. *Politics in Hard Times.* Ithaca, N.Y.: Cornell University Press, 1986.

Grant, Wyn, ed. *The Political Economy of Corporatism.* London: Macmillan, 1985.

Green, Diana. *Managing Industrial Change? French Policies to Promote Industrial Adjustment.* London: HMSO, 1981.

Hall, Peter. "Socialism in One Country: Mitterrand and the Struggle to Define a New Economic Policy for France." In P. G. Cerny and M. A. Schain, eds., *Socialism, the State and Public Policy in France.* New York: Methuen, 1985.

———. *Governing the Economy: The Politics of State Intervention in Britain and France.* New York: Oxford University Press, 1986.

Hall, Stuart, and Martin Jacques, eds. *The Politics of Thatcherism.* London: Lawrence and Wishart, 1983.

Harrigan, K. R. *Strategies for Declining Business.* Lexington, Mass.: Lexington Books, 1980.

Harrison, B. "The International Movement for Prenotification of Plant Closures." *Industrial Relations* 23 (Fall 1984): 387–409.

Hastings, Sue, and Hugo Levie, eds. *Privatisation?* Nottingham: Spokesman, 1983.

Hayward, Jack. *The State and the Market Economy: Industrial Patriotism and Economic Intervention in France.* Sussex: Harvester, 1986.

Heald, David. *Public Expenditure: Its Defence and Reform.* Oxford: Martin Robertson, 1983.

Hilferding, Rudolf. *Finance Capital.* London: Routledge and Kegan Paul, 1981.

Holmes, Martin. *The First Thatcher Government, 1979–1983: Contemporary Conservatism and Economic Change.* Brighton: Wheatsheaf Books, 1985.

Huntington, Samuel P. "The United States." In M. Crozier, S. P. Huntington, and J. Watanuki, *The Crisis of Democracy: Report on the Governability of Democracies to the Trilateral Commission.* New York: New York University Press, 1975.

Johnson, Chalmers. *MITI and the Japanese Miracle.* Stanford: Stanford University Press, 1982.

Katz, Harry C., and Charles F. Sabel. "Industrial Relations and Industrial Adjustment in the Car Industry." *Industrial Relations* 24 (Fall 1985): 295–315.

Katzenstein, Peter. *Corporatism and Change: Austria, Switzerland, and the Politics of Industry.* Ithaca, N.Y.: Cornell University Press, 1984.

———. *Small States in World Markets.* Ithaca, N.Y.: Cornell University Press, 1985.

———. *Policy and Politics in West Germany: The Growth of a Semisovereign State.* Philadelphia: Temple University Press, 1987.

———. ed. *Between Power and Plenty: Foreign Economic Policies of Advanced Industrial States.* Madison: University of Wisconsin Press, 1978.

Katznelson, Ira. "Considerations on Social Democracy." *Comparative Politics* 11 (October 1978): 77–100.

Kay, John, and D. J. Thompson. "Privatisation: A Policy in Search of a Rationale." *Economics Journal* 96 (March 1986): 18–32.

Kay, John, Colin Mayer and David Thompson, eds. *Privatisation and Regulation: The UK Experience.* Oxford: Clarendon Press, 1986.

Keegan, William. *Mrs. Thatcher's Economic Experiment.* Harmondsworth: Penguin, 1984.

Keeler, John T. S. "Situating France on the Pluralism-Corporatism Continuum: A Critique and Alternative to the Wilson Perspective." *Comparative Politics* 17 (January 1985): 229–49.

Kesselman, Mark. "Prospects for Democratic Socialism in Advanced Capitalism: Class Struggle and Compromise in Sweden and France." *Politics and Society* 11 (1982): 397–438.

Kesselman, Mark, and Guy Groux, eds. *The French Workers' Movement: Economic Crisis and Political Change.* London: George Allen and Unwin, 1984.

Krasner, Stephen. "State Power and the Structure of International Trade." *World Politics* 28 (April 1976): 317–43.

———. "Approaches to the State: Alternative Conceptions and Historical Dynamics." *Comparative Politics* 16 (January 1984): 223–46.

Krieger, Joel. *Reagan, Thatcher, and the Politics of Decline.* New York: Oxford University Press, 1986.

Kuhn, Thomas S. *The Structure of Scientific Revolutions.* 2nd ed. Chicago: University of Chicago Press, 1970.

Kurzweil, E. *Italian Entrepreneurs: Rearguard of Progress.* New York: Praeger, 1983.

Labour Research Department. *Privatisation: Who Loses, Who Profits.* London: LRD, 1983.

Lash, Scott. "The End of Neo-corporatism?: The Breakdown of Centralised Bargaining in Sweden." *British Journal of Industrial Relations* 23 (July 1985): 215–39.

Lauber, Volkmar. *The Politics of Economic Policy: France 1974–1982.* New York: Praeger, 1983.

Lawrence, R. Z. "Is Trade Deindustrializing America? A Medium Term Perspective." *Brookings Papers on Economic Activity* 1 (1983): 129–71.

———. *Can America Compete?* Washington, D.C.: Brookings, 1984.

LeGrand, Julian, and Ray Robinson, eds. *Privatisation and the Welfare State.* London: George Allen and Unwin, 1984.

Lehmbruch, Gerhard, and Philippe Schmitter, eds. *Patterns of Corporatist Policy-Making.* Beverly Hills: Sage, 1982.

Leurez, Jacques. *Economic Planning and Politics in Britain.* translated by Martin Harrison. London: Martin Robertson, 1975.

Lindblom, Charles. *Politics and Markets: The World's Political-Economic Systems.* New York: Basic Books, 1977.

Lowi, Theodore. "American Business, Public Policy, Case-Studies, and Political Theory." *World Politics* 16 (July 1964): 677–715.

———. "Four Systems of Policy, Politics, and Choice." *Public Administration Review* 33 (July-August 1972): 298–310.

———. *The End of Liberalism.* 2nd ed. New York: W. W. Norton, 1979.

Lustig, R. J. "The Politics of Shutdown: Community, Property, Corporatism." *Journal of Economic Issues* 19 (March 1985): 123–52.

McArthur, John H., and Bruce R. Scott. *Industrial Planning in France.* Boston: Harvard University School of Business Administration, 1969.

McConnell, Grant. *Private Power and American Democracy.* New York: Alfred A. Knopf, 1967.

March, James G., and Johan P. Olsen. "The New Institutionalism: Organizational Factors in Political Life." *American Political Science Review* 78 (September 1984): 734–49.

Markovits, Andrei. *The Politics of the West German Trade Unions.* Cambridge, Eng.: Cambridge University Press, 1986.

Markovits, Andrei, and Christopher S. Allen. "Trade Unions and the Economic Crisis: The West German Case." In Peter Gourevitch et al., *Unions and Economic Crisis: Britain, West Germany and Sweden.* London: George Allen and Unwin, 1984.

Martin, Andrew. "Is Democratic Control of Capitalist Economies Possible?" In L. Lindberg et al., eds., *Stress and Contradiction in Modern Capitalism.* Lexington, Mass.: D. C. Heath, 1975.

Martin, Ross. "Pluralism and the New Corporatism." *Political Studies* 31 (March 1983): 68–102.

Masi, Anthony C. "The Relationship Between National Industrial Strategy and Regional Economic Development Programs for the Mezzogiorno: Some Lessons from the Case of Nuova Italsider-Taranto." *Journal of Regional Policy/Mezzogiorno d'Europa* 8 (January-March 1988):11–30.

Meny, Yves, and Vincent Wright, eds. *The Poliltics of Steel: Western Europe and the Steel Industry in the Crisis Years (1974–1984).* New York: De Gruyter, 1987.

Miliband, Ralph. *Marxism and Politics.* New York: Oxford University Press, 1977.

Nolan, Mary, and Charles F. Sabel. "Class Conflict and the Social Democratic Reform Cycle in Germany." *Political Power and Social Theory* 3 (1982): 145–73.

Nordlinger, Eric. *On the Autonomy of the Democratic State.* Cambridge, Mass.: Harvard University Press, 1981.

Norton, R. D. "Industrial Policy and American Renewal." *Journal of Economic Literature.* 24 (March 1986): 1–40.

O'Connor, James. *The Fiscal Crisis of the State.* New York: St. Martin's Press, 1973.

Offe, Claus. "Corporatism as Macro-structuring." *Telos* 65 (Fall 1985): 97–111.

Offe, Claus, and Helmut Wiesenthal. "The Two Logics of Collective Action—Theoretical Notes on Social Class and The Political Form of Interest Representation." *Political Power and Social Theory* 1 (1979): 67–115.

O'Higgins, Michael. "Privatisation and Social Security." *Political Quarterly* 55 (April-June 1984): 129–39.

Olson, Mancur. *The Rise and Decline of Nations: Economic Growth, Stagflation, and Social Rigidities.* New Haven: Yale University Press, 1982.

Panitch, Leo. "Recent Theorizations of Corporatism: Reflections on a Growth Industry." *British Journal of Sociology* 31 (June 1980): 159–87.

———. "Trade Unions and the Capitalist State." *New Left Review* 125 (January-February 1981): 21–44.

Piore, Michael, and Charles Sabel. *The Second Industrial Divide: Possibilities for Prosperity.* New York: Basic Books, 1984.

Poggi, Gianfranco. *The Development of the Modern State: A Sociological Introduction.* Stanford: Stanford University Press, 1978.

Poulantzas, Nicos. *Political Power and Social Classes.* London: New Left Books, 1973.

Pryke, Richard. *The Nationalized Industries: Policies and Performance Since 1968.* Oxford: Martin Robertson, 1981.

Quick, Perry D. "Reagan's Industrial Policy." In J. L. Palmer and I. V. Sawhill, eds., *The Reagan Record.* Cambridge, Mass.: Ballinger, 1984, pp. 287–316.

Reich, Robert. *The Next American Frontier.* New York: Penguin, 1983.

Riddell, Peter. *The Thatcher Government.* Oxford: Martin Robertson, 1983.

Riemer, Jeremiah M. "Alterations in the Design of Model Germany: Critical Innovations in the Policy Machinery for Economic Steering." In Andrei S. Markovits, ed., *The Political Economy of West Germany: Modell Deutschland.* New York: Praeger, 1982.

———. "West German Crisis Management: Stability and Change in the Post Keynesian Age." In Norman J. Vig and Stephen E. Schier, eds., *Political Economy in Western Democracies.* New York: Holmes and Meier, 1985.

Robinson, Joan. *Economic Heresies: Some Old Fashioned Questions in Economic Theory.* New York: Basic Books, 1971.

Ross, George. "Nicos Poulantzas, Eurocommunism, and the Debate on the Theory of the Capitalist State." *Socialist Review* 9 (March-April 1979): 143–58.

———. "The Perils of Politics: French Unions and the Crisis of the 1970s." In Peter Lange, George Ross, and Maurizio Vannicelli, *Unions, Change and Crisis: French and Italian Union Strategy and the Political Economy, 1945–1980.* London: George Allen and Unwin, 1982.

Sabel, Charles. *Work and Politics: The Division of Labor in Industry.* Cambridge, Eng.: Cambridge University Press, 1982.

———. "Struktureller Wandel der Produktion und neue gewerkschaftliche Strategien." *Prokla* 62 (March 1986): 41–60.

Schmenner, Roger W. "Industrial Location and Urban Public Management." In Arthur P. Solomon, ed., *The Prospective City.* Cambridge, Mass.: MIT Press, 1980.

Schmitter, Philippe. "Still the Century of Corporatism?" *Review of Politics* 36 (January 1974): 85–131.

———. "Democratic Theory and Neo-corporatist Practice." *Social Research* 50 (Winter 1983): 885–928.

Schmitter, Philippe, and Gerhard Lehmbruch, eds. *Trends Toward Corporatist Intermediation.* Beverly Hills: Sage, 1979.

Scholten, Ilja, ed. *Political Stability and Neo-corporatism: Corporatist Integration and Societal Cleavages in Western Europe.* London: Sage, 1987.

Schultze, Charles. "Industrial Policy: A Dissent." *Brookings Review* (Fall 1983): 3–12.

Schumpeter, Joseph. *Capitalism, Socialism, and Democracy.* New York: Harper and Row, 1976.

Sengenberger, Werner. "West German Employment Policy: Restoring Worker Competition." *Industrial Relations* 23 (Fall 1984): 323–43.

Sheehan, M. F. "Plant Closings and the Community: The Instrumental Value of Public Enterprise in Countering Corporate Flight." *American Journal of Economics and Sociology* 44 (October 1985): 423–33.

Shonfield, Andrew. *Modern Capitalism: The Changing Balance of Public and Private Power.* New York: Oxford University Press, 1965.

Silvia, Stephen J. "The West German Labor Law Controversy: A Struggle for the Factory of the Future." *Comparative Politics* 20 (January 1988): 155–76.

Steel, David, and David Heald. "Privatising Public Enterprise: An Analysis of the Government's Case." *Political Quarterly* 53 (April-June 1982): 333–49.

———. "The Privatization of Public Enterprises, 1979–83." In Peter Jackson, ed., *Implementing Government Initiatives: The Thatcher Administration 1979–1983.* London: Royal Institute of Public Administration, 1985, pp. 69–91.

———. eds. *Privatizing Public Enterprises.* London: Royal Institute of Public Administration, 1984.

Streeck, Wolfgang. "Qualitative Demands and the Neo-corporatist Manageability of Industrial Relations." *British Journal of Industrial Relations* 19 (July 1981): 149–69.

———. "Co-determination: The Fourth Decade." In B. Wilpert and A. Sorge, eds., *International Perspectives on Organizational Democracy.* New York: Wiley, 1984.

Streeck, Wolfgang, and Philippe C. Schmitter, eds. *Private Interest Government: Beyond Market and State.* London: Sage, 1985.

Suleiman, Ezra N. *Elites in French Society.* Princeton, N.J.: Princeton University Press, 1978.

———. *Les notaires: Le pouvoir d'une corporation.* Paris: Seuil, 1987.

Thurow, Lester. *The Zero-Sum Society.* New York: Penguin, 1980.

Tokunaga, Shigeyoshi, and Joachim Bergmann, eds. *Industrial Relations in Transition: The Cases of Japan and the Federal Republic of Germany.* Tokyo: University of Tokyo Press, 1984.

Vogel, David. "Why Businessmen Distrust Their State: The Political Consciousness of American Corporate Executives." *British Journal of Political Science* 8 (January 1978): 45–78.

Wilensky, Harold. *The "New Corporatism," Centralization, and the Welfare State.* Beverly Hills: Sage, 1976.

Wilkinson, Frank, ed. *The Dynamics of Labor Market Segmentation.* London: Academic Press, 1981.

Wilson, Frank L. "Alternative Models of Interest Intermediation: The Case of France." *British Journal of Political Science* 12 (April 1982): 173–200.

———. "French Interest Group Politics: Pluralist or Neocorporatist?" *American Political Science Review* 77 (1983): 895–910.

———. "The French Left in Power." *Western Political Quarterly* 38 (June 1985): 334–45.

Wolfe, Joel D. "Corporatism and Union Democracy: The British Miners and Incomes Policy, 1973–74." *Comparative Politics* 17 (July 1985): 421–36.

———. "Class Formation and Democracy: The Decline of Working-Class Power in Britain." *West European Politics* 9 (July 1986): 343–61.

———. "Varieties of Participatory Democracy and Democratic Theory." *Political Science Reviewer* 16 (Fall 1986): 1–38.

Wolin, Sheldon. "Paradigms and Political Theories." In P. King and B. C. Parekh, eds., *Politics and Experience: Essays Presented to Michael Oakeshott.* Cambridge, Eng.: Cambridge University Press, 1968, pp. 125–52.

Young, Stephen. "The Nature of Privatisation in Britain, 1979–85." *West European Politics* 9 (April 1986): 235–52.

Zysman, John. *Political Strategies for Industrial Order.* Berkeley and Los Angeles: University of California Press, 1977.

———. *Government, Markets and Growth: Financial Systems and the Politics of Industrial Change.* Ithaca, N.Y.: Cornell University Press, 1983.

Index

About the Editors and Contributors

CHRISTOPHER S. ALLEN is Assistant Professor of Political Science at the University of Georgia.

ANTHONY DALEY is Assistant Professor of Government and Science in Society at Wesleyan University.

HARVEY B. FEIGENBAUM is Associate Professor of Political Science at George Washington University.

RICHARD E. FOGLESONG is Associate Professor of Politics at Rollins College, Florida.

ANTHONY C. MASI is Associate Professor of Sociology at McGill University.

JEREMIAH M. RIEMER is Assistant Professor in the School of Advanced International Studies at Johns Hopkins University.

KATHLEEN THELEN is Assistant Professor of Politics at Princeton University.

JOEL D. WOLFE is Associate Professor of Political Science at the University of Cincinnati.